AMENITY GRASSLAND
An Ecological Perspective

All grassland in lowland Britain is held in a state of plagioclimax. These photographs of Kingley Vale NNR taken in 1954 (top) and 1973 (bottom) show the dramatic effect that the removal of rabbit-grazing has had on the character of the vegetation. See also Plate 11.1(a)–(d)

AMENITY GRASSLAND
An Ecological Perspective

Edited by

I. H. RORISON

and

RODERICK HUNT

Unit of Comparative Plant Ecology,
(Natural Environment Research Council),
Department of Botany,
The University of Sheffield, UK

A Wiley–Interscience Publication

JOHN WILEY & SONS
Chichester · New York · Brisbane · Toronto

British Library Cataloguing in Publication Data

Amenity grassland: An ecological perspective
   1. Turf management—Congresses
   2. Grounds maintenance—Great Britain—Congresses
   I. Rorison, Ian Henderson
   II. Hunt, Roderick
   635.9'64   SB433   79-40823

ISBN 0 471 27666 9

Typeset by Preface Ltd., Salisbury, Wilts
Printed and bound in Great Britain
at The Pitman Press, Bath

List of contributors

BRADSHAW, A. D., *Department of Botany, The University of Liverpool, Liverpool L69 3BX, England.*

CANAWAY, P. M., *Sports Turf Research Institute, Bingley, West Yorkshire, BD16 1AU, England.*

ESCRITT, J. R., *Sports Turf Research Institute, Bingley, West Yorkshire, BD16 1AU, England.*

GREEN, B. H., *Countryside Planning Unit, School of Rural Economics and Related Studies, Wye College, Nr. Ashford, Kent TN25 5AH, England.*

GRIME, J. P., *Unit of Comparative Plant Ecology (NERC), Department of Botany, The University, Sheffield S10 2TN, England.*

HAGGAR, R. J., *ARC Weed Research Organization, Begbroke Hill, Yarnton, Oxford OX5 1PF, England.*

HELLIWELL, D. R., *Waterloo Mill, Wooton-under-Edge, Gloucestershire, GL12 7JN, England.*

HUMPHREYS, M. O., *Welsh Plant Breeding Station, Plas Gogerddan, Nr. Aberystwyth, SY23 3EB, Wales.*

PARKER, J. C., *Kent County Council, Estates and Valuation Department, Springfield, Maidstone, Kent ME14 2LL, England.*

RORISON, I. H., *Unit of Comparative Plant Ecology (NERC), Department of Botany, The University, Sheffield S10 2TN, England.*

SHILDRICK, J. P., *Sports Turf Research Institute, Bingley, West Yorkshire, BD16 1AU, England.*

SNAYDON, R. W., *Department of Agricultural Botany, The University, Reading RG6 2AS, England.*

STEWART, V. I., *Soil Science Unit, University College of Wales, Aberystwyth SY23 3DE, Wales.*

WELLS, T. C. E., *Institute of Terrestrial Ecology, Monks Wood Experimental Station, Abbots Ripton, Huntingdon PE17 2LS, England.*

Contents

Preface

Although for many years British amenity grassland was thought of only in terms of intensively managed turfgrass, a meeting of experts convened by the Natural Environment Research Council in 1971 revealed a more widespread interest than this. A need for a review of research needs was also evident and this was carried out during 1973–6 by a committee set up by NERC and funded by the Department of the Environment. A report was published by NERC at the end of 1977 under the title *Amenity Grasslands—the Needs for Research*. Amenity grassland was defined as 'all grass with recreational, functional or aesthetic value and of which agricultural productivity is not the primary aim.'

The report provided enough evidence to show that amenity grassland forms not only a significant part of the landscape in the UK, but is also the basis of a multi-million pound industry. In addition, it recognized that there is a significant amount of semi-natural vegetation that has largely been ignored in the amenity context but which is important for at least two reasons: (1) increasingly it acts as a vital overspill for the more intensively-used amenity areas—particularly on urban fringes; (2) no less importantly, its study provides information about the methodology of low-cost/low-maintenance—very relevant in the present days of escalating costs.

In order to extend the debate, members of the 'Amenity Grass Committee' initiated a discussion meeting for research workers in December 1976 which was jointly organized by the University of Liverpool's Department of Botany and the Sports Turf Research Institute, Bingley. Over 30 short papers were presented at Liverpool, mainly on current topics of research, and they illustrated a great diversity of interest. A record of the meeting appeared in *The Journal of the Sports Turf Research Institute* **53**, 93–117 (1977).

A second meeting, entitled 'Amenity Grassland Research—An Ecological Perspective', was held at the University of Sheffield on 11–13 December, 1978. This meeting offered a further opportunity to discuss amenity grassland, particularly in the light of the NERC report which had been widely circulated. The aim of this meeting was to provide not so much a kaleidoscope of research activity as a concise review of current knowledge, highlighting pressing needs for study. The 14 main contributions to the meeting are

reproduced in this volume. The chapters cover aspects on which the inter-
change of ideas between turfgrass specialists, ecologists, and managers is
deemed timely and productive.

The structure of the volume (shown in the figure below) does not provide the coverage of a comprehensive textbook. This already exists for the
intensively-managed turfgrass of North America in A. A. Hanson and F. V.
Juska's *Turfgrass Science* (1969) and J. B. Beard's *Turfgrass: Science and Culture*
(1973), while semi-natural British grassland is covered by E. Duffey and col-
leagues in *Grassland Ecology and Wildlife Management* (1974). Rather, we aim to
relate the disciplines, both of intensively managed turfgrass and of the more
extensive semi-natural grassland, through emphasis on ecological principle

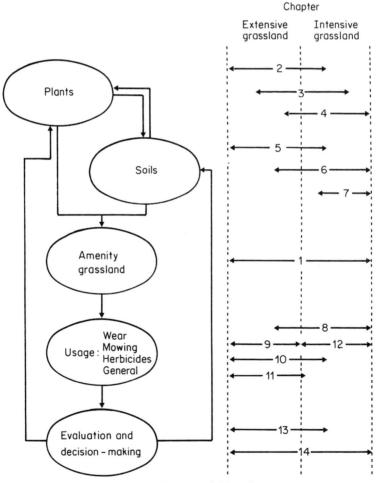

A schematic view of this volume

relevant to both. The degree to which this has been achieved has depended upon the background of each contributor.

We include no separate coverage of climate because this all-pervading subject is mentioned in several chapters, from which an idea of its importance may be judged. Although not considered a major factor in the relatively protected sphere of intensively managed turfgrass, its demonstrable effects on a more general scale warrant further consideration.

There are gaps between research and development as there are between the approach of the turfgrass manager and the conservationist. Unevenness in the scope of the 'poster' contributions at the meeting (which make up the final section of the book) merely reflects the variable degrees of interest and progress in the field.

We hope that the approach taken by this volume, and the challenge that it offers, will stimulate the co-operation of all interested in amenity grassland, both in the UK and abroad.

Throughout, we have adopted the SI system of units (*Système International d'Unités*) with imperial equivalents given in brackets. Authorities are quoted for the scientific names of plant species only where these are not listed in A. R. Clapham, T. G. Tutin, and E. F. Warburg's *Flora of the British Isles* (2nd ed., 1962). Common names of plants are given in brackets at the first mention in the text of each chapter; wherever possible, these also are the names listed in the *Flora*.

We are indebted to many for contributions made to the success of this venture: Professor A. D. Bradshaw, Dr J. P. Grime, and Mr J. P. Shildrick each helped in the planning of the meeting, which was executed with the assistance of Mrs H. J. Hucklesby, Mrs N. Ruttle, Mrs R. E. Spencer, and Mr G. Woods; the University of Sheffield provided residential and conference facilities at Tapton Hall of Residence and the Crookesmoor Building; Mrs N. Ruttle carried out all the typing necessary for the meeting and for this volume; Mr G. Woods performed many photographic services; Professor A. J. Willis welcomed the participants and assisted at the proof stage. Finally, the permissions granted by the authors and publishers of the various illustrative examples are gratefully acknowledged.

I. H. RORISON

Sheffield, March 1979   RODERICK HUNT

Part I
INTRODUCTION

Amenity Grassland: An Ecological Perspective
Edited by I. H. Rorison and R. Hunt
© 1980 John Wiley & Sons Ltd

1

The current challenge for research and development

I. H. R O R I S O N *Unit of Comparative Plant Ecology (NERC), Department of Botany, The University, Sheffield, England*

Introduction

Amenity grassland has been defined as all grassland which has recreational, functional, or aesthetic value, but which is not used primarily for agricultural production (NERC, 1977). It may consist of pure stands of grasses or, typically in semi-natural areas, of mixtures of forbs and of grasses. It is widely scattered over some 4 per cent of the surface of the British Isles and is mainly situated at less than *c.* 350 m (1150 ft) above sea level. It is now recognized as a major national resource with considerable potential for exploitation and its current annual cost demands efficient management. This in turn requires the employment of sound ecological principles gained through adequate research and applied through adequate development. Nor should it be thought of in isolation for it has many problems in common with the establishment and maintenance of grassland on marginal land, both agricultural and urban, and on reclaimed industrial waste. Something of the variety of grasslands involved may be seen among the plates that illustrate the present volume.

Extent and scope

The areas involved in each major functional category may be seen from Table 1.1. They represent an approximate gradient from intensive to extensive management; from heavy to light usage; and from high- to low-cost maintenance. It should be noted that over half the total area comprises semi-natural grassland, the maintenance costs of which in 1973 represented less than 10 per cent of total expenditure (NERC, 1977).

The greatest overall expenditure is on urban parks (Plate 1.1), domestic lawns, and playing fields (Plate 7.1), although the highest cost per unit area is likely to be for bowling and golf greens (Plates 1.2 and 12.2). Table 1.2 indicates the types of amenity grassland and the types of maintenance operations that are the most costly.

Table 1.1   Amenity grass—categories, areas, and costs of maintenance in 1973 (from NERC, 1977)

Categories	Area (km²)†	Cost (£m)
Intensively managed areas	*c.* 1100	57
School playing fields and lawns	490	
Armed services sports pitches and lawns	70	
Other football and hockey pitches	90	
Golf fairways	348	
Golf greens	17	
Golf tees	9	
Cricket grounds (privately owned)	62	
Bowling greens	5	
Horse race tracks	5	
Greyhound tracks	0.2	
Field sports stadia } No separate figures		
Tennis courts }		
Trampled open spaces		
Man-made	*c.* 2700	66
Urban parks and open spaces	1345	
Domestic lawns	900	
Urban and suburban road verges	250	
Armed services sports outfields	190	
Semi-natural	*c.* 4070	12.5
Rural road verges	1010	
National Trust land	922	
Nature reserves	630	
'Common land'	526	
Golf 'rough'	497	
Miscellaneous County Council land	300	
Caravan and picnic sites, nature trails	70	
Waterway banks	49	
Country parks	60	
Untrampled open spaces	*c.* 630	1.5
Military airfields	259	
Railway embankments	202	
Civil airports	110	
Motorway embankments	56	
Dam faces	0.8	
	c. 8500	£137m

†1 km² = 247.106 acres.

The overwhelming expenditure on mowing and fertilizing is central to every budget of intensively managed turfgrass, but an understanding of each ecosystem can lead to a reduction in costs. For example, a knowledge of nutrient cycling at the ecosystem level could help in the regulation of

Plate 1.1 Urban parks managed at about the same intensity as domestic lawns together account for *c*. 40 per cent of the country's annual expenditure on amenity grassland (photograph by I. H. Rorison)

Plate 1.2 A bowling green, the ultimate in uniformity of production and maintenance
(photograph by Ransomes, Sims & Jefferies Ltd, Ipswich, England)

Table 1.2   The most costly areas and operations. Costs as percentages of £137m, the whole year's budget in 1973 (from NERC, 1977)

Areas	%	Operations	%
Urban parks	24	Mowing (including machinery)	66
Domestic lawns	18	Fertilizing (including materials)	16
School playing fields	16	Weed control	5
Golf courses	14	Disease and pests	2
Others	28	Others	11

fertilizer input while ensuring adequate plant growth. A knowledge of the phenology of the component plants could ensure the best timing and height at which to cut the grass in order to minimize the number of mowings needed each season.

The main priorities for research listed by the Amenity Grass Committee (NERC, 1977) were:

(1) standards of management and measurement;
(2) establishment and renovation;
(3) species and cultivar selection;
(4) mowing and growth control;
(5) fertilizing;
(6) wear;
(7) weed control;
(8) use of semi-natural areas.

This list reflects the emphasis of interest today, and the primary concern over the past 50 years, with the problems of intensively used turf. An extensive body of knowledge and expertise has been accumulated already (Hanson & Juska, 1969; Beard, 1973) and it is now important to consider how far the principles involved may be applied in less heavily managed areas. For, increasingly, some of the considerable areas of semi-natural grassland and of urban dereliction (Plate 1.3) are being pressed into service to satisfy growing amenity needs and their carrying capacity must be assessed. Compared with intensively managed areas, environmental conditions are often extreme, sites more extensive, usage less intensive, and funds less available.

It is in such areas where urban and country parks (Plate 1.4) are being developed. Here, the expertise both of the turfgrass scientist and of the grassland ecologist can be brought to bear and there has already been fruitful co-operation (Lowday & Wells, 1977). An understanding of the ecology of suitable vegetation cover is particularly valuable in order to achieve both functional and aesthetic success.

Compared with the conditions required for the acceptable growth of turfgrass, soil or spoil conditions in these areas may be very different both physically and chemically. There are already a number of studies in which such areas are described and their amelioration is considered (Chadwick & Goodman, 1975; Wright, 1977). Sites may also contain a variety of slopes and aspects (Plate 1.5) which give rise to different microclimates (Rorison & Sutton, 1976). These can have a marked effect on plant growth and species composition (Ward, 1969). So, although climate is an uncontrollable variable and many turfgrasses have a fairly wide climatic tolerance (Chapter 3), field trials should be designed to detect its influence. Finally, human pressures and types of usage may differ throughout an area, adding to its heterogeneity.

Alternative strategies

It is important to specify precisely the role of each area to be developed or managed. The standard prescription is to modify the environment to suit the species to be introduced (Schmidt & Blaser, 1969). For, if wear is likely to be heavy, the use of tolerant turfgrass species is at present the only choice. The operator is thus committed to additional expenditure to produce an environment suitable for the selected species.

There are two possible alternatives, the first of which is to introduce species adapted to the unaltered environment. Enough is already known to prescribe the native species and populations which are likely to thrive in any workable set of environmental conditions. In terms of the physical aspects, such as drainage and moisture supply (discussed in Chapter 6), there are plants adapted to dry, sandy heath or duneland communities on the one hand, and plants of temporarily waterlogged bog and fen communities on the other. In terms of chemical factors (Plate 5.1), considered in Chapter 5, there are the plants adapted to generally infertile soils and others adapted to soils which suffer chemical imbalance through being either acidic or alkaline (Rorison, 1979). There are also plants adapted to soils containing high levels of toxic materials such as heavy metals (Gemmell, 1977). The relative lack of tolerance to wear of these plants is the main limitation to their extensive use. This is particularly true in physically unstable sites such as sand dunes, heathland, and colonized scree slopes.

In such places where the native sward can be trampled away relatively easily, the growth medium is inadequate to support wear-resistant species and site modification is too expensive. Erosion may then become a major problem. Some attempts have been made to use turfgrass species for renovation but, because of poor growth and their colour and texture, they fail to blend with the surroundings.

The most ecologically sound and aesthetically pleasing way of re-establishing vegetation is to use native species adapted to the area and in

Plate 1.3 Urban restoration on the slopes of the Don Valley in Sheffield. Background, many hectares of open slope to be contoured and grassed; foreground, small-scale grassing of domestic surrounds (photograph by I. H. Rorison)

Plate 1.4 A lowland country park overlying Bunter Sandstone at Clumber, Nottinghamshire showing multiple land use including amenity grassland (from the Cambridge University Collection of Aerial Photography)

Plate 1.5 Semi-natural grassland in a Carboniferous Limestone dale incised some 80 m (250 ft) into a plateau at 300 m OD (*c.* 1000 ft). The pattern of vegetation and soil type varies with aspect and slope (from the Cambridge University Collection of Aerial Photography)

Plate 1.6 A plastic mat laid over a wet and unstable section at the southern end of the Pennine Way, an experiment since discontinued in favour of faggot rafts (photograph by the Peak National Park)

Plate 1.7 A successful diversion. A disused railway track running through areas of Carboniferous Limestone grassland and used by walkers, cyclists and horseriders (photograph by the Peak National Park)

some way to channel the feet of users away from it and on to specially prepared surfaces. These could be 'hardened up' surfaces of local materials or, in less stable areas such as the wet peatlands of the Pennine Way, a plastic mat (Plate 1.6). Wear could also be diverted by the use of adjacent bridle ways or abandoned railway lines (Plate 1.7).

The second alternative is to breed species which are tolerant both of wear and also of the relatively extreme or impoverished environmental conditions. The tapping of the enormous natural variation which exists in adaptation to climate, soil type, and management is considered in Chapter 3. It will be particularly interesting to see how much of the adaptive material from the broader spectrum of semi-natural grasslands can be utilized to reduce maintenance costs in the turfgrass sector and how much material from the standard 16 turfgrasses considered in Chapter 4 can be utilized beyond the turfgrass sector into low-maintenance areas.

My main proposition is that because the cost of manipulating the environment is so great, it is important that we explore the possibility of using species and populations that are adapted to the conditions of existing environments and that we do not persist in all cases—regardless of subsequent maintenance costs—in using the existing, and adequate, supplies of traditional species, cultivars, and mixtures. It is part of the long-recognized fact that inadequate (low-cost) site preparation leads to expensive long-term maintenance. The overriding importance of physical and chemical factors is stressed in Chapter 7, but the part played by the species that is sown should not be overlooked. An extreme case concerns the use of cultivars of *Lolium perenne* (perennial ryegrass) which are very wear-resistant and have high relative growth-rates. They require high inputs of fertilizer to maintain vigour and, unless heavily-worn, require frequent mowing or the application of growth retardants to ensure that swards are maintained in a suitable condition.

If heavy wear is not the primary criterion, the use of species and cultivars better adapted to low maintenance should be explored. It may involve an extra initial expense but it could be one that is repaid many times over by subsequent savings in maintenance costs. Site preparation and maintenance may be considered by land managers under different budgetary headings but, ecologically, they are inseparably part of the same system.

Dynamics of processes

From the identification of critical environmental factors and the selection of suitable plant material we move to the dynamics of establishment and renovation. Can a consideration of the strategies for survival found in plants help to provide guidelines for the management of different types of amenity grassland? Certainly, an understanding of regeneration in gaps is as important to amenity grass managers as to ecologists, with gaps ranging in size from a penny piece to a derelict site of several hectares (Plate 1.3). The importance of change in growth in both time and space is already appreciated. The conceptual developments outlined in Chapter 2 provide a sound basis for many of the forms of management which are dealt with in Chapters 8–11. The roles of each of the major management tools: mowing, growth control via herbicides, growth retardants, burning, and grazing, might well be modified to advantage in the light of knowledge of plant strategies.

Some of these tools appear less useful than others. For example, at first sight, the use of growth retardants appears to be a retrograde step. Do they merely suppress the growth of inherently fast growers which should not have been planted in the first place? Or have growth retardants a genuine place in the management system and if so, what? No doubt they are valuable in places where it is undesirable or impractical to use any other method, as on central reservations of motorways, steep banks, and other inaccessible places. On the other hand, these are just the places to act as refugia for slow-growing species which are intolerant of wear.

As a physiologist I would also be concerned that growth retardants slow both root and shoot growth and that this might affect the ultimate survival of the sward (Elkins *et al.*, 1977). Perhaps their true worth, like that of herbicides, lies in the manipulation of species diversity as outlined in Chapter 10.

Conclusions

With intensive management, we are moving towards a balance between the minimum growth for maximum wear-resistance on the one hand and the minimum of fertilizer application and mowing on the other. Having welcomed the acceptance of a philosophy of minimum maintenance, ecologists are keen to further the case of the species adapted to specialized environments, i.e. the infertile, the wet, the dry, the sunny or the shady slope, the acidic, or the calcareous (Duffey *et al.*, 1974). Can these tolerances be blended with resistance to wear or merely utilized to help plants cover areas where wear is restricted?

Seed production

In any case, potential users will say, 'Give us the seed and we will finish the job.' We know that for restricted areas the seed banks in existing topsoil will provide an adequate cover (Thompson & Grime, 1979), but for larger projects seed production on a commercial scale will be vital.

A research programme based on the known skills of our agronomists has already achieved some success (Hebblethewaite & Ahmed, 1978) and its techniques should now be extended to native species. Valuable pilot work has been done showing that commercial production of certain species is feasible and that present costs ranging from £10 per kilo for seeds of *Zerna erecta* (upright brome) to £2400 per kilo for *Campanula rotundifolia* (harebell) could be significantly reduced (Wells, 1978). It has been estimated (1978) that over 90 per cent of all amenity grass seed is imported into the UK at a current cost of *c.* £9 million per annum. It would seem both economically and scientifically wise to encourage local growers to provide seed of the required turfgrasses and also to develop production lines of selected native species (Chapter 3). The need is now to draw up a list of species for specific purposes that would be acceptable to users and producers alike and one is currently in preparation (Bradshaw *et al.*, 1979).

Evaluation and decision-making

To achieve an overall balance-sheet we need to consider land-use in general and also how amenity grassland stands in relation to agriculture, forestry, mining, and urban renovation. Such an evaluation is not easy. Economic aspects have been considered by several authors and the discussion of aesthetics in Chapter 13 is a brave attempt to extend our understanding of a difficult problem.

Such evaluations must be made to convince decision-makers at the national level of the importance of amenity grassland. The problems facing local authorities at middle-management level have been outlined in Chapters 7 and 12. It is generally agreed that there is a need for education based on the results of research to date as well as a need for further research in the areas indicated.

In all this the ecological perspective should ensure effective development and management of amenity grass environments both economically and aesthetically. Ways in which this may be achieved are explored in Chapter 14.

References

Beard, J. B. (1973). *Turfgrass: Science and Culture*, Prentice-Hall Inc., Englewood Cliffs, N.Y.
Bradshaw, A. D., Holliday, R. J. H. & Bell, R. M. (1979). *The Grassing of Countryside Recreation areas*, Countryside Commission, Cheltenham (in press).
Chadwick, M. J. & Goodman, G. T. (eds) (1975). *The Ecology of Resource Degradation and Renewal*, Blackwell Scientific Publications, Oxford.
Duffey, E., Morris, M. G., Sheail, J., Ward, L. K., Wells, D. A. & Wells, T. C. E. (1974). *Grassland Ecology and Wildlife Management*, Chapman & Hall, London.
Elkins, D. M., Vandeventer, H. W. & Briskovich, M. A. (1977). 'Effect of chemical growth retardants on turfgrass morphology', *Agronomy Journal*, **69**, 458–61.

Gemmell, R. P. (1977). *Colonization of Industrial Wasteland*, Studies in Biology no. 80, Edward Arnold, London.

Hanson, A. A. & Juska, F. V. (eds) (1969). *Turfgrass Science*, American Society of Agronomy, Madison, Wisc.

Hebblethwaite, P. D. & Ahmed, M. el H. (1978). 'Production of amenity grass seeds in the United Kingdom', *Acta horticulturae*, **83**, 43–8.

Lowday, J. E. & Wells, T. C. E. (1977). *The Management of Grassland and Heathland in Country Parks*, Countryside Commission, Cheltenham.

NERC (1977). *Amenity Grasslands—the Needs for Research*, Natural Environment Research Council, Publications Series 'C', no. 19, London.

Rorison, I. H. (1979). 'The effects of soil acidity on nutrient availability and plant response', in *The Effects of Acid Precipitation on Terrestrial Ecosystems* (T. C. Hutchinson, ed.), Plenum Publishing, New York, pp. 283–304.

Rorison, I. H. & Sutton, F. (1976). 'Climate, topography and germination', in *Light as an Ecological Factor II* (G. C. Evans, R. Bainbridge, & O. Rackman, eds), Blackwell Scientific Publications, Oxford, pp. 361–83.

Schmidt, R. E. & Blaser, R. E. (1969). 'Ecology and turf management', in *Turfgrass Science* (A. A. Hanson & F. V. Juska, eds), American Society of Agronomy, Madison, Wisc., pp. 217–39.

Thompson, K. & Grime, J. P. (1979). 'Seasonal variation in the seed banks of herbaceous species in ten contrasting habitats', *Journal of Ecology*, **67** (in press).

Ward, C. Y. (1969). 'Climate and adaptation', in *Turfgrass Science* (A. A. Hanson & F. V. Juska, eds), American Society of Agronomy, Madison, Wisc., pp. 27–79.

Wells, T. C. (1978). *Establishment of Herb Rich Swards*, Interim Report to the Nature Conservancy Council, London, March 1978.

Wright, M. J. (ed.) (1977). *Plant Adaptation to Mineral Stress in Problem Soils*, Cornell University Press, New York.

Part II
PLANTS

Amenity Grassland: An Ecological Perspective
Edited by I. H. Rorison and R. Hunt
© 1980 John Wiley & Sons Ltd

2

An ecological approach to management

J. P. GRIME *Unit of Comparative Plant Ecology (NERC), Department of Botany, The University, Sheffield, England*

Introduction

For certain types of amenity grassland, and in some reclamation projects, sufficient funds may be available to allow the construction and maintenance of grasslands of sown species. In these circumstances vegetation structure and species composition are under close control and management involves the extension and adaptation of concepts and techniques employed in agriculture and horticulture (see particularly Chapters 4, 6, and 7).

Over the very large area of infertile and/or relatively neglected grassland, wasteland, and scrub, however, such strict control is neither economic nor desirable. Here the processes controlling vegetation characteristics are more complex and management can be most usefully informed by ecological methods and theories. This is to suggest that in this part of the landscape our objective should be to understand the major ecological processes and to seek to manipulate them.

Attempts to use ecological information in the management of amenity grassland present the ecologist with two basic problems. The first is to decide what kind of data should be collected, whilst the second is to distil this information into succinct, usable forms which can be relayed to those engaged in management.

Sources of ecological information

Surveys

One way in which to gain information concerning the ecology of grassland plants is to conduct surveys in which estimates of the species composition of vegetation samples are collected in association with measurements of topography, soil characteristics, and land-use. Particularly valuable are surveys which sample at random the full range of habitats represented in each geographical region and include not only established vegetation but also areas which have been recently and severely disturbed and exhibit different stages of recolonization. The main advantage of this type of comprehensive survey is that it allows us to examine the various contributions to the landscape made by particular types of plants (e.g. grasses, legumes, composites, sedges, rushes). From this type of survey it is also possible to obtain standardized descriptions of the field distribution of individual species (Grime & Lloyd, 1973) and to make some inferences concerning the effects of environment and management upon their ecology. As an illustration of the contribution which surveys can make to the comparative study of grassland plants, diagrams have been drawn in Appendix 2.1(a) summarizing, for a number of common grasses, data obtained in an unpublished survey conducted in part of North Derbyshire, Nottinghamshire, and South Yorkshire. From these data it is apparent that although the species concerned are all familiar constituents of intensively-managed amenity grassland there are major differences with regard to their capacities to exploit the full range of habitats colonized by herbaceous vegetation. It is clear that whereas certain species, e.g. *Agrostis tenuis* (common bent-grass), *Festuca rubra* (red fescue), and *Holcus lanatus* (Yorkshire fog), are virtually ubiquitous, grasses such as *Cynosurus cristatus* (crested dog's-tail), *Lolium perenne* (perennial ryegrass), and *Phleum pratense* (Timothy) are much more restricted in their distribution in the landscape at large.

Surveys may also provide more specific data on the ecology and habitat requirements of individual plants and in Appendices 2.1(b)–(h) examples are

Table 2.1   Some common species of the British flora classified with respect to their ability to accumulate persistent reserves of buried seeds in the soil

With persistent seed banks	Without persistent seed banks
Agrostis canina ssp. *canina*[2,3,5,7]	*Arrhenatherum elatius*[7]
Agrostis stolonifera[2,3,5]	*Cynosurus cristatus*[3]
Agrostis tenuis[2,3,5,7]	*Dactylis glomerata*[2,3]
Anthoxanthum odoratum[4,7]	*Deschampsia flexuosa*[7]
Deschampsia cespitosa[7]	*Festuca ovina*[2,3,6,7]
Holcus lanatus[3,6,7]	*Festuca rubra*[2,3,6,7]
Plantago lanceolata[2,3,6,7,8]	*Helictotrichon pratense*[6,7]
Poa annua[1,2,3,7]	*Lolium perenne*[2,3,7]
Poa pratensis[2]	*Nardus stricta*[3,5,7]
Poa trivialis[2,3,7]	*Phleum pratense*[2]

Key to authorities: 1, Brenchley & Warington (1930); 2, Champness & Morris (1948); 3, Chippendale & Milton (1934); 4, King (1976); 5, Milton (1939); 6, Spray, M. (unpublished); 7, Thompson & Grime (1979); 8, Wesson & Wareing (1969).

provided of various types of additional information which can be abstracted from surveys and used as a guide to the selection of species for particular renovation projects.

It may be important to bear in mind that surveys of established vegetation do not take account of buried seeds and in consequence often provide an incomplete assessment of a grassland flora. The results of field studies such as those summarized in Table 2.1 have established that there are consistent differences between common grassland species with regard to their capacity to accumulate reserves of seeds in the soil.

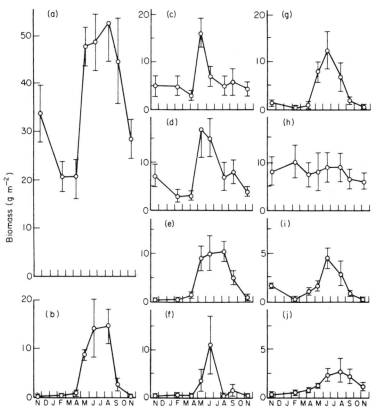

Figure 2.1 Seasonal changes in shoot biomass of the main components of the vegetation in an area of derelict grassland, subject to occasional burning, on a very shallow calcareous soil in South Yorkshire. The vertical lines represent standard errors. (a) *Brachypodium pinnatum*, (b) *Trifolium medium*, (c) *Carex caryophyllea*, (d) *Briza media*, (e) *Centaurea nigra*, (f) *Lotus corniculatus*, (g) *Leontodon hispidus*, (h) *Carex flacca*, (i) *Hieracium lachenalii*, (j) *Campanula rotundifolia* (from Al-Mufti *et al.*, 1977)

Phenological and demographic studies

Surveys are concerned essentially with the spatial distribution of plant species and vegetation types and provide few direct insights into the events in the life-histories and population dynamics of plants which actually determine vegetation composition and the success or failure of constituent species and genotypes. In order to examine these vegetation processes it is necessary to conduct more intensive studies involving a series of measurements at the same site.

One of the most useful investigations of this type is that in which, at regular intervals of time, samples of the total above-ground biomass are removed to the laboratory and sorted into constituent species (Plate 2.1), dried and weighed. Measurements of this type allow seasonal changes in the composition of grassland to be described quantitatively (Figure 2.1) and have revealed a number of consistent phenological patterns of interest to grassland

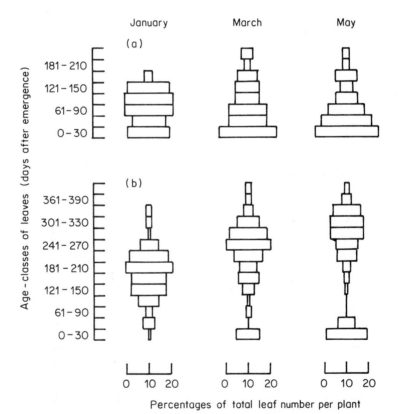

Figure 2.2   A comparison of the age-structure of the leaf canopies of (a) *Anthoxanthum odoratum* and (b) *Carex flacca* established in the same area of derelict calcareous grassland (from Sydes, 1979)

Plate 2.1 Phenological studies: a turf 250 mm (9.8 in) square was taken from species-rich calcareous grassland in June. In the laboratory the turf was sorted into the 35 components seen above. Total plant litter is in the bottom right compartment and living bryophyte material is at the bottom left. The tray measures 460 mm × 295 mm (photograph by G. Woods)

[*facing page 16*

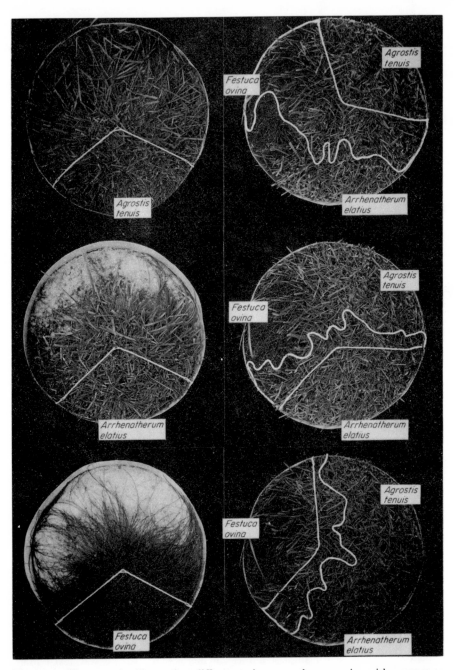

Plate 2.2 Photographs illustrating differences between three species with respect to their ability for lateral spread over bare soil (left) and into a clipped sward (right). All treatments were clipped every 3 days at 60 mm (2.4 in) and the photographs were taken after 4 months (Mahmoud, 1973). Left: three monocultures in which the sector in each pot marks the area initially sown with the species. Right: three photographs of one container, initially sown in equal sectors with *Arrhenatherum elatius, Agrostis tenuis*, and *Festuca ovina*. The photographs show in turn the extent of the original sector and the area over which shoots of each particular species have extended laterally
(photograph by G. Woods)

managers. From a number of investigations (Getz, 1960; Golley, 1960, 1965; Mehinick, 1967; Barrett, 1968; Precsenyi, 1969; Shure, 1971; Mellinger & McNaughton, 1975; Al-Mufti *et al.*, 1977) there is evidence that in pastures and unmanaged grasslands the peak biomass of the grass component occurs in advance of that due to the forbs. It is also apparent from these studies that differences in soil fertility and grassland productivity are consistently related to differences with respect to the shoot phenology of the dominant species. Whereas, under highly fertile conditions the vegetation tends to consist of species (e.g. *Lolium perenne, Holcus lanatus, Arrhenatherum elatius* (oat-grass)) capable of rapid expansion of the leaf canopy to a peak during the spring and summer, the majority of the plants occurring in infertile grasslands whether calcareous (e.g. *Helictotrichon pratense* (meadow oat), *Koeleria cristata* (crested hair-grass)) or acidic (e.g. *Deschampsia flexuosa* (wavy-hair grass), *Nardus stricta* (mat-grass)) are evergreens with much less pronounced seasonal variation in shoot biomass.

In recent research, such as that of Williamson (1976) and Sydes (1979), phenological studies have been complemented by more detailed seasonal investigations in which the life-span of individual leaves has been determined. From the resulting data it is possible to describe the age structure of the population of leaves on each species at various times during the year. In Figure 2.2 a comparison is drawn between two species established in the same area of derelict calcareous grassland. Over the period of study the canopy of one species, *Anthoxanthum odoratum* (sweet vernal-grass), was found to be composed exclusively of leaves aged <270 days. In contrast, the shoots of the strongly evergreen sedge, *Carex flacca* (carnation-grass), included, on each sampling occasion, a high proportion of older (>270 days) leaves.

It is not difficult to foresee the value of such phenological and demographic information to grassland management. Knowledge of the seasonal patterns of shoot growth and of the timing of leaf appearance and senescence are particularly relevant to the design of mowing regimes (Chapter 9) and to assessments of seasonal variation in carrying capacity and response to trampling damage (Chapter 8).

Seasonal studies have been applied also to the reproductive biology of plants and investigations following the fate of seeds and seedlings are yielding data applicable to several aspects of grassland management. Of particular interest are studies of seasonal variation in the numbers of detached readily-germinable seeds in various plant communities. From these investigations it has been possible to recognize four basic types of seed banks (Figure 2.3) and to begin to use this information (see page 29) to explain differences between species with respect to their ability to regenerate and to persist under particular grassland conditions and management regimes.

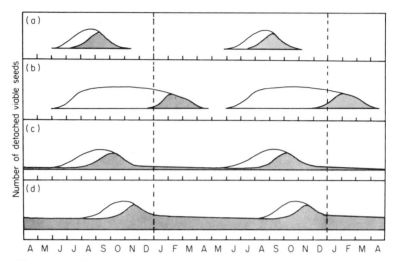

Figure 2.3 Scheme describing four types of seed banks of common
occurrence in temperate regions. Shaded area: seeds capable of
germinating immediately after removal to suitable laboratory conditions.
Unshaded area: seeds viable but not capable of immediate germination.
(a) Annual and perennial grasses of dry or disturbed habitats (e.g.,
Hordeum murinum, *Lolium perenne*, *Catapodium rigidum*); (b) annual and
perennial herbs colonizing vegetation gaps in early spring (e.g., *Impatiens
glandulifera*, *Anthriscus sylvestris*, *Heracleum sphondylium*); (c) annual and
perennial herbs, mainly germinating in the autumn but maintaining a
seed bank (e.g. *Arenaria serpyllifolia*, *Poa trivialis*, *Holcus lanatus*); (d) annual
and perennial herbs and shrubs with large, persistent seed banks (e.g.
Stellaria media, *Origanum vulgare*, *Calluna vulgaris*)

Screening experiments

There are many circumstances where field studies cannot by themselves lead
to an understanding of *how* management and the physical environment
determine vegetation structure and the fate of particular species and
genotypes. Scrutiny of plants growing under natural conditions is unlikely to
expose the influences of climate and soil which inhibit the growth of
seedlings and established plants of certain species and cause them to be
vulnerable to phenomena such as desiccation, predation, and competitive
exclusion. In order to recognize these more subtle effects, comparative
studies involving the growth of plants in controlled environments may be
necessary. There is also a wider justification for such studies. This is related
to the recent development of 'predictive ecology', i.e. the approach whereby
comparative studies under standardized conditions are used to document the
characteristics of groups of species and genotypes of contrasted ecology. By
this method it is possible to recognize attributes of germination, growth,

stress-physiology, and reproductive biology which are consistently associated with particular types of ecology. This, in turn, may lead to explanations of features of a plant's ecology and may allow prediction to be made regarding the conditions of environment and management under which it will be most successful in the field. At present there is a major requirement for programmes of research which involve the screening of species and genotypes in experiments conducted in standardized, simplified environments (e.g.

Table 2.2   Estimates of the relative rate of dry matter production in the seedling phase in a range of grasses (Grime & Hunt, 1975 and unpublished)

	R_{max}	$\bar{R}$
(a) Species of common occurrence in sown grasslands		
Agropyron repens	1.21	1.21
Agrostis stolonifera	1.48	1.48
Agrostis tenuis	1.36	1.36
Cynosurus cristatus	1.54	1.54
Dactylis glomerata	1.31	1.31
Deschampsia cespitosa	1.45	1.45
Festuca rubra	1.18	1.18
Holcus lanatus	2.01	1.56
Lolium multiflorum	2.00	1.34
Lolium perenne × multiflorum		
(var. sabrina)	1.44	1.10
Lolium perenne	1.30	1.30
Plantago lanceolata	1.70	1.40
Poa annua	2.70	1.74
Poa pratensis	1.26	1.26
(b) Species mainly restricted to unsown grasslands		
Agrostis canina ssp. canina	1.41	1.41
Anthoxanthum odoratum	0.94	0.94
Arrhenatherum elatius	1.30	1.30
Deschampsia flexuosa	0.81	0.81
Festuca ovina	1.00	1.00
Helictotrichon pratense	0.75	0.75
Nardus stricta	0.71	0.71
Sesleria albicans	0.75	0.75
Sieglingia decumbens	0.60	0.60

The values tabulated are the maximum (R_{max}) and average ($\bar{R}$) relative growth rates attained during the period 2–5 weeks after germination in a standardized, productive environment (g g^{-1} week^{-1}). (Note: 1 g g^{-1} week^{-1} = 1 lb lb^{-1} week^{-1}.)

Grime & Hunt, 1975). Because such experiments can be repeated wherever there are adequate facilities, data for different species or genotypes, and from different laboratories, can be directly compared. Information collected in this way not only allows the possibility of recognizing the major avenues of ecological specialization (i.e. primary strategies) in grassland plants (see pages 21–29) but is also likely to suggest specific objectives for plant breeding programmes related to amenity grassland.

Screening experiments of potential value to grassland management are those involving measurement of relative growth rates under fertile conditions (Table 2.2), studies of the capacity of established plants for vegetative spread (Plate 2.2) and investigations of plant responses to a wide range of standardized experimental treatments including various forms and intensities of defoliation and exposure to low temperatures, moisture stress, shade, nutrient deficiencies, and mineral toxicities.

Additional screening experiments are necessary in order to investigate the dormancy mechanisms and germination requirements of seeds. Considerable progress has been made in the design and interpretation of germination experiments and, as explained elsewhere (Grime, 1979), it is now possible to recognize different sets of laboratory characteristics which are predictably related to phenomena such as autumn germination, spring germination, and the tendency to develop buried seed banks.

Distillation and use of ecological information

One way in which to assemble ecological data for the purpose of grassland management is to compile biographies of the more important species. Although often lacking in quantitative data and in standardization, the 'Biological Floras' published by the *Journal of Ecology* exemplify this approach. However, it is doubtful whether information in this detailed form can be assimilated into management plans and, as pointed out in Chapter 12, the exigencies of amenity grassland management often call for extremely simple guidelines.

An alternative framework in which to deploy ecological information arises from current efforts to recognize the major types of plant strategies which have evolved in land plants and to describe the role of these strategies in vegetation processes. An explanation of the relevance to vegetation management of theories relating to plant strategies is attempted opposite in the form of a series of propositions (left) together with their practical implications (right).

ECOLOGICAL THEORIES	IMPLICATIONS FOR MANAGEMENT

(a) Definition of strategies

Although, on first inspection, terrestrial plants appear to represent an infinite variety of forms, life-histories, and physiologies, comparisons between groups of plants from contrasted habitats reveal that threats to the existence of plants (i.e. forms of natural selection) and adaptation to survive them (i.e. strategies) fall into a small number of basic types.[1]

[1]Knowledge concerning plant strategies may be more valuable than detailed taxonomic expertise for the purposes of grassland management.

Strategies may be defined as groupings of similar or analogous genetic characteristics which recur widely among species or populations and cause them to exhibit similarities in ecology.

Juvenile and mature stages in the life-cycle of a plant may be subject to different forms of natural selection or, because of differences in size and function, they may respond in different ways to the same selection force. In consequence, it is necessary, in order to understand the ecology of a plant, to examine the strategies adopted during both the established (mature) and regenerative (immature) phases of its life-cycle.[2]

[2]Information concerning the characteristics and habitat requirements of seedlings and vegetative offspring is relevant not only to the establishment of sown species but also to the management of permanent grasslands.

(b) Types of established strategies

(1) The intensity of competition between established plants reaches a maximum in the circumstances allowing the rapid development of a large biomass of plant material, i.e. where there is high productivity and minimal damage to the vegetation. Under these conditions, the species which prevail are usually those which are best equipped to capture resources and to maximize production. High competitive ability is represented, therefore, by a combination of genetic

ECOLOGICAL THEORIES

characteristics which, by maximizing production, facilitate the exclusive occupation of fertile, relatively undisturbed environments[3] (see (8)). Competitive herbs are perennials, and possess in common such features as a dense canopy of leaves, the production of which coincides with an extended period[4] when environmental conditions are conducive to high productivity. High competitive ability above ground depends upon the development of a large mass of shoot material, which itself depends upon high rates of uptake of mineral nutrients and water. Hence, although the mechanism of competition may culminate in above ground competition for space and light, the outcome may be influenced or even predetermined by earlier competition below ground.

(2) The factors which limit the plant biomass in any habitat and reduce the intensity of competition may be classified under two headings—stress and disturbance. Stress consists of the phenomena which restrict production, e.g. shortages of light, water, and mineral nutrients and suboptimal temperatures. These shortages may be an inherent characteristic of the environment, or they may be induced or intensified by the vegetation itself. The most widespread forms of plant-induced stress arise from shading and from reduction in the levels of mineral nutrients in the soil (as a result of their accumulation in the plant biomass).[5] Disturbance arises from the partial or total destruction of living or dead components of the vegetation, by the activities of herbivores, pathogens, and man (trampling, mowing, ploughing,

IMPLICATIONS FOR MANAGEMENT

[3] Reduced vegetation disturbance in productive habitats (e.g. derelict pastures and unmown road verges) encourages the expansion of large perennial grasses, tall forbs, and shrubs.

[4] In Britain, the peaks of biomass in competitive plants occur between May and August. Management designed to suppress these plants may be most effective when applied during this period.

[5] Reductions in vegetation productivity and related changes in species composition can be brought about by removal of grass clippings and plant litter and by scrub clearance (see implication [25] in this column).

ECOLOGICAL THEORIES

IMPLICATIONS FOR MANAGEMENT

etc.), and by phenomena such as wind-damage, frosting, desiccation, soil erosion, and fire.

(3) The effects of both stress and disturbance change according to their severity. At low intensities, both function as modifiers of competition,[6] whereas at high intensities each is capable of exercising a dominant and direct impact upon species-composition and vegetation structure.

This impact involves the elimination or debilitation[7] of species of high competitive ability, and the selection of species which are of lower competitive ability but are capable of surviving under the prevailing forms of stress or disturbance.

(4) No plants are capable of surviving severe stress *and* continuous disturbance. This is because, in highly disturbed habitats, the effect of stress is to prevent a sufficiently rapid recovery or re-establishment of the vegetation.[8]

(5) Stress and disturbance exercise different forms of natural selection, and at severe intensities each has evoked a distinct strategy in herbaceous plants.

Stress-tolerant plants exhibit a range of features which are adaptations to continuously unproductive conditions. These features include morphological reductions, inherently slow rates of growth, an evergreen habit, long-lived organs, sequestration and slow turnover of carbon, mineral nutrients, and water, low phenotypic plasticity, infrequent flowering, the presence of mechanisms which allow the plant to capture resources during temporarily favourable conditions, and low palatability to unspecialized herbivores.[9]

The most consistent feature of species

[6]In productive grassland the effect of a low intensity of grazing or mowing is to cause tall competitors (e.g. *Arrhenatherum elatius*) to be displaced by short competitors (e.g. *Agrostis tenuis*) which produce a dense leaf canopy close to the ground surface.

[7]Grasslands frequently contain stunted specimens of potentially productive species. These plants may remain inconspicuous until increases in soil fertility or relaxation of grazing or mowing regimes allow them to expand in size and vigour.

[8]Where environments are subject to high intensities of both stress and disturbance (e.g., paths on forest floors or mountain tops), efforts to maintain vegetation cover are unlikely to be successful. In recent years much effort ·has been wasted in efforts to revegetate such 'impossible habitats'. However, where stress is due to mineral nutrient deficiency, the carrying capacity may be increased by application of fertilizers, and maintenance of more productive vegetation.

[9]Because of their comparatively slow growth rates, low seed

ECOLOGICAL THEORIES	IMPLICATIONS FOR MANAGEMENT

adapted to persistently and severely disturbed habitats is the tendency for the life-cycle to be that of the ephemeral, a specialization clearly adapted to exploit environments intermittently favourable for rapid plant growth. A related characteristic of many ruderals is the capacity for high rates of dry matter production, a feature which appears to facilitate rapid completion of the life-cycle and maximizes seed production.[10]

(6) It is suggested, therefore, that in herbaceous plants there are three primary strategies, each of which may be identified by reference to a number of characteristics, including morphological

production, and reduced palatability, grasses of unproductive habitats are unsuitable for intensive forms of agriculture. In consequence they are rarely available from seed merchants and many excellent opportunities to employ these species in landscape reclamation and revegetation have been ignored. [10]Where repeated severe damage to turf is unavoidable (paths, sportsfields, recreation areas) ephemeral grasses such as *Poa annua* (annual poa) make a valuable contribution to the maintenance of vegetation cover.

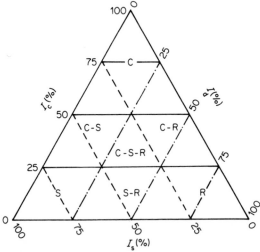

Figure 2.4　Model describing the various equilibria between competition, stress, and disturbance in vegetation and the location of primary and secondary strategies. I_c, relative importance of competition (——); I_s, relative importance of stress (- - -); I_d, relative importance of disturbance (- · - · -). A key to the symbols for the strategies is included in the text (from Grime, 1974)

ECOLOGICAL THEORIES	IMPLICATIONS FOR MANAGEMENT

features, resource allocation, phenology, and response to stress. The competitive strategy prevails in productive, relatively undisturbed vegetation, whereas the stress-tolerant strategy is associated with continuously unproductive conditions, and the ruderal strategy is characteristic of severely disturbed but potentially productive habitats. These three strategies are, of course, extremes. The genotypes of the majority of plants appear to represent compromises between the conflicting selection pressures associated with particular equilibria between competition, stress and disturbance.[11] A simple model describing the range of equilibria is illustrated in Figure 2.4. At their respective corners of the triangle, competitors, stress-tolerators, and ruderals become the exclusive constituents of the vegetation and the remaining zones of the model correspond to conditions favourable to four types of intermediate or secondary strategy consisting of:

(a) competitive-ruderals (C–R), adapted to circumstances in which there is a low impact of stress and competition is restricted to a moderate intensity by disturbance;[12]

(b) stress-tolerant ruderals (S–R), adapted to lightly-disturbed, unproductive habitats;[13]

(c) stress-tolerant competitors (C–S), adapted to relatively undisturbed conditions experiencing moderate intensities of stress;[14]

(d) 'C-S-R strategists', adapted to habitats in which the level of competition is restricted by

[11]Adjustments of the *intensities* of stress and disturbance allow manipulation of the structure and productivity of vegetation. Fine control of species composition depends upon the *kinds* of stress and disturbance operating in the habitat and their periodicity.

[12]The tall biennial umbellifers, *Anthriscus sylvestris* (cow parsley) and *Heracleum sphondylium* (hogweed) which contribute to the visual attractiveness of roadsides and meadows often depend for their persistence upon occasional mowing which restricts the vigour of larger perennial species.

[13]Survival of the small, slow-growing annuals and biennials which often occur in large numbers in some unproductive grasslands depends upon local disturbance of the turf by factors such as drought, hoofmarks, mole-hills, ant-hills, rabbit-scrapes, and worm-casts.

[14]When unproductive grasslands are allowed to become derelict there is a tendency for them to become overgrown by large, relatively slow-growing grasses such as *Brachypodium pinnatum* (tor grass), *Festuca arundinacea* (tall fescue), and robust varieties of *Festuca rubra*.

ECOLOGICAL THEORIES

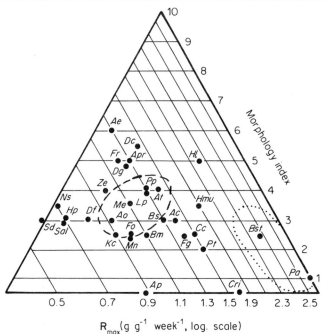

$$R_{max}(g\ g^{-1}\ week^{-1},\ log.\ scale)$$

Figure 2.5   A triangular ordination of some common grasses of contrasted ecology. The morphology index (M) was calculated from the formula $M = (a + b + c)/2$, where a, estimated maximum height of leaf canopy (1, <120 mm; 2, 120–250 mm; 3, 250–370 mm; 4, 370–500 mm; 5, 500–620 mm; 6, 620–750 mm; 7, 750–870 mm; 8, 870–1000 mm; 9, 1000–1120 mm; 10, >1120 mm); b, lateral spread (0, small therophytes; 1, robust therophytes; 2, perennials with compact unbranched rhizome or forming small (<100 mm diameter) tussock; 3, perennials with rhizomatous system or tussock attaining diameter 100–250 mm; 4, perennials attaining diameter 260–1000 mm; 5, perennials attaining diameter >1000 mm); c, estimated maximum accumulation of persistent litter (0, none; 1, thin, discontinuous cover; 2, thin, continuous cover; 3, up to 10 mm in depth; 4, up to 50 mm in depth; 5, >50 mm depth). (Note 1 mm = 0.039 in.) Key to species: Ac, *Agrostis canina* ssp. *canina*; Ae, *Arrhenatherum elatius*; Ao, *Anthoxanthum odoratum*; Ap, *Aira praecox*; Apr, *Alopecurus pratensis*; At, *Agrostis tenuis*; Bm, *Briza media*; Bs, *Brachypodium sylvaticum*; Bst, *Bromus sterilis*; Cc, *Cynosurus cristatus*; Cri, *Catapodium rigidum*; Dc, *Deschampsia cespitosa*; Df, *Deschampsia flexuosa*; Dg, *Dactylis glomerata*; Fg, *Festuca gigantea*; Fo, *Festuca ovina*; Fr, *Festuca rubra*; Hl, *Holcus lanatus*; Hmu, *Hordeum murinum*; Hp, *Helictotrichon pratense*; Kc, *Koeleria cristata*; Lp, *Lolium perenne*; Me, *Milium effusum*; Mn, *Melica nutans*; Ns, *Nardus stricta*; Pa, *Poa annua*; Pp, *Poa pratensis*; Pt, *Poa trivialis*; Sal, *Sesleria albicans*; Sd, *Sieglingia decumbens*; Ze, *Zerna erecta*. The ordinations refer to single populations sampled in the vicinity of Sheffield. As a reminder of the extent to which genetic variation must be taken into account lines have been drawn indicating the hypothetical strategic range of two genetically variable grasses, *Agrostis tenuis* (- - -) and *Poa annua* (· · ·)

ECOLOGICAL THEORIES

IMPLICATIONS FOR MANAGEMENT

moderate intensities of both stress and disturbance.[15]

(7) The triangular model provides a basis upon which to attempt to classify plants with respect to their established strategies and data such as those in Figure 2.5 suggest that ordination can be based upon plant morphology and potential relative growth-rate. The positions ascribed to species in Figure 2.5 refer only to the populations investigated. On the basis of field observations and population studies, it may be predicted as indicated by the broken lines in Figure 2.5 that, in certain species, genetic variation is sufficient to enlarge considerably both the strategic and ecological range.[16]

(c) Dominance

(8) Dominance in vegetation is the process by which the resources in certain habitats are monopolized by one species or by a small number of species. Dominance arises from a positive feedback between (a) the mechanisms whereby the dominant plants achieve a size larger than that of their neighbours and (b) the deleterious effect which large plants may exert upon the fitness of smaller neighbours. The mechanism of (a) varies according to which strategy is favoured by the habitat conditions. In contrast, (b) does not vary substantially according to habitat or strategy and consists principally of various forms of plant-induced stress such as those due to shading, deposition of leaf litter, release of toxins, and depletion of the levels of mineral nutrients and water in the soil.

Because of the variable nature of (a) different types of dominance may be

[15]The British Flora includes a large number of small tussock grasses, small creeping plants and tap-rooted forbs. These perennial plants are most abundant in unproductive calcareous pastures and tend to disappear when conditions encourage the expansion of larger herbs.

[16]Where species of wide ecological amplitude such as *Agrostis tenuis* and *Festuca rubra* are employed in landscape reclamation selection of appropriate genotypes may be of critical importance.

ECOLOGICAL THEORIES	IMPLICATIONS FOR MANAGEMENT

recognized. Competitive dominants (e.g. *Arrheratherum elatius, Urtica dioica* (stinging nettle), achieve large stature in productive, undisturbed habitats through exceptionally high rates of resource capture and growth. Stress-tolerant dominants (e.g. many evergreen dwarf shrubs), depend upon the ability to sustain slow rates of growth under limiting conditions over long periods of time. Ruderal dominance such as that exercised by *Lolium multiflorum* (Italian ryegrass) in leys is characteristic of productive habitats subject to seasonally predictable disturbance and usually arises from the synchronous germination of a dense population of seeds followed by rapid development of a dense population of short-lived plants of comparable age and maturity.

(d) Regenerative strategies
(9) The impact of a dominant plant may be exerted upon neighbours at various stages of their life-cycles. Mineral nutrient depletion and shading, together with the physical and chemical effects of litter may reduce the seed output of established plants and cause premature mortalities. The most profound effects of dominance, however, are exerted upon juvenile plants. Because of their relatively small size, the seedlings and vegetative offspring of plants often differ very substantially from their parents with respect to their ability to compete for resources and to tolerate or evade stress conditions. Particularly in productive, relatively undisturbed vegetation, the most potent threats to the survival of seedlings and vegetative offspring are due to the variety of stresses which arise from close proximity to established plants.[17]

[17]Where there is a continuous cover of herbaceous vegetation, seedling establishment by trees and shrubs may be severely restricted. For this reason, foresters have found it advisable, when planting into grassland, to check the growth of established herbs by spot applications of herbicide.

ECOLOGICAL THEORIES

IMPLICATIONS FOR MANAGEMENT

In many circumstances, successful regeneration depends upon exploitation of local conditions in which the cover of established plants and litter has been disturbed.[18] Regenerative strategies have evolved primarily through the development of mechanisms whereby the juvenile stages in life-histories tolerate or evade the potentially dominating effects of established plants. Differences in the intensity, periodicity, and spatial distribution of vegetation disturbance have provided the major selective forces in the differentiation of regenerative strategies.[19] On this basis, types of regenerative strategy (described in detail by Grime, 1979) may be classified as follows:

Regenerative strategy	Habitat conditions to which strategy appears to be adapted
1. Vegetative expansion by persistent stolons, rhizomes or suckers.	Productive or unproductive habitats subject to low intensities of disturbance.
2. Seasonal regeneration[20] (from seed or vegetative propagules) in vegetation gaps.	Habitats subjected to seasonally predictable disturbance by climate or biotic factors.
3. Regeneration involving a bank of persistent, (usually buried) seeds.[21]	Habitats subjected to temporally unpredictable disturbance.
4. Regeneration involving numerous widely-dispersed seeds or spores.[22]	Habitats subjected to spatially unpredictable disturbance.
5. Regeneration involving a bank of persistent seedlings and immature plants.	Unproductive habitats subjected to low intensities of disturbance.

[18]Where the objective of turf management is to maintain a uniform monoculture, e.g. lawns, bowling greens, cricket squares, it is desirable to restrict the frequency of vegetation gaps to a minimum and to encourage the growth of grasses, e.g. *Festuca rubra*, *Agrostis tenuis*, which produce a dense, 'rapidly-repaired' leaf canopy close to the ground surface.

[19]Where the objective of turf management is to maintain a species-rich plant community, e.g. picnic areas, road-verges, parkland, nature reserves, it may be helpful to 'disturb' the established vegetation by occasional grazing, mowing, or harrowing in order to create gaps in which regeneration of the component species can take place. Variation in the extent, type, and timing of this disturbance allows manipulation of species composition (see Chapter 11).

[20]Seeds of sown grasses such as *Lolium perenne*, *L. multiflorum*, *Dactylis glomerata* (cock's foot), *Festuca rubra*, and *Phleum pratense* germinate soon after they are shed. Because these species do not accumulate reservoirs of seeds in the soil they are poorly-adapted to regenerate from seed in turf subjected to continuous forms of disturbance.

[21]Native grasses which invade sown swards e.g. *Poa annua*, *P.*

ECOLOGICAL THEORIES

(10) Although many plants have only one regenerative strategy,[23] it is not unusual for the same plant to exhibit two or more regenerative strategies. Such multiple regeneration may be expected to enlarge the range of conditions in which regeneration can occur and is characteristic of some of the most widely successful plant species.[24]

(e) Vegetation dynamics
(11) Information concerning established and regenerative strategies provides a basis for understanding the sequence and rate of successional and cyclical changes in vegetation and for predicting vegetation responses to changes in management.

Following the clearance of vegetation from a productive environment, the usual sequence of recolonization is: (1) ruderals → competitors, (2) competitors → stress tolerators. Step (1) in this sequence is due to competitive exclusion whilst step (2) is the result of resource depletion arising from the development of a large plant biomass. The rate of vegetation change in this succession is initially rapid but falls progressively with the incursion of slow-growing, long-lived plants and declining opportunities for regeneration. Succession in unproductive environments proceeds more slowly and the role of competitors is condensed or occluded.[25]

(12) In landscapes subject to occasional and spatially unpredictable vegetation clearance, ruderal and competitive species lead a fugitive existence and the most effective regenerative strategy is that involving the

IMPLICATIONS FOR MANAGEMENT

trivialis (rough-stalked meadow-grass), *Agrostis stolonifera* (fiorin), *A. tenuis*, *Holcus lanatus*, and *Deschampsia cespitosa* (tufted hair-grass), are all capable of developing banks of persistent buried seeds. Germination and seedling establishment in these species is encouraged by soil disturbance and exposure of the turf to intense wear.

[22]In parts of the landscape where major vegetation disturbance is limited to infrequent events such as tree felling, road construction, pipe laying, and accidental fires, species such as *Chamaenerion angustifolium* (rose-bay willow-herb) and *Senecio squalidus* (Oxford ragwort) which produce numerous widely-dispersed seeds will play an important role in vegetation recolonization.

[23]Some rare plants, including many orchids, appear to possess only one method of regeneration. In order to conserve these plants it is necessary to identify the regenerative strategy and to provide conditions which allow its success.

[24]The widespread occurrence of grasses such as *Holcus lanatus* and *Agrostis tenuis* (see Appendix 2.1(a)) and their persistence under fluctuating management conditions may be due in part to the variety of mechanisms by which these species regenerate.

ECOLOGICAL THEORIES	IMPLICATIONS FOR MANAGEMENT

production of numerous widely dispersed seeds or spores.[22]

Where clearance occurs relatively frequently in the same place the process of vegetation-change is cyclical rather than successional. The effect of frequent clearance is not merely to arrest succession but to bring into prominence those among the ruderal and competitive species which regenerate by means of persistent seed banks.[21]

[25]Where the objective of landscape management or reclamation is to minimize costs it may be advantageous *either* to create an unproductive grassland environment which will require infrequent mowing and scrub clearance *or* to encourage, by tree planting, rapid succession to a relatively stable woodland ecosystem.

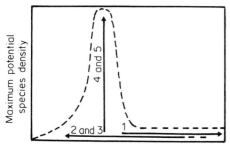

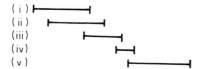

Figure 2.6 A model summarizing the impact of five processes upon the species density in vegetation: 1, dominance; 2, stress; 3, disturbance; 4, niche-differentiation; 5, ingress of suitable species or genotypes. The horizontal lines describe the range of contingencies encompassed by a number of familiar vegetation types: (i) paths, (ii) grazed rock outcrops with discontinuous soil cover, (iii) infertile pastures, (iv) fertilized pastures, (v) derelict fertile pastures (from Grime, 1979)

ECOLOGICAL THEORIES

IMPLICATIONS FOR MANAGEMENT

(f) Control of species density in herbaceous vegetation

(13) As described under (c), where conditions allow the development of a large, relatively undisturbed biomass, there is a tendency for the more robust species to dominate the vegetation and to suppress the growth and regeneration of other plants. Where this process is allowed to continue unchecked vegetation may approach a state of monoculture. It follows that the maintenance of vegetation of high species density (i.e. >20 species per square metre) depends upon conditions in which stress and/or disturbance limit the vigour of potential dominants. However, under extremes of stress and/or disturbance, not only are the dominants eliminated, but an environment is created in which few species can survive.

These relationships may be summarized in the form of the 'hump-backed' model (Figure 2.6) in which the potential species density is plotted against the annual maximum in standing crop plus litter. This model is tentative particularly with regard to the exact location of the 'corridor' of potentially high species density which in temperate herbaceous vegetation appears to extend between 350 and 750 g m^{-2} (0.6–1.4 lb yd^{-2}).[26]

(14) Two major factors which influence the actual species densities attained in particular 'corridor environments' may be identified. The first is the degree of niche-differentiation, i.e. the extent to which spatial and temporal variation in stress and disturbance permit co-existence between species with complementary types of

[26]In circumstances where a uniform species-poor sward is required it is usually necessary to provide conditions in which the peak biomass of shoots plus litter exceeds 750 g m^{-2} (1.4 lb yd^{-2}) (see also implication[18]).

Where a species-rich turf is desirable one objective of management should be to maintain the seasonal peak in biomass of shoots plus litter within the range of approximately 350–750 g m^{-2} (0.6–1.4 lb yd^{-2}). In order to encourage diversity further, other procedures may be adopted (see implications[19],[27], and[28]).

ECOLOGICAL THEORIES

IMPLICATIONS FOR MANAGEMENT

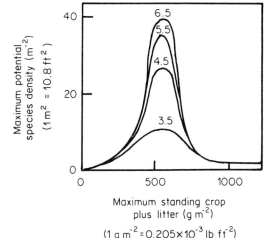

Figure 2.7 A diagram summarizing the relationship between surface soil pH (values given on the curves), seasonal maximum biomass in standing crop plus litter and maximum potential species density in British herbaceous vegetation (from Grime, 1979)

[27]Small-scale variation in soil features such as depth, texture, and acidity often allows plants of different types to grow together. However, soil variation will not lead to the development of species-rich vegetation if the intensity of grazing or mowing is insufficient to prevent litter accumulation and lateral projection of the shoots by the larger plants rooted in pockets of more fertile soil.

[28]Where species-rich vegetation is to be developed in a species-poor landscape, rates of natural colonization may be too slow. Particularly in species with intermittent seed production and ineffective mechanisms of dispersal, transplanting and deliberate sowing of seeds may be necessary.

[29]On very acidic soils, species density will remain low regardless of the management regime.

growth and regeneration.[27] The second is the rate of ingress of species from the surrounding landscape. It is clear that in vegetation of recent origin species densities often remain low because of the small reservoir of suitable species[28] in the immediate vicinity of the site. 'Reservoir effects' operating on a larger scale appear to limit species density in vegetation established on acidic soils.[29] The relationships between soil pH, maximum standing crop plus litter, and maximum potential species density in Britain are summarized in Figure 2.7.

Conclusions

Although information concerning the distribution, life-histories, phenology, reproductive biology, and physiology of herbaceous plants is relevant to the management of amenity grassland, many of these data are too detailed and specific to be applied directly. An alternative approach is to use the information to classify species, cultivars, and populations with respect to their ecological strategies. Recognition of the major types of strategies provides an insight into the processes controlling the structure, species composition, and dynamics of vegetation and this, in turn, suggests a number of guidelines for management.

References

Al-Mufti, M. M., Sydes, C. L., Furness, S. B., Grime, J. P. & Band, S. R. (1977). 'A quantitative analysis of shoot phenology and dominance in herbaceous vegetation', *Journal of Ecology*, **65**, 759–91.

Barrett, G. W. (1968). 'The effects of an acute insecticide stress on a semi-enclosed grassland ecosystem', *Ecology*, **49**, 1019–35.

Brenchley, W. E. & Warington, K. (1930). 'The weed seed population of arable soil. 1. Numerical estimation of viable seeds and observations on their natural dormancy', *Journal of Ecology*, **18**, 235–72.

Champness, S. S. & Morris, K. (1948). 'The population of buried viable seeds in relation to contrasting pasture and soil types', *Journal of Ecology*, **36**, 149–73.

Chippendale, H. G. & Milton, W. E. J. (1934). 'On the viable seeds present in the soil beneath pastures', *Journal of Ecology*, **22**, 508–31.

Getz, L. L. (1960). 'Standing crop of herbaceous vegetation in southern Michigan', *Ecology*, **41**, 393–5.

Golley, F. B. (1960). 'Energy dynamics of a food chain of an old-field community', *Ecological Monographs*, **30**, 187–206.

Golley, F. B. (1965). 'Structure and function of an old-field broomsedge community', *Ecological Monographs*, **35**, 113–37.

Grime, J. P. (1974). 'Vegetation classification by reference to strategies', *Nature, London*, **250**, 26–31.

Grime, J. P. (1979). *Plant Strategies and Vegetation Processes*, John Wiley, London.

Grime, J. P. & Hunt, R. (1975). 'Relative growth rate: its range and adaptive significance in a local flora', *Journal of Ecology*, **63**, 383–422.

Grime, J. P. & Lloyd, P. S. (1973). *An Ecological Atlas of Grassland Plants*, Edward Arnold, London.

King, T. J. (1976). 'The viable seed content of ant-hill and pasture soil', *New Phytologist*, **77**, 143–7.

Mahmoud, A. (1973). 'A laboratory approach to ecological studies of the grasses *Arrhenatherum elatius* (L.) Beauv. *ex* J. and C. Presl, *Agrostis tenuis* Sibth. and *Festuca ovina* L.', PhD thesis, University of Sheffield.

Mehinick, E. F. (1967). 'Structure, stability and energy flow in plants and arthropods in a *Sericea lesedza* stand', *Ecological Monographs*, **37**, 255–72.

Mellinger, M. V. & McNaughton, S. J. (1975). 'Structure and function of successional vascular plant communities in Central New York', *Ecological Monographs*, **45**, 161–82.

Milton, W. E. J. (1939). 'The occurrence of buried viable seeds in soils at different elevations and on a salt marsh', *Journal of Ecology*, **27**, 149–59.

Precsenyi, I. (1969). 'Analysis of the primary production (phytobiomass) in an *Artemisio-Festucetum pseudovinae*. *Acta biologica hungarica*, **15**, 309–25.

Shure, D. J. (1971). 'Insecticide effects on early succession in an old-field ecosystem', *Ecology*, **52**, 271–9.

Sydes, C. L. (1979). 'An investigation of competition and coexistence in various types of herbaceous vegetation', Ph.D. thesis, University of Sheffield.

Thompson, K. & Grime, J. P. (1979). 'Seasonal variation in the seed banks of herbaceous species in ten contrasting habitats', *Journal of Ecology*, **67** (in press).

Wesson, G. & Wareing, P. F. (1969). 'The role of light in the germination of naturally occurring populations of buried weed seeds', *Journal of Experimental Botany*, **20**, 402–13.

Williamson, P. (1976). 'Above-ground primary production of chalk grassland allowing for leaf death', *Journal of Ecology*, **64**, 1059–75.

Appendix 2.1
This section gives characteristics of the field ecology of some common grassland species. Data were drawn from surveys performed by the Unit of Comparative Plant Ecology in North Derbyshire, Nottinghamshire, and South Yorkshire over the period 1965–73.

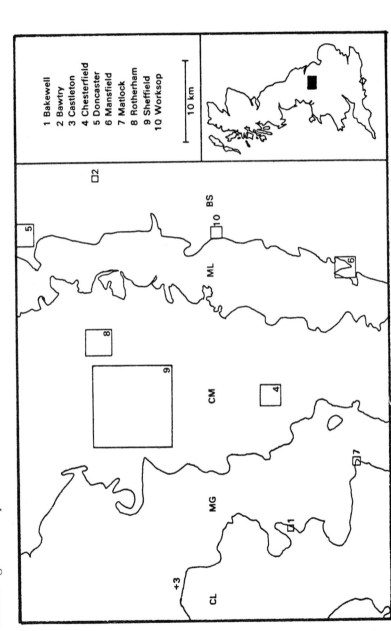

1 Bakewell
2 Bawtry
3 Castleton
4 Chesterfield
5 Doncaster
6 Mansfield
7 Matlock
8 Rotherham
9 Sheffield
10 Worksop

10 km

The UCPE survey area. The approximate extent of urban development is shown by numbered squares. Geological substrata are CL, Carboniferous Limestone; MG, Millstone Grit; CM, Coal Measures; ML, Magnesian

(a) *Habitat ranges*

In the following six figures each small box represents a habitat or group of habitats.

Numbers indicate per cent of samples from the habitat which were found to contain the species.

Numbers in bold type indicate that the species is found in at least 25 per cent of samples.

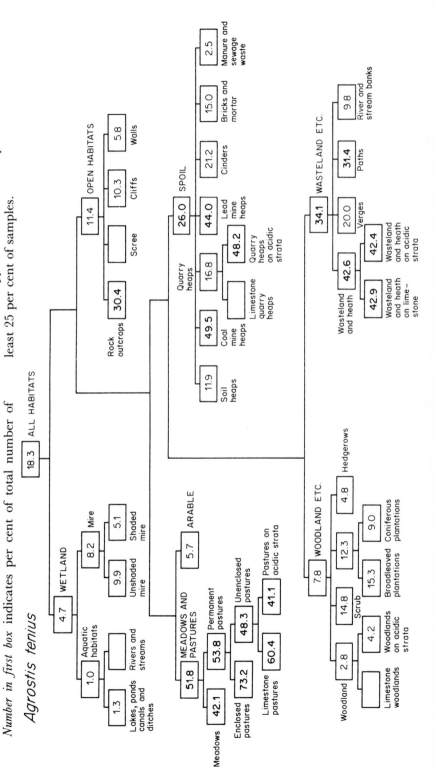

Agrostis tenuis

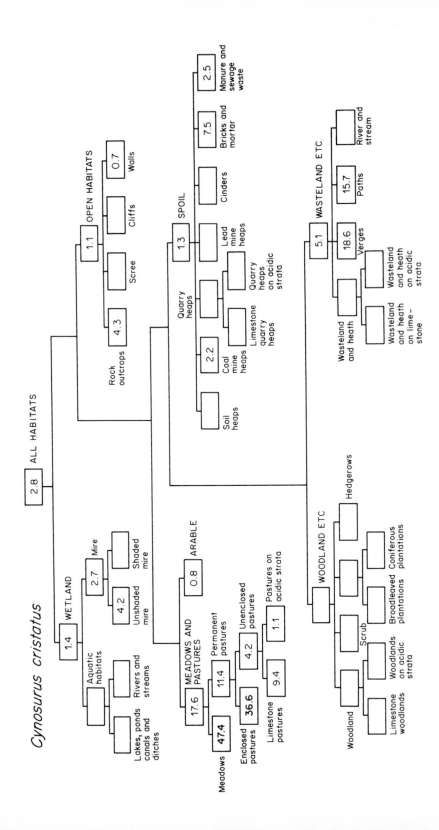

Cynosurus cristatus

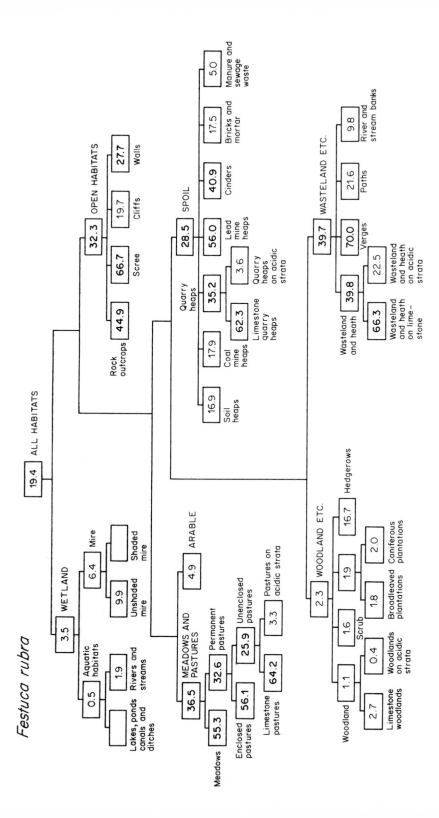

Festuca rubra

Holcus lanatus

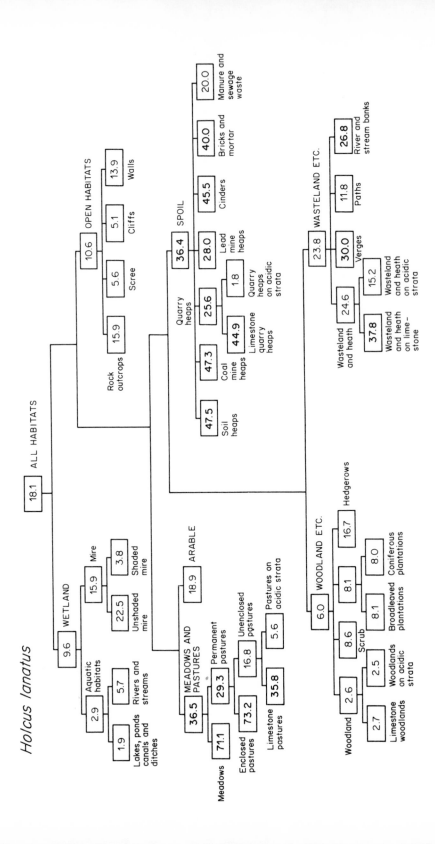

Lolium perenne

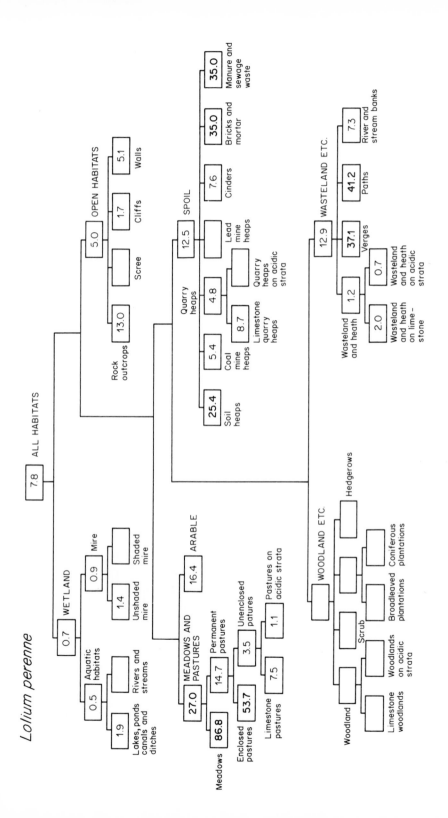

Phleum pratense

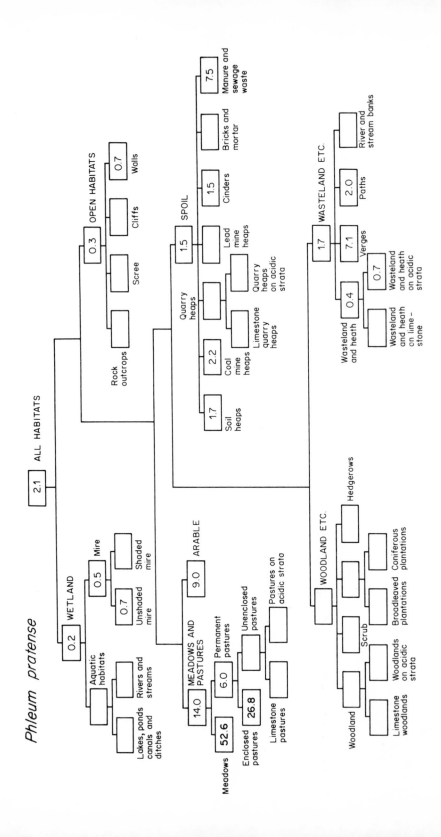

Each quadrant of 1 m² (1.2 yd²) area was subdivided into a hundred 100 mm × 100 mm (3.9 in × 3.9 in) subsections and for each species the number of subsections containing rooted specimens was counted. By examining the total number of quadrats in which a species occurs, it is possible to determine the type of contribution which it makes to herbaceous vegetation. It is clear, for example, that *Festuca rubra* often occurs as a minor component of the vegetation but can also form extensive patches. In contrast *Senecio jacobaea* is almost always represented by isolated individuals.

	Frequency classes									
	1–10	11–20	21–30	31–40	41–50	51–60	61–70	71–80	81–90	91–100
(1) Species of intensively managed grasslands										
Agropyron repens	49.4	14.6	9.1	5.9	3.2	5.5	3.6	2.0	2.4	4.3
Agrostis stolonifera	45.4	15.7	7.5	6.9	5.2	4.6	2.6	3.4	3.4	5.2
Agrostis tenuis	39.2	12.9	4.4	4.0	7.6	4.2	4.4	3.4	6.2	13.9
Anthoxanthum odoratum	49.2	18.6	10.9	6.6	6.6	3.3	1.6	1.1	1.6	0.5
Cynosurus cristatus	48.1	16.9	3.9	6.5	5.2	3.9	1.3	3.9	6.5	3.9
Dactylis glomerata	61.5	18.7	8.6	4.5	3.7	0.8	1.0	0.8	0.2	0.2
Deschampsia cespitosa	58.7	14.5	9.9	7.6	2.9	1.2	1.7	0.6	2.3	0.6
Festuca rubra	29.3	9.4	7.5	5.8	6.0	4.9	4.7	5.6	6.0	20.8
Holcus lanatus	53.9	9.5	8.0	6.4	3.2	3.4	3.4	3.0	3.4	5.6
Lolium perenne	45.5	14.6	8.5	3.8	2.8	3.3	3.8	3.8	5.2	8.9
Phleum pratense	51.7	17.2	8.6	10.3	5.2	3.4	3.4	—	—	—
Plantago lanceolata	57.8	14.1	9.9	5.7	1.5	3.0	2.7	0.4	2.3	2.7
Poa annua	46.6	14.0	8.7	7.8	5.4	3.9	2.4	3.6	2.1	5.7

| | Frequency classes | | | | | | | | | |
	1–10	11–20	21–30	31–40	41–50	51–60	61–70	71–80	81–90	91–100
Poa pratensis	43.3	13.8	9.9	4.8	4.6	5.3	4.8	4.1	3.6	5.6
Poa trivialis	48.6	13.2	5.8	5.5	6.0	3.3	3.3	2.3	3.5	8.6
Ranunculus repens	57.3	13.3	6.2	6.2	1.3	4.9	4.4	2.2	0.9	3.1
Rumex obtusifolius	86.4	8.5	1.7	0.8	0.8	—	0.8	0.8	—	—
Senecio jacobaea	92.0	5.2	1.7	—	—	—	1.1	—	—	—
Stellaria media	65.3	11.0	11.6	2.3	1.7	1.7	2.3	1.2	0.6	2.3
Trifolium repens	47.2	12.8	6.4	4.2	4.5	3.8	4.5	4.5	4.2	7.9
(2) Species of less intensively managed grasslands										
Agrostis canina†	36.4	15.2	8.1	6.1	3.0	2.0	5.1	2.0	10.1	12.1
Arrhenatherum elatius	51.3	13.4	9.0	4.9	5.7	4.4	3.9	3.9	1.5	2.1
Deschampsia flexuosa	18.7	4.8	5.7	3.4	5.0	5.9	5.2	6.3	41.5	—
Festuca ovina	24.3	10.7	7.4	4.2	4.2	4.9	5.8	8.7	7.4	22.3
Helictotrichon pratense	54.5	16.4	12.7	9.1	5.5	—	1.8	—	—	—
Nardus stricta	29.5	17.0	19.3	6.8	4.5	6.8	8.0	4.5	2.3	1.1

†Includes *A. canina* ssp. *canina* and *A. canina* ssp. *montana*.

the species in each category.

	Altitude (m)†				
	<100	100–199	200–299	300–399	400+
(1) Species of intensively managed grasslands					
Agropyron repens	12.1	11.3	5.1	6.0	—
Agrostis stolonifera	24.2	22.4	8.7	12.1	—
Agrostis tenuis	12.9	15.6	23.8	26.4	28.9
Anthoxanthum odoratum	1.3	4.6	14.0	8.6	24.4
Cynosurus cristatus	1.5	3.4	3.5	3.2	2.2
Dactylis glomerata	18.5	20.6	16.0	15.2	2.2
Deschampsia cespitosa	5.2	7.9	5.2	6.6	6.7
Festuca rubra	15.2	17.7	24.7	24.7	13.3
Holcus lanatus	19.1	20.0	15.8	15.5	15.6
Lolium perenne	8.1	10.0	6.4	4.9	—
Phleum pratense	0.7	3.1	2.0	3.4	—
Plantago lanceolata	9.1	9.8	10.3	10.1	—
Poa annua	14.7	14.5	8.4	8.3	4.4
Poa pratensis	12.6	15.6	16.4	17.8	8.9
Poa trivialis	20.9	30.9	18.1	11.8	8.9
Ranunculus repens	8.3	10.5	6.7	5.7	2.2
Rumex obtusifolius	5.8	4.4	2.9	3.4	—
Senecio jacobaea	5.7	3.7	11.5	5.5	—
Stellaria media	8.0	7.8	3.8	4.0	—
Trifolium repens	8.1	9.9	10.7	11.5	4.4
(2) Species of less intensively managed grasslands					
Agrostis canina (2 ssp.)	1.8	1.2	6.7	5.2	26.7
Arrhenatherum elatius	12.5	11.5	22.2	11.2	—
Deschampsia flexuosa	8.8	11.8	28.1	48.6	64.4
Festuca ovina	5.1	2.2	23.5	22.4	35.6
Helictotrichon pratense	0.1	1.2	5.7	2.0	—
Nardus stricta	0.6	0.5	2.6	13.2	35.6

Note: 1 m = 3.28 ft.

(d) Distribution in relation to slope

All samples in the survey have been classified into ten groups according to the angle of slope. The values tabulated refer to the percentage of the samples in each category in which the frequency of the species exceeds 20 per cent. Slope categories greater than 50° mainly correspond to rock outcrops, cliffs, walls and embankments.

	Slope categories									
	0–9	10–19	20–29	30–39	40–49	50–59	60–69	70–79	80–89	90+
(1) Species of intensively managed grasslands										
Agropyron repens	4.2	4.7	2.3	1.7	2.1	—	—	—	—	—
Agrostis stolonifera	11.8	4.4	1.6	2.1	2.1	—	—	—	1.2	—
Agrostis tenuis	8.5	11.9	14.2	9.1	9.6	4.5	—	—	—	—
Anthoxanthum odoratum	1.4	2.6	5.2	4.5	4.3	—	—	—	—	—
Cynosurus cristatus	1.5	0.9	1.0	—	—	—	—	—	—	—
Dactylis glomerata	4.4	2.3	2.3	6.3	5.3	9.1	—	—	—	—
Deschampsia cespitosa	2.2	1.6	2.9	1.0	—	—	—	—	—	—
Festuca rubra	9.8	11.2	15.9	19.9	27.7	13.6	8.7	5.8	7.2	—
Holcus lanatus	7.3	7.7	5.8	7.0	12.8	—	—	—	—	—
Lolium perenne	4.9	2.3	1.9	1.0	—	—	—	—	—	—
Phleum pratense	1.3	0.2	0.3	—	—	—	—	—	—	—
Plantago lanceolata	2.1	2.8	3.9	7.3	3.2	—	4.3	—	—	—
Poa annua	8.4	3.3	1.0	1.0	—	—	—	—	—	—
Poa pratensis	6.8	7.0	7.4	6.3	8.5	9.1	4.3	1.4	—	2.3
Poa trivialis	11.8	11.5	3.6	2.4	5.3	—	4.3	4.3	—	—

Ranunculus									
repens	3.7	1.9	0.6	0.3	2.1	4.5	—	—	—	—
Rumex									
obtusifolius	0.4	0.2	—	—	—	—	—	—	—	—
Senecio jacobaea	0.1	0.5	—	0.7	—	—	—	—	—	—
Stellaria media	2.6	0.2	0.3	1.4	—	4.5	—	—	—	—
Trifolium repens	6.2	2.3	3.2	1.0	1.1	—	—	—	—	—

(2) Species of less intensively managed grasslands

Agrostis canina									
(2 ssp.)	1.7	3.0	2.9	0.7	2.1	—	—	—	1.2	—
Arrhenatherum									
elatius	2.5	3.5	10.4	14.3	14.9	9.1	—	1.4	—	—
Deschampsia									
flexuosa	10.3	20.6	25.9	25.2	31.9	31.8	8.7	1.4	2.4	2.3
Festuca ovina	3.7	9.4	13.9	15.7	16.0	13.6	13.0	4.3	3.6	—
Helictotrichon									
pratense	—	0.2	1.9	2.8	1.1	—	—	—	—	—
Nardus stricta	1.4	3.0	1.3	2.1	2.1	4.5	—	—	1.2	—

(e) Distribution in relation to aspect

Under 'present' the numbers tabulated refer to the percentage of the samples on north-facing (315–45°) and south-facing (135–225°) slopes which contained the species.

Under 'abundant' the numbers refer to the percentage of occurrences in which the frequency within the quadrat exceeded 19 per cent.

	Present		Abundant	
	N-facing	*S-facing*	*N-facing*	*S-facing*
(1) Species of intensively managed grasslands				
Agropyron repens	8.7	5.8	40.9	38.5
Agrostis stolonifera	9.4	13.9	29.2	29.0
Agrostis tenuis	20.1	29.1	62.7	42.2
Anthoxanthum odoratum	15.4	6.3	48.7	35.7
Cynosurus cristatus	1.6	1.8	50.0	50.0
Dactylis glomerata	24.8	33.2	14.3	18.9
Deschampsia cespitosa	4.7	2.7	16.7	16.7

Festuca rubra	41.3	30.9	62.9	60.0
Holcus lanatus	21.7	23.3	29.1	36.5
Lolium perenne	7.5	10.8	36.8	20.8
Phleum pratense	1.6	1.8	0.0	25.0
Plantago lanceolata	14.6	22.0	18.9	32.7
Poa annua	8.7	8.5	13.6	21.1
Poa pratensis	21.7	26.0	36.4	37.9
Poa trivialis	18.9	17.0	27.1	31.6
Ranunculus repens	4.3	6.7	27.3	26.7
Rumex obtusifolius	5.5	4.0	0.0	0.0
Senecio jacobaea	13.4	12.1	2.9	0.0
Stellaria media	3.9	4.9	20.0	27.3
Trifolium repens	10.6	9.0	37.0	15.0
(2) Species of less intensively managed grasslands				
Agrostis canina (2 ssp.)	3.5	3.1	55.6	57.1
Arrhenatherum elatius	28.3	24.2	37.5	40.7
Deschampsia flexuosa	31.1	24.7	87.3	80.0
Festuca ovina	20.9	22.4	79.2	68.0
Helictotrichon pratense	7.5	4.9	36.8	18.2
Nardus stricta	7.9	4.0	45.0	66.7

(f) Distribution in relation to soil pH

The survey samples are classified with respect to the pH at field capacity of samples removed from the surface 30 mm (1.18 in) of the soil profile. The values tabulated refer to the percentage of the samples in each category in which the frequency of the species exceeds 20 per cent.

					Categories of soil pH						
	<3.5	3.5–3.9	4.0–4.4	4.5–4.9	5.0–5.4	5.5–5.9	6.0–6.4	6.5–6.9	7.0–7.4	7.5–7.9	8.0+
(1) Species of intensively managed grasslands											
A. repens	—	0.3	0.6	3.1	2.5	6.2	4.5	2.8	5.8	7.5	2.9
A. stolonifera	—	0.8	0.6	4.9	6.8	16.1	9.0	10.3	10.7	12.2	8.8
A. tenuis	5.9	9.3	17.1	25.0	16.8	14.3	7.0	6.3	1.9	—	—
A. odoratum	—	1.3	2.4	6.7	6.2	6.8	1.0	2.5	0.9	—	—
C. cristatus	—	—	—	—	1.9	1.9	3.5	3.1	0.9	—	—
D. glomerata	—	—	0.3	2.7	7.5	8.1	5.5	3.4	5.6	7.1	—
D. cespitosa	—	0.5	2.1	4.0	5.0	1.9	2.5	1.9	0.7	0.8	—
F. rubra	—	1.3	3.6	12.1	19.9	19.3	13.6	15.9	16.9	20.1	8.8
H. lanatus	1.0	2.3	3.9	7.6	16.8	18.0	8.5	9.7	4.7	5.5	2.9
L. perenne	—	—	—	0.4	4.3	6.8	6.5	7.5	4.5	2.0	5.9

P. pratense	—	0.8	0.4	1.3	3.5	2.5	0.6	—	—	—	—
P. lanceolata	—	5.1	4.3	4.7	2.0	6.2	5.6	0.9	0.3	—	—
P. annua	—	10.6	7.1	6.9	7.5	6.2	6.2	1.3	—	—	—
P. pratensis	29.4	7.5	9.0	5.0	10.1	8.7	9.3	10.7	3.6	1.3	—
P. trivialis	11.8	10.6	12.2	17.2	16.1	15.5	9.3	2.7	1.5	0.8	—
R. repens	5.9	2.8	2.6	5.9	6.0	3.1	3.7	0.9	—	0.3	—
R. obtusifolius	—	0.4	0.4	—	—	1.2	0.6	—	—	—	—
S. jacobaea	—	0.4	0.6	—	—	0.6	—	—	—	—	—
S. media	—	3.5	2.8	2.8	2.5	1.9	1.2	—	—	—	—
T. repens	—	4.7	5.8	5.9	5.5	12.4	6.8	2.2	—	—	—

(2) Species of less intensively managed grasslands

A. canina (2 ssp.)		—	—	0.3	0.5	1.2	2.5	5.8	4.2	3.8	72.3
A. elatius	5.9	10.6	7.9	4.1	8.5	6.2	5.6	4.9	1.2	0.5	—
D. flexuosa	—	—	0.2	0.3	1.0	2.5	5.0	12.5	32.0	51.0	—
F. ovina	—	8.3	5.1	3.8	4.5	6.2	6.2	10.3	8.7	13.9	9.9
H. pratense	—	1.2	0.6	1.3	—	1.2	—	1.3	0.3	—	—
N. stricta	—	—	—	—	—	1.2	—	1.3	2.1	5.6	12.9

(g) Distribution in relation to bare ground

Each quadrat was classified according to the number of 100 mm × 100 mm (3.9 in × 3.9 in) subdivisions on which the cover of bare ground exceeded 50 per cent. The numbers tabulated refer to the percentage occurrence of the species in each category.

	Extent of bare ground					
	Nil	1–10	11–25	26–50	51–75	76–100
(1) Species of intensively managed grasslands						
Agropyron repens	2.9	4.3	3.9	4.1	7.8	8.4
Agrostis stolonifera	5.4	4.6	11.2	9.1	7.8	12.9
Agrostis tenuis	8.4	12.2	10.5	14.9	4.7	3.5
Anthoxanthum odoratum	2.2	3.3	2.0	0.8	—	0.3
Cynosurus cristatus	1.7	1.3	0.7	—	—	0.3
Dactylis glomerata	4.1	5.9	3.9	5.8	3.1	2.8
Deschampsia cespitosa	1.5	3.9	5.3	—	—	0.7
Festuca rubra	12.8	17.4	20.4	13.2	14.1	1.4
Holcus lanatus	7.1	7.6	5.9	9.9	3.1	4.5

Lolium perenne	4.1	4.6	4.6	3.3	3.1	3.1
Phleum pratense	1.1	0.7	0.7	—	1.6	0.7
Plantago lanceolata	2.5	5.3	4.6	3.3	6.3	1.4
Poa annua	8.2	6.6	12.5	19.0	18.8	49.0
Poa pratensis	6.4	11.2	9.2	7.4	1.6	1.7
Poa trivialis	7.4	7.2	19.1	12.4	12.5	10.8
Ranunculus repens	1.6	1.6	2.0	1.7	—	3.8
Rumex obtusifolius	0.2	0.3	—	—	—	0.7
Senecio jacobaea	0.2	0.3	—	0.8	—	—
Stellaria media	0.2	—	1.3	2.5	1.6	11.9
Trifolium repens	4.7	5.3	7.9	4.1	6.3	1.7

(2) Species of less intensively managed grasslands

Agrostis canina (2 ssp.)	1.5	1.6	—	—	—	—
Arrhenatherum elatius	7.1	4.3	5.3	5.8	—	—
Deschampsia flexuosa	20.4	18.8	13.2	14.0	12.5	2.1
Festuca ovina	5.4	12.5	10.5	8.3	4.7	0.3
Helictotrichon pratense	0.1	1.3	0.7	—	—	—
Nardus stricta	1.2	1.6	0.7	—	—	—

(h) Associated species density

The samples containing the species have been divided into ten classes by reference to the frequency of the species. The values tabulated refer to the mean number of species (per square metre) present in the samples in each class. The results show that some species (e.g. *Deschampsia flexuosa*) consistently occur in species-poor vegetation, others (e.g. *Plantago lanceolata*) tend to be associated with high species densities.

	Frequency of the species										Mean
	1–10	11–20	21–30	31–40	41–50	51–60	61–70	71–80	81–90	91–100	
(1) Species of intensively managed grasslands											
A. repens	13.6	12.3	11.8	15.1	14.5	13.4	12.1	10.4	8.2	10.0	12.14
A. stolonifera	12.8	16.8	13.9	15.7	17.4	15.2	16.7	13.8	14.6	11.9	14.88
A. tenuis	11.3	11.9	10.8	14.9	11.7	12.0	12.2	10.5	13.7	11.4	12.04
A. odoratum	16.5	19.9	19.7	19.3	18.8	18.5	23.3	21.0	15.3	10.0	18.23
C. cristatus	18.4	21.2	21.7	16.8	25.5	25.3	24.0	17.7	22.4	18.3	21.13
D. glomerata	14.7	17.5	18.8	19.5	18.1	19.3	17.4	13.3	15.0	8.0	16.16
D. cespitosa	13.1	14.8	10.6	9.5	9.4	14.0	13.0	11.0	10.8	10.0	11.62
F. rubra	14.2	14.0	14.6	14.3	15.3	17.7	17.5	17.2	16.2	17.6	15.86

H. lanatus	14.1	18.0	17.1	15.0	17.5	14.0	18.3	16.0	16.6	13.3	16.00
L. perenne	16.5	16.4	15.3	18.3	14.7	18.0	16.6	14.5	17.7	14.3	16.23
P. pratense	17.9	20.0	19.0	14.8	17.0	15.0	13.0	—	—	—	16.67
P. lanceolata	19.0	21.8	20.6	21.4	28.8	23.4	22.9	31.0	21.2	19.6	22.97
P. annua	13.9	16.4	16.0	17.1	14.2	16.5	17.3	10.4	8.3	11.2	14.13
P. pratensis	14.7	17.2	15.3	17.7	13.9	16.9	14.4	15.9	13.0	12.8	15.18
P. trivialis	12.0	13.9	15.2	17.4	14.8	14.4	13.1	13.9	13.1	14.5	14.23
R. repens	15.3	16.8	12.6	22.0	9.7	16.2	21.9	19.0	9.0	15.9	15.84
R. obtusifolius	17.0	17.1	18.5	9.0	23.0	—	16.0	15.0	—	—	16.51
S. jacobaea	18.9	23.8	25.7	—	—	—	23.5	—	—	—	22.98
S. media	13.3	15.1	20.2	16.8	24.3	23.3	18.3	12.0	15.0	14.3	17.26
T. repens	17.8	19.9	19.5	18.5	17.8	16.9	18.4	17.8	16.7	18.2	18.15

(2) Species of less intensively managed grasslands

A. canina (2 ssp.)	11.6	15.1	16.8	12.3	9.7	12.5	12.6	21.5	9.7	9.9	13.17
A. elatius	12.8	12.8	15.4	13.7	12.7	14.8	14.0	12.8	11.0	11.8	13.18
D. flexuosa	6.6	5.2	6.1	7.4	5.2	5.0	4.9	5.4	5.3	4.4	5.50
F. ovina	10.3	10.2	10.9	13.9	11.4	12.5	9.9	15.0	15.8	14.0	12.39
H. pratense	21.4	24.1	27.7	26.6	22.0	—	14.0	—	—	—	22.63
N. stricta	7.8	5.6	6.7	8.7	8.8	8.8	5.4	5.8	12.5	—	7.17

Amenity Grassland: An Ecological Perspective
Edited by I. H. Rorison and R. Hunt
© 1980 John Wiley & Sons Ltd

3
Grass breeding: objectives, principles, and potentials

M . O . H U M P H R E Y S *Welsh Plant Breeding Station, Plas Gogerddan, nr Aberystwyth, Wales*

Introduction

At least half of all maintenance costs for amenity grassland are met from public funds, mainly local authorities, so it is in everyone's interest to ensure that these areas are maintained as efficiently as possible. This Chapter aims to discuss the purpose and value of breeding amenity cultivars in the light of the information on maintenance costs presented in Table 1.2. In so doing, it is intended to identify those areas in which further research will enable the breeder to make a more effective contribution to efficiency in amenity grasslands

Objectives

The basic aim of amenity grass breeding must be to produce cultivars which keep maintenance costs to a minimum while maintaining, and possibly improving, standards. It follows that the greatest impact of purpose-bred amenity cultivars is in intensively managed areas where maintenance costs are highest. Sward requirements are reasonably well defined in such areas and it is possible to formulate fairly precise breeding objectives. At present there is little economic justification in breeding for semi-natural amenity grasslands which, although occupying half the total amenity area, cost relatively little to maintain. In such areas improvement in the near future probably depends more on advances in management techniques. Thus it is more useful to concentrate resources in these areas on studies of the establishment and management of semi-natural swards possessing high carrying capacities (see Chapter 2). Techniques of harvesting and utilizing local seed sources of naturally adapted species which normally are not commercially available should be investigated further (Rorison, 1977).

Precise objectives in breeding for fairly intensively managed amenity areas depend on usage, environmental stresses, management, and various ecological factors. The relative importance of objectives such as low seed costs, good seedling establishment, low sward growth, persistence under close mowing, wear tolerance, general appearance and colour throughout the year, low fertilizer requirements, and resistance to pests and diseases varies accordingly. It is not feasible to breed cultivars specifically for every kind of amenity situation. Thus it is desirable to breed for wide adaptability and versatility as well as for specific attributes such as wear tolerance.

Principles

To achieve objectives such as those outlined above, the grass breeder uses as his raw material the natural genetic variability that exists within species. Early grassland studies (Gregor & Sansome, 1927; Stapledon, 1928) demonstrated the great range of variability that exists within species in relation to differences in climatic, edaphic, and biotic factors. Stapledon (1933) recognized the potential of naturally adapted ecotypes in the rapid production of improved agricultural cultivars. In addition, full appreciation of genetic principles in developing a technique of selection, breeding and strain-building at Aberystwyth (Jenkins, 1931) enabled the products of natural selection to be selected uniformly and to be made commercially available through seed multiplication without genetic deterioration (Plates 3.1 and 3.2). As a result, a number of very useful improved agricultural cultivars were produced and several are still of importance today. Some of the cultivars, such as S.23 *Lolium perenne* (perennial ryegrass), S.59 *Festuca rubra* (red fescue), and S.50 *Phleum pratense* (timothy) have also long been used for amenity purposes. Recently, more attention has been paid by some breeders to the development of cultivars specifically for amenity use. Many such cultivars are now available (STRI, 1978); some from abroad, particularly Holland (see Chapter 4). The approach used in producing new amenity cultivars is essentially that used in the early agricultural grass-breeding work, i.e. the direct exploitation of naturally adapted ecotypes. Success in this approach depends on the breeder's ability to identify habitats where natural selection pressures have produced material which is also adapted for amenity use.

Some of the characteristics found in perennial ryegrass populations collected for amenity breeding purposes from a restricted range of grazed semi-natural and natural grassland areas in the U.K. are shown in Tables 3.1 and 3.2. The populations are ranked according to a subjective habitat rating, based mainly on an assessment of grazing intensity.

The importance of grazing in producing characteristic plant types was emphasized in the early studies previously cited. Later work by Breese & Charles (1962) demonstrated a close link between heading date and 'management-rating' in *Lolium perenne*. Populations from habitats with a high frequency of cutting for hay or silage were earlier heading than those from

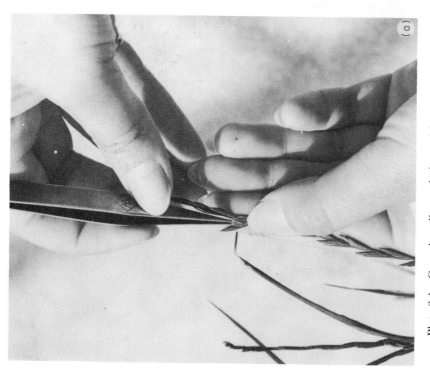

Plate 3.1   Grass breeding techniques (a) emasculation, (b) pollination (photographs by the Welsh Plant Breeding Station)

Plate 3.2   Plants of *Lolium perenne* being grown for individual assessment (photograph by the Welsh Plant Breeding Station)

Table 3.1 Perennial ryegrass populations collected in 1972

Accession	Number of plants collected†	Habitat rating‡	Heading class §	Mean height ¶	Mean diameter ¶	Percentage of green leaf ‖ mown at 20 mm
N723	50	1	Late	15.3c	23.9a	62.2b
N725	27	1	Late	15.0bc	24.0a	
N720	37	2	Late	12.3d	23.6ab	
N724	93	2	Late	17.9a	25.0a	62.2b
N721	100	2	Late	17.2ab	23.6ab	65.3ab
N726	27	2	Medium-late	17.4ab	22.0c	
N722	96	3	Medium-late	15.8abc	22.2bc	66.2a
N727	37	4	Medium-early	17.9a	20.8cd	
N729	41	4	Early	15.6bc	21.1cd	
N728	63	4	Early	13.8cd	19.6d	
Manhattan	—	—	—	—	—	64.8ab
S.23	—	—	—	—	—	53.7c

Duncan's multiple range test was applied at $P < 0.05$. Numbers bearing the same letter do not differ significantly.
†Each plant was split into two, and these clonal replicates were then grown separately.
‡Based mainly on grazing intensity (see text).
§As defined in NIAB lists.
¶Measured in millimetres during the period 31 January to 5 February 1974. (1 mm = 0.03937 in.)
‖Measured by 100 point quadrats per square metre.

continuously grazed habitats. The results given for various populations in Table 3.1 indicate that a similar relationship exists even with a smaller range of grazing intensities. N723 and N725 are both from very old, intensively sheep-grazed, upland pastures, N720, N724, N721, and N726 are from sheep pastures subjected to slightly less intensive grazing. N722 is horse-grazed and N727 is cattle-grazed. N729 and N728 are from sand-dune, golf-course roughs. The populations in Table 3.2 produce a similar picture although the material was assessed at a different time. Again, populations from intensively sheep-grazed pastures (habitat rating 1) are later heading than those from cattle-grazed pastures (habitat rating 4). The other populations derive from less intensively sheep-grazed pastures and rabbit-grazed cliff-tops. Relationships between plant growth habit (height and diameter) and habitat rating are less clear, although there is a tendency for the populations from intensively sheep-grazed pastures to be more prostrate and spreading. No doubt edaphic and climatic factors (e.g. degree of 'exposure') can play a large part in determining plant growth in addition to biotic (grazing) factors (see also Breese & Charles, 1962).

The kind of information presented above for *Lolium perenne* and by Bradshaw (1959) for *Agrostis tenuis* (common bent) is a valuable guide to the

Table 3.2 Perennial ryegrass populations collected in 1973

Accession	Number of plants collected†	Habitat rating‡	Heading class§	Mean height¶	Mean diameter¶	Percentage of green leaf ‖ mown at 20 mm
N730	38	1	Late	5.7c	16.2a	
N732	86	1	Medium-late	5.8c	15.5ab	57.5b
N739	46	2	Medium-late	5.7c	14.1cd	72.0a
N736	42	2	Medium-late	7.5b	15.0abc	60.3b
N738	43	2	Medium-late	7.7b	16.0a	
N733	33	3	Medium-early	7.7b	14.9abc	
N737	61	3	Early	7.7b	13.2d	
N731	42	3	Early	8.5ab	15.5ab	
N734	39	4	Early	7.6b	13.5cd	
N735	32	4	Early	9.7a	13.7cd	
Manhattan	—	—	—	—	—	62.35b
S.23	—	—	—	—	—	45.75c

Duncan's multiple range test was applied at $P < 0.05$.
¶Measured in millimetres during the period 3 March to 5 March 1974. (1 mm = 0.03937 in.)
Other notes as in Table 3.1.

location of suitable basic breeding material. Thus, material from intensively sheep-grazed pastures is very likely to persist under regular close mowing. Characteristics important in aiding survival can be identified in such material, e.g. late heading with a prostrate, spreading growth habit. If a breeder is not sure of the material best suited to meet his objectives, or even of which species he should use, an ecologically orientated exploration will form an important first stage in his breeding programme.

Breeding for wear tolerance is another example. Observations on naturally worn areas show that *Lolium perenne* is usually the most persistent species, except in some upland areas where *Poa annua* (annual meadowgrass) often predominates. Most breeding for wear tolerance is done with *Lolium perenne*. Perhaps, despite inherent difficulties, more attention should be paid to the potential of *Poa annua*. In the absence of critical information on selection criteria, collections from adjacent worn and unworn areas (Tyler & Chorlton, 1975) provide extremely useful information on the characters which are probably important in natural adaptation to this particular stress condition. Much more research is needed on the kind of natural adaptations that exist and their potential uses in grass breeding.

To summarize, it has been argued that ecological studies, which provide information on (a) species attributes, (b) ecotypic variation, including specific adaptations to environmental and user stress, and (c) sources of useful basic breeding material, form an important and necessary preliminary to amenity grass breeding programmes.

Potentials

The success of the 'ecological' approach has been well demonstrated by the development of heavy-metal-tolerant cultivars for use in reclamation (Humphreys & Bradshaw, 1976). 'Merlin' *Festuca rubra* was developed from a single, old mine-tip population with the minimum of artificial selection (Smith & Bradshaw, 1972). It possesses tolerance of high levels of lead and zinc and has been grown successfully on soils having a total lead content of 12 000 ppm and a total zinc content of 35 000 ppm. Some of this cultivar's other attributes, e.g., tolerance of low nutrient levels and drought tolerance (Humphreys, 1978) are also easily identified as natural adaptations to a mine waste environment. However, 'Merlin' also has characteristics, very advantageous in a general amenity cultivar, which to some extent were not expected on the basis of previous knowledge of mine waste adaptations. For example, it produces a fine, dense turf under close mowing and requires relatively few cuts per year. Also very few flowering heads are produced in fairly dense, well-established swards which, therefore, retain a 'tidy' appearance throughout the year even in low-maintenance areas such as roadside verges. It is apparent that there is always an element of luck involved in collecting basic breeding material even when plenty of ecological information is available.

Identification of suitable collecting sites is relatively straightforward in the case of adaptation to stress conditions such as heavy metal toxicity and salt spray. Table 3.3 shows the tolerance to salt spray of five coastal populations of hexaploid *Festuca rubra* and three control cultivars. At 15 weeks old, plants

Table 3.3 Salt and drought tolerance in hexaploid *Festuca rubra*

| Population | Salt | | Drought |
	Per cent green leaf[†]	Regression coefficient for yield[‡]	Regression coefficient for yield [§]
1	22.36a	0.43 ± 0.04	0.11 ± 0.20
2	22.30a	0.79 ± 0.10	0.21 ± 0.24
3	15.99b	1.07 ± 0.10	0.93 ± 0.21
4	15.66b	0.90 ± 0.07	1.62 ± 0.21
5	12.53c	0.95 ± 0.05	1.28 ± 0.19
S.59	8.17d	1.23 ± 0.09	1.37 ± 0.18
'Merlin'	5.55de	0.79 ± 0.05	0.10 ± 0.12
'Highlight'	4.42e	1.84 ± 0.02	2.50 ± 0.66

Duncan's multiple range test was applied at $P < 0.01$.
[†]Mean for all treatments and replicates.
[‡]See Figure 3.1.
[§] See Figure 3.2.

were given six doses of 17 g m^{-2} (0.03 lb yd^{-2}) or 68 g m^{-2} (0.13 lb yd^{-2}) sodium chloride as a foliar spray in two concentrations (430.5 or 861 ml m^{-2} (2.5 or 5.1 gill yd^{-2})) over 2 weeks. Tolerance was measured in two ways: (a) as the percentage green leaf remaining at the end of the experiment and (b) as the regression of population mean yield (over three replicates) on the mean yield of all eight populations/cultivars for each of the ten treatments/harvests (two salt levels in two concentrations and a 'no-salt' control, two 50 mm (2-in) cut harvests). The treatment/harvest mean yields essentially provide a measure of the severity of the salt treatments in biological terms (Finlay & Wilkinson, 1963). A large regression coefficient indicates a rapid decline in growth rate and a high susceptibility to salt damage (see Figure 3.1 and Table 3.3).

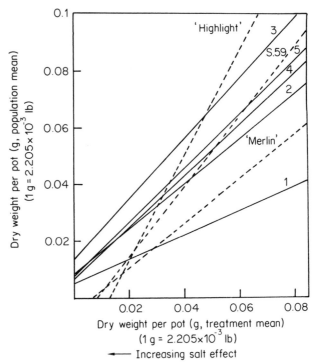

Figure 3.1 The effect of salt on populations of *F. rubra*. Coastal populations: solid lines; control cultivars: broken lines. Mean values were obtained from three replicate pots of ten plants each and represent the weekly yield of clippings cut at 50 mm (2 in) height. There were ten treatments/harvests. Steep regression lines indicate high susceptibility to salt

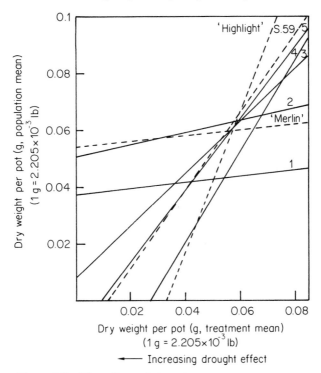

Figure 3.2 The effect of drought on populations of *F. rubra*. Coastal populations: solid lines; control cultivars: broken lines. Mean values were obtained from three replicate pots of ten plants each and represent the weekly yield of clippings cut at 50 mm (2 in) height). There were 12 treatments/harvests. Steep regression lines indicate high susceptibility to drought

Both measures of tolerance indicate that the coastal populations are less susceptible to salt than the control cultivars. Although 'Merlin' does not survive high salt levels, its decrease in yield with increasing salt levels is gradual, as shown by a low regression coefficient. This may be associated with its drought tolerance as shown in Figure 3.2 in which population mean yield (over three replicates) is plotted against treatment mean yield for 12 treatments/harvests (zero, 1291.5 or 2583 ml m^{-2} week^{-1} (7.6 or 15.2 gill yd^{-2} week^{-1}) over 4 weeks). Again, treatment mean yield may be regarded as a measure of the severity of the drought treatments. Significant differences between the regression coefficients for the populations/cultivars are indicated in Table 3.3. 'Merlin' and the highly salt-tolerant populations (which are also drought-tolerant) have generally a low relative growth rate, a characteristic often found in tolerance to environmental stress

(Grime & Hunt, 1975). From an amenity point of view such a relationship is extremely useful.

It is relatively easy to devise fairly simple screening techniques to select out tolerance to stress factors such as salt or heavy metal toxicity. However, even in these cases the relevance of selection techniques to breeding objectives must be carefully tested in practice. For example, when screening grasses for SO_2 tolerance the results obtained when plants are given high levels of SO_2 for short periods (acute treatment) can differ from the results obtained when plants are given low levels of SO_2 for prolonged periods (chronic treatment) which is more laborious but perhaps more relevant to natural conditions (J. N. B. Bell, personal communication).

It is much more difficult to identify suitable collecting sites and to devise simple, rapid, and relevant screening techniques for more complex characters such as wear tolerance. Likewise, in agricultural grass breeding it is difficult to identify simple selection criteria which are relevant in terms of animal production. Much more research work is needed into the development of screening techniques for amenity purposes. The production and assessment of experimental selections based on individual plant characteristics can be a very valuable aid to this kind of work (Wilson, 1976; Cooper, 1974). The kind of ecological work discussed earlier also provides useful clues.

Fortunately, at present, natural ecotypes are still able to provide the basis for superior cultivars without the need for sophisticated methods of artificial selection. Naturally adapted populations of *Lolium perenne* can produce swards with a green leaf cover (important for persistence under mowing and wear) much higher than that of S.23 and similar to the 'Manhattan' cultivar, which is known to be very wear-tolerant (see Tables 3.1 and 3.2). However, there is bound to be a time in the future when further improvement will not be obtained using 'straight' ecotypes.Results of research into selection criteria will then be vital.

Another important research need is to look into the 'adaptability' of cultivars and to discover ways of building this into breeding programmes (Breese, 1976). For some cultivars bred specifically for the most intensively managed sports turf, it may be possible, and often desirable, to specify precisely the management required to achieve the best results. However, in the majority of amenity areas, precise management is often not possible and there is a need for versatile and adaptable cultivars.

The old agricultural cultivars such as S23 *Lolium perenne* achieve fairly wide adaptability by virtue of their inherent genetic heterogeneity. They possess a very wide genetic base, having a large number of parent plants which, although of similar morphological type, derive from a range of sites. With the introduction of the Plant Varieties and Seeds Act 1964, and the granting of plant breeders' rights based on statutory trials for distinctiveness, uniformity, and stability, it is likely that newly bred cultivars of outbreeding grass species (including most amenity species apart from *Poa pratensis,* which is a facultative apomict) may possess a more limited degree of genetic variability. The genetic bases of the new cultivars appear to be much narrower than in older ones, e.g. 'Manhattan' *Lolium perenne* is based on 16 parental clones but 'Yorktown' is based on only five. The degree of reduction in potential variability that this may produce, and its consequences, require further investigation. If genetic heterogeneity is limited in modern cultivars, then it may be possible to restore adaptability through the use of cultivar blends and species mixtures, with the possibility of breeding for co-adaptation. This is another area which requires more research. Investigations into adaptation through phenotypic plasticity are also needed, including the possibilities of using versatile species hybrids as in agriculture (Breese, 1976). Such work may also help to solve the problems involved in attempting to combine biologically conflicting characteristics into single cultivars, e.g. rapid establishment/low sward growth, winter growth/winter hardiness, seed production/vegetative performance.

Conclusions

Despite a lack of basic research, new amenity cultivars have been developed which are beginning to make valuable contributions to the production of efficient amenity grasslands. Although they have rather higher initial seed costs compared with older (and essentially agricultural) cultivars, the value of the new amenity cultivars in terms of reduced management costs is gradually becoming appreciated. Of course, seed costs cannot totally be ignored by breeders who must regard good seed production as an important general breeding objective. The extent to which vegetative performance should be sacrificed for increased seed yield is open to debate. In choosing cultivars the user *must* set seed costs against subsequent management costs. To aid in this decision-making, the rapid distribution and easy access of relevant research information, as in the present volume, are essential.

In this Chapter the importance of the 'ecological' approach to amenity grass breeding has been stressed. The value of natural and semi-natural grassland in terms of genetic conservation cannot be over-emphasized. Its rapid disappearance through increasing urban expansion and changes in farm practice is cause for concern (NCC, 1977). Investigations into methods of collecting material and its storage in gene banks for possible use in future breeding work must continue. The importance of preserving local ecotypic differences as well as larger-scale geographical differences must be appreciated and methods of collecting and storing relevant ecological data worked out.

Most of the principles and potentials discussed in this paper in relation to grasses also apply to breeding in other species which are of amenity importance. Legumes, in particular, deserve more attention (Chapter 5). Research work in progress in New Zealand on species such as *Lotus corniculatus* (birdsfoot trefoil) for hill land use (DSIR, 1978) is obviously very relevant in this context. Similar work in the UK would be very valuable.

In the long term, it is the breeders' task to take information from many areas of activity and translate it into improved cultivars by means of appropriate breeding objectives and selection criteria. An active breeding programme often serves to identify areas requiring further research and some of these are outlined in this paper. Only if basic research information is available will long-term progress be possible towards the production of efficient amenity grasslands which are able to meet the needs of an increasingly leisure-conscious society.

References

Bradshaw, A. D. (1959). 'Population differentiation in *Agrostis tenuis*. I. Morphological differentiation', *New Phytologist*, **58**, 208–27.

Breese, E. L. (1976). 'Breeding for adaptability in grasses', in *Breeding Methods and Variety Testing in Forage Plants* (B. A. Dennis, ed.), Report of Meeting of Fodder Crops Section, EUCARPIA, Roskilde, 7–9 September 1976, pp. 81–6.

Breese, E. L. & Charles, A. H. (1962). 'Population studies in ryegrass,' *Report of the Welsh Plant Breeding Station for 1961*, 30–4.

Cooper, J. P. (1974). 'The use of physiological criteria in grass breeding', *Report of the Welsh Plant Breeding Station for 1973*, 95–102.

DSIR (1978). *Grasslands Division Research Report 1978*, DSIR Information Series No. 132, Wellington, New Zealand.

Finlay, K. W. & Wilkinson, G. N. (1963). 'The analysis of adaptation in a plant-breeding programme', *Australian Journal of Agricultural Science*, **14**, 742–54.

Gregor, J. W. & Sansome, F. W. (1927). 'Experiments on the genetics of wild populations. Part 1. Grasses', *Journal of Genetics*, **17**, 349–64.

Grime, J. P. & Hunt, R. (1975). 'Relative growth-rate: its range and adaptive significance in a local flora', *Journal of Ecology*, **63**, 393–422.

Humphreys, M. O. (1978). 'The possibilities of breeding resistance to environmental factors of roadsides', in *Proceedings of a Symposium on The Impact of Road Traffic on Plants*, Transport and Road Research Laboratory, Crowthorne.

Humphreys, M. O. & Bradshaw, A. D. (1976). Genetic potentials for solving problems of soil mineral stress: Heavy metal toxicities', *Proceedings of a Workshop on Plant Adaptation to Mineral Stress in Problem Soils*, (M. J. Wright, ed.), Cornell University Press, Ithaca, N.Y., pp. 95–105.

Jenkin, T. J. (1931). 'The method and technique of selection, breeding and strain building in grasses.' *Bulletin of the Bureau of Plant Genetics, Aberystwyth*, **3**, 1–34.

NCC (1977). *Nature Conservation and Agriculture*, Nature Conservancy Council, London.

Rorison, I. H. (1977). 'Selection and establishment of species in relation to soil conditions', *Journal of the Sports Turf Research Institute*, **53**, 103–4.

Smith, R. A. H. & Bradshaw, A. D. (1972). 'Stabilisation of toxic mine wastes by the use of tolerant plant populations', *Transactions/Section A of the Institution of Mining and Metallurgy*, **81**, 230–7.

Stapledon, R. G. (1928). 'Cocksfoot grass (*Dactylis glomerata* L.): ecotypes in relation to the biotic factor', *Journal of Ecology*, **16**, 71–104.

Stapledon, R. G. (Ed.) (1933). 'An account of the organization and work of the station from its foundation in April 1919 to July 1933', published by Cambrian News Ltd for the Welsh Plant Breeding Station, Aberystwyth.

STRI (1978). *Choosing Turfgrass Seed in 1978*, The Sports Turf Research Institute, Bingley.

Tyler, B. F. & Chorlton, K. H. (1975). 'Ecotypic differentation in *Lolium perenne* populations', *Report of the Welsh Plant Breeding Station for 1975*, 14–15.

Wilson, D. (1976). 'Physiological and morphological selection criteria', in *Breeding Methods and Variety Testing in Forage Plants* (B. A. Dennis, ed.), Report of meeting of fodder crops section, EUCARPIA, Roskilde, 7–9 September 1976, pp. 81–6.

Amenity Grassland: An Ecological Perspective
Edited by I. H. Rorison and R. Hunt
© 1980 John Wiley & Sons Ltd

4
Species and cultivar selection

J. P. SHILDRICK *Sports Turf Research Institute, Bingley, West Yorkshire, England*

Introduction

This paper deals principally with turfgrasses. Admittedly, even the most intensively-managed turf is unlikely to consist entirely of grass, and many broad-leaved species are important for the quality and diversity of grassland—and may even be essential for establishing the vegetation cover on some soils. Nevertheless, the grasses are both biologically and commercially the principal ground-cover plants in the UK, particularly where the cover is managed to give a natural surface for a special purpose—sport, play, erosion control, or aesthetic satisfaction in gardens and landscaping.

Choice of species

The turfgrasses of the UK are listed in Table 4.1, with an indication of their persistence under close mowing (for fine sports turf or ornamental lawns), low growth (for less-intensively managed areas requiring good appearance for the least possible maintenance), and wear tolerance (for heavily-worn sports and recreation areas). This summary, like all such summaries, suffers from over-simplification or in some respects from lack of information, but it reflects views in several other European countries as well as in the UK and is a reasonably sound starting-point. The final column of the table indicates relative importance. *Lolium perenne* (perennial ryegrass) and *Festuca rubra* (red fescue) are the two main species. Some of the less important species are restricted for reasons of seed availability (*Phleum bertolonii*, cat's tail) or limited usefulness (*Cynosurus cristatus*, crested dog's tail) or both (*Agrostis canina* ssp. *canina*, brown bent-grass). Some were prominent in the past because seed was readily available but are now less conspicuous in the mixtures for intensive use (*Cynosurus cristatus* and *Poa trivialis*, rough-stalked meadowgrass), though still perhaps to be considered for special areas of

Table 4.1   The relative merits and use of the main turfgrasses (adapted from STRI, 1978) with some alternative common names

Turfgrass	Persistence under close mowing (5 = most persistent)	Low growth (5 = lowest growing)	Tolerance of heavy wear (5 = most tolerant)	UK seed use in year 1975–6 (tonnes)
Velvet bent (*Agrostis canina* ssp. *canina*)	5	4	2	
Browntop bent				
European cultivars (*A. tenuis*)	5	4	2	461
'Highland' (*A. castellana*)	5	3	2	
Creeping bent (*A. stolonifera*)	5	4	2	
Fine-leaved sheep's fescue (*Festuca tenuifolia*) and sheep's fescue (*F. ovina*)	3	3	2	14
Hard fescue (*F. longifolia*)	4	3	2	
Red fescue (*F. rubra*)				
Chewings fescue (ssp. *commutata*)	4	3	2	1493
Slender creeping red fescue (ssp. *litoralis*, etc.)	4	3	2	2284
Strong creeping red fescue (ssp. *rubra*)	3	2	1½	
Rough-stalked meadow-grass (*Poa trivialis*)	2	3	1	53
Annual meadow-grass (*Poa annua*)	3–5	4–5	3–5	0†
Smooth-stalked meadow-grass (*Poa pratensis*)	3	2–4	4	588
Crested dogstail (*Cynosurus cristatus*)	2	3	2	98
Small-leaved timothy (*Phleum bertolonii*)	3	3	4	48‡
Large-leaved timothy (*Phleum pratense*)	2	2–3	4	
Perennial ryegrass (*Lolium perenne*)	1–2	1–2	5	4716‡

†No official figures are published for this species: a very small amount of seed may be sold for use. In practice the species can readily be sown by spreading cuttings.
‡Estimated.

semi-natural or natural grassland. Others have come to the fore through intensive breeding work (e.g. *Poa pratensis*, smooth-stalked meadow-grass).

A few other grass species deserve brief mention, as being of possible future interest, though—as far as can be predicted—no substantial value. *Festuca arundinacea* (tall fescue) is useful for heavy-duty turf in parts of the USA just outside the optimum area for *Lolium perenne*: but the UK is so ideal for the latter that *F. arundinacea* seems unlikely to have value except perhaps in a rather hot, dry environment in special conditions. *Dactylis glomerata* (cock's-foot) is relatively important in agriculture but seems to have almost no amenity value at present. *Poa supina* Schrad., a putative parent of *Poa annua* (annual poa), has attracted interest in West Germany, but in the UK the offspring is so ubiquitous and adaptable that it is doubtful whether there is any need to develop and sow the parent. *Poa compressa* (flattened poa) and *Festuca pseudovina* (no common name) are two species that may have value for inland areas with special problems of dryness or salinity, while *Elymus arenarius* (lyme-grass) and *Ammophila arenaria* (marram grass) are important on the coast. Some other grasses from North America and Europe might also meet specialized needs.

Outside the grasses, and therefore the range of this paper, there is a wide range of legumes—*Trifolium* (clover), *Lotus* (trefoil), and *Medicago* (lucerne) spp.—which can be considered for reclamation but which are not suitable for inclusion in Table 4.1. Various other broad-leaved species might also be used either to create or to restore natural grassland, but only a few curiosities such as *Chamaemelum nobile* (chamomile) have been adopted for relatively intensive use.

Within the grass species mentioned, there is a large array of cultivars, and the possibility of innumerable permutations in mixtures. The next two main sections of this paper deal with cultivars and mixtures. Although in practice the user would first choose his mixture and then his cultivars, it is easier to consider the simpler units first—this corresponding to the present state of knowledge and understanding.

Choice of cultivar

There are already several precedents in European countries with conditions comparable to those in the UK, for the presentation of cultivar information. The appendix gives brief notes on the Danish, Dutch, and West German publications. It also outlines the current practice in UK agriculture, particularly the slightly different systems of England and Wales (with the Recommended Lists of the National Institute of Agricultural Botany) and of Scotland (with a classification by the Scottish Agricultural Colleges).

The following section deals first of all with the information required by users and advisers, and the information currently being supplied by testing organizations. It then considers the requirements for Recommended Lists for turfgrasses in the UK and suggests one form which they might take. Next, it reviews what is possible at present, with the necessity of drawing on data from other sources in the UK and abroad, and what should be the next steps by researchers and technicians. Finally, it stresses the need for information to be translatable into financial terms.

The information required

There have been various attempts to list the characters of importance in assessing turfgrass merit: some recent ones have been by Beard (1973), Escritt & Daniel (1974), and Shildrick (1977*a*). These are incorporated into Table 4.2, which ignores morphological or other features which may be needed for assessing distinctness, uniformity, and stability, but tries to

Table 4.2   A check-list of turfgrass qualities and some determining factors

A. Turfgrass qualities
   (i) Establishment
        Speed of initial establishment
        Spread of rhizomes or stolons
        Sward closure (*Narbenschluss*)
        Competitiveness
  (ii) Persistence, i.e. survival of stresses
     (a) Man-made stresses
         Tolerance of, or persistence under, mowing (especially
           frequent or close mowing)
         Durability under wear or trampling =
           (1) tolerance of wear while it takes place, plus
           (2) recovery after wear
     (b) Natural stresses
         Freedom from weeds
         Tolerance of, or resistance to,
            pests,
            diseases,
            salinity,
            drought,
            shade, etc.
     (c) Certain generalized or abstract qualities related to persistence
         Competitiveness
         Compactness (sward density)
 (iii) Fitness for purpose
     (a) Intensive (mainly sport)
         Texture
         Speed
         Evenness of surface (smoothness, predictability of bounce)
         Shear strength, 'grip'
         Absence of excess fibre (litter, thatch)
     (b) Low maintenance
         Ease of cutting
         Reduced frequency of cutting (time of heading is related to some
           aspects of infrequent cutting)

Table 4.2   *continued*

(iv) Good appearance
        Dark or light colour
        Uniformity of colour
        Absence of seasonal variation in colour (dead leaf, yellowing, etc.)
        Absence of seed heads
        Cleanness of cut
B. Determining factors (relative importance often depends on levels of water and nutrient availability)
  (i) Fortuitous seed characters
        Seed size (within species range)
        Germination vigour
        Final germination percentage
  (ii) Morphological characters
        Plant size
        Number of rhizomes and stolons
        Number and density of shoots
        Leaf size, angle, number per shoot
        Leaf structure and mechanical strength
        Crown location
        Root distribution, structure, and mechanical strength
  (iii) Physiological characters
        Growth rate
        Amount and distribution of
          (a) structural carbohydrates
          (b) reserves
        Response to light and temperature; hence, duration and pattern of growing season, and bulk of dry matter production (biomass above and below ground)
        Time and amount of heading

indicate the main features relevant to merit, and to group them in a meaningful way. In the upper part of this table are the qualities, as conventionally described by users or advisers, which either define certain aspects of users' requirements or indicate broad desiderata. These can be put into four main categories.

(1) rapid establishment (the sown grass must cover the ground as quickly as possible);
(2) persistence (it must remain there);
(3) fitness for purpose (it must provide not merely plant cover, but plant cover satisfactory to the users—players, children, etc.—and to the people looking after it);
(4) good appearance (it should, if possible, be attractive as well).

'Persistence' includes a group of qualities more or less important in agricultural assessments, but also includes other qualities which are particular to amenity uses of various kinds. It is a word much argued over. Agriculturalists define it as survival of the sown species, although they link to it the maintenance of yield. In turf use, persistence can be considered the quantitative aspect of the survival of a sward which must at the same time survive qualitatively, i.e. retain fitness for its purpose. The stresses which reduce persistence—defoliation, wear (or treading), and such natural antagonists as pests and diseases—are very roughly the same in turf as in agriculture: sometimes more serious, sometimes less, but sufficiently linked to justify inter-disciplinary collaboration.

In the lower part of Table 4.2 are some of the morphological and physiological features which can be examined and quantified, and which will lead to useful predictions of the qualities listed in the upper part. The first aim is to separate out those quantifiable features such as shoot density, which are most often mentioned alongside, or confused with, the more abstract qualities in the upper part. The second aim is to define the often-ignored effects of those seed characters which are not genetically determined but which may have some influence in the early stages of establishment and could, perhaps, be more exploited than at present. The list in the lower part of Table 4.2 is obviously only partial, and no attempt is made to link each item to the qualities it affects.

The heading of the lower part of Table 4.2 emphasizes that water and nutrient availability will often decide to what extent the desired qualities can be obtained.

Some qualities and factors are known to be important only at the cultivar level: others are at present only important at species level, although this will no doubt change with increasing knowledge. Table 4.2 is not intended as a programme for more and more exhaustive cultivar testing, but as an attempt to lead to:

(1) the confirmation by users of their requirements; and
(2) the understanding of what plant characters contribute to these, which will in turn lead to:
(3) simplified testing in more-or-less controlled conditions to replace at least some, and perhaps most, of the present assessment under variable field conditions.

What information is being supplied?

The data principally available on turfgrass cultivars in this country and three other European countries are summarized in Table 4.3.

The items for the three foreign countries are more or less standard in their Recommended Lists or equivalent publications. Those listed for the UK

Table 4.3 Turfgrass characters on which information is currently published

Character	Ratings given (as appropriate for various species) by			
	Netherlands (RIVRO, 1978)	West Germany (Bundessortenamt, 1977)	Denmark (Jensen & Thuesen, 1978)	UK (Journal of the Sports Turf Research Institute; all reported characters)
	('Standard' characters: see text)			
Establishment				
Rate of germination (G: *Aufgang*) and initial establishment		×		×
Rhizome formation		×		×
Sward closure (G: *Narbenschluss*)		×		
Persistence, etc.				
Persistence under close mowing				×
Wear tolerance (D: *Resistentie tegen betreding*)	×			×
Weed incursion (G: *Verunkrautung*)		×	×	×
Susceptibility to various diseases	×	×	×	×
Winter hardiness, winterkill	×		×†	×
Drought resistance	×		×	×
Gappiness (G: *Lückigkeit*)		×		
Compactness or sward density (D: *Zodedichtheid*; G: *Narbendichte*)	×	×‡		×
Number of shoots per unit area			×	

Table 4.3 *continued*

Character	Ratings given (as appropriate for various species) by			
	Netherlands (RIVRO, 1978)	West Germany (Bundessortenamt, 1977)	Denmark (Jensen & Thuesen, 1978)	UK (*Journal of the Sports Turf Research Institute*; all reported characters)
	('Standard' characters: see text)			
Fitness for purpose				
Leaf width or fineness	X	X		X
Earliness of spring growth		X		X
Growth rate, vigour of growth (D: *Groeisnelheid*; G: *Wüchsigkeit*)	X	X		X
Time of heading	X	X	X	X
Height at maturity		X		X
Growth form at maturity		X		X
Appearance				
Colour (dark or light)	X	X		X
Lack of uniformity		X		X
Poor colour after mowing (G: *Schnittflächenverfärbung*)		X		X
Seasonal variation in colour				X
Winter appearance	X	X	X†	X
Freedom from heading shoots				X
Cleanness of cut				X
General impression		X§	X¶	X

D = Dutch term; G = German term.

†Winter character, judged at the end of winter, mainly according to winterkill, colour, and fungal attack.

‡'Good sward density generally denotes good wear tolerance and good competitiveness in mixtures.'

§A comprehensive evaluation over the whole period of growth.

¶The aggregate of scores for uniformity, freedom from weeds, colour, density, disease attack, and drought resistance.

have all been reported for at least one or two trials but are not necessarily always recorded or reported. The main items are discussed briefly below.

(1) Persistence under mowing or artificial wear is most easily measured when there is a substantial proportion of bare ground or weeds. Then, estimates or point quadrat (first-hit) assessments of ground cover are related to the state of the sward sufficiently closely to be satisfactory, especially if the essential requirement is a comparison with a control cultivar. When a sward is more or less complete and undamaged, first-hit ground-cover is a less satisfactory measure. Perhaps here it becomes necessary to measure or estimate above-ground biomass. 'Verdure' and the German term *Narbensubstanz* are two estimates of this type. Verdure is the living grass above the ground (green plant material) not removed by mowing. *Narbensubstanz* comprises both green material and thatch.

(2) Shoot number per unit area has the merit of being a precisely defined variable and, in general, high numbers are considered meritorious. It is reflected in good texture and other qualities for intensive sports use: it may also be relevant for tolerance of wear.

(3) Compactness is primarily an expression of shoot number, although it must be admitted that visual estimates may also reflect subjective impressions of biomass and ground cover. (Sward density is an alternative term, although density in the dictionary sense of 'closeness of substance: crowded state' may be confused with its more specialized meaning of the number of individuals per unit area, and is therefore perhaps best avoided.) Compactness and sward density are expressive terms to the layman but need to be used with care because of possible imprecision. Table 4.4, taking *Festuca rubra* as an example, illustrates how ratings for various aspects of performance combine into a reasonably coherent pattern.

(4) Tolerance of, or resistance to, diseases is generally a reflection of the abundance of readily visible symptoms, and might be expected to be an indication more of likely disfigurement than of loss of sward. Nevertheless, for some diseases at least, there is a clear connection between disease and loss of ground cover. For example, Shildrick (1978) demonstrated a correlation ($r = 0.49$; $P < 0.001$) between percentage ground cover of *Poa pratensis* cultivars in mown plots and the general consensus of ratings for those cultivars for freedom from *Drechslera poae* (Baudys) Shoem. (leaf spot disease).

(5) Growth rate (vigour of growth) is a guide to the required frequency of cutting. This may be based on a few measurements at the peak of the growing season or on regular measurements of growth increments between cuts.

Table 4.4 Comparison of turf qualities of *Festuca rubra* (red fescue) sub-species and cultivars, from various sources (adapted from Shildrick, 1976)

Sub-species and cultivar	Wear tolerance				Compactness (shoot density)			Persistence under mowing	
	Dutch rating	French rating		UK per cent cover	UK rating	Dutch rating	West German rating	UK per cent cover	
		Light wear	Medium wear					1 year after sowing	3 years after sowing
	(0–9)†	(0–9)	(0–9)		(0–9)	(0–9)	(0–9)		
F. rubra ssp. *commutata*	5								
Waldorf		8.9	6.6	7	6.7	8½	9	94	79
Famosa		8.8	4.7						
Highlight		8.8	4.7	7	7	8	8	86	76
Flevo		8.6	4.5	4	6	7½	8	83	50
Koket		8.1	4.6	4	5.8	8	8		
F. rubra ssp. *litoralis*	6								
Dawson		8.7	7.0	2		8	8		
Golfrood		7.0	2.8	1	5	7½	7	83	33
F. rubra ssp. *rubra*	5								
Novorubra		7.5	2.3	2	2.9	6	6		
Cottage		6.6	2.6		2	6½	6	49	10
Gracia		5.9	—	1	4				
Rubina Roskilde		5.9	—	1	3			60	20
Bergere		3.6	0					40	—

†Scores or ratings on 0–9 scale, 9 best.

(6) Colour may be described for normal conditions, for winter, and for drought. The lack of objective techniques for colour assessment is often lamented, although in practice the information is probably little needed.

(7) General impression is liable to be a subjective assessment, simple for the assessor and also for the user, if he is prepared to trust the assessor, but not easily usable by anyone else trying to build up an accurate composite picture of a cultivar.

What form should Recommended Lists take?

The old-fashioned liberal way with technical information—to give it to the user and leave him to make up his own mind on the basis of common sense and his knowledge of his needs—is obsolete for the 1980s. The majority of amenity grass users have insufficient knowledge, and neither the time nor the inclination, to do much more than read cultivar names off a list in order of preference. The descriptive notes in the current booklet of the Sports Turf Research Institute (STRI, 1978), which provides separate ratings for various features, go some way, but not far enough, to satisfy the users. They ask for Recommended Lists, i.e. lists of cultivars recommended for different purposes. In these the evaluation of the various data, and the weighting to compensate for some features being more important than others, are left to experts or committees, or both. The user demands of them the identification of different uses and the recommendation of appropriate cultivars; preferably only one, but certainly no more than two or three, within each species. This is in fact not as tall an order as it might seem, because of the separate distribution 'networks' within the seed trade in the UK. If a group of cultivars recommended for a certain use includes one cultivar from each 'network', the purchaser only has to decide which tender to accept, or which retail seedsman to go to, and all but one of the possible cultivars are eliminated. Such grouping is not only commercially convenient but also the most sensible way of dealing with the majority of cultivars. It takes a bold and very well-informed person (or committee) to draw up a list of names in an order of merit which will stand the test both of time and of new information, especially if several aspects of plant performance are to be taken into account. It is easier (though by no means simple) to divide cultivars into a few groups, for example, 'good', 'satisfactory', and 'poor' (A, B, and C). A Recommended List might show the first two groups, with special sub-divisions for the promising, but not fully tested, new cultivars. A possible pattern for the cultivars of any one species, for any one type of use, might be as shown in Table 4.5.

It might also be necessary to have a sub-division of B for cultivars becoming outclassed and likely to be demoted to C, to give adequate

Table 4.5   Possible cultivar groupings

Normal first-choice range	A Confirmed good cultivars	A(N) New cultivars, apparently good
Acceptable substitutes if shortage or price rule out Group A	B Confirmed satisfactory cultivars	B(N) New cultivars, apparently only satisfactory
	C Cultivars not included in merit lists, although legally marketable	

warning of such changes. The influence of the procedures of the National Institute of Agricultural Botany and the Scottish Colleges can be seen in these proposals.

This pattern is suggested only as a framework for what is to follow, and is the easiest part to devise or alter. The problems arise when allotting cultivars to their groups. Four steps are needed:

(1) to decide which characters are relevant to the use in question;
(2) to assign weightings to each;
(3) to assemble trial information, convert it to a common numerical basis, such as 0–9 scores, and complete the calculations with a single weighted value for each cultivar;
(4) to draw the boundaries of the groups.

It is not appropriate to enter into specific details here, but an imaginary example is given in Table 4.6. In this example the imaginary cultivar 'X' gets the higher total for heavy winter wear while cultivar 'Y' is better for more general ornamental or landscaping use. Cultivar 'Y' might be in Group A in the Recommended List for close mowing but relatively little wear, but only in B for heavy winter wear.

What is possible at present?

It would obviously be almost impossible to conduct trials in the UK to obtain information within a reasonable time on all the characters listed in Table 4.3 for all the cultivars that ought to be considered, as Table 4.7 indicates. In practice, the trials currently made by the Sports Turf Research Institute are on two levels:

(1) preliminary trials (at Bingley);
(2) main trials, currently supported by a contract from the Natural Environment Research Council (at Bingley and other centres).

Table 4.6 An example of cultivar comparison in *Lolium perenne* (perennial ryegrass) (imaginary data)

(a) Heavy winter wear	Weighting	Cultivar 'X'		Cultivar 'Y'	
		Actual score	Weighted score	Actual score	Weighted score
(i) Durability under wear	×5	9	45	6	30
(ii) Freedom from *Corticium fuciforme* (Berk.) Wakef.	×2	7	14	8	16
(iii) Winter greenness	×1	6	6	7	7
Totals			65		53

(b) Close mowing but relatively little wear	Weighting	Cultivar 'X'		Cultivar 'Y'	
		Actual score	Weighted score	Actual score	Weighted score
(i) Persistence when mown at 20 mm	×3	8	24	9	27
(ii) Short growth	×2	7	14	8	16
(iii) Freedom from *Corticium*	×2	7	14	8	16
(iv) Absence of seasonal variation in colour	×1	7	7	6	6
(v) Cleanness of cut	×1	8	8	8	8
Totals			67		73

Table 4.7   Numbers of cultivars at the end of 1977 (STRI, 1978). For common names, see text

Species	On National List or EEC Common Catalogue	Seed declared to be available in 1978
Lolium perenne (all diploid cultivars)	92	73
Lolium perenne (persistent diploid cultivars†)	60	49
Festuca rubra	64	39
Poa pratensis	54	36
Agrostis spp.	29	20

†Cultivars bred for turf and those showing good or fairly good persistence for agriculture.

The first set of main trials under the contract dealt with *Lolium perenne*, and were completed in 1978. Results have been reported in detail elsewhere (Laycock & Shildrick, 1979), but in spite of their comprehensive nature they could deal with only 21 of the 49 persistent cultivars which are available. Later trials of *Poa pratensis* and *Festuca rubra* have each been restricted to 16 cultivars, representing the most that could reasonably be dealt with. Even if the preliminary trials at Bingley were used as a source of information for all the potentially available cultivars which could not be accommodated in main trials, it would be unlikely that all the required information could be obtained from them; in any case a single trial would not be a sufficient basis in itself for something as important as a Recommended List.

It is clear therefore, that

(1) The number of qualities to be taken into account should be as few as possible, perhaps no more than six to eight.

(2) Unless the UK turfgrass trial system is to be considerably expanded, it will be necessary to draw on as much data as possible from other sources in the UK or abroad, as is already done in, for example, STRI (1978). Such data must of course be used with discretion, having regard to differences in such variables as mowing heights, fertility levels, and climate.

The most important qualities for turfgrass in the UK are perhaps the following, shown in the same order as in Table 4.3:

(1) persistence under close mowing;
(2) durability under wear;
(3) disease tolerance;
(4) compactness;

(5) slow vertical growth (i.e. shortness desirable, in general, to reduce mowing);

(6) good winter colour;

(7) cleanness of cut.

All these qualities would have to be considered in relation to the likely intensity of maintenance and level of fertility. They would not apply equally in all species, and some other qualities would be important for certain uses. A major omission is rate of establishment which would be important if it could be shown to be a predictable attribute of certain cultivars. Until it can be, it would be misleading to include it in the shortlist.

The next steps for research workers and technical specialists

If there is a consensus among users and advisers on a shortlist of important qualities for each species, research workers and technical specialists will then have three tasks:

(1) To ensure that all available information is collated and made into a reliable foundation of knowledge and understanding.

(2) To fill important gaps by special trials, e.g. to gain information on durability under wear.

(3) To devise the simplest possible system of routine screening for new material, making use as far as possible of morphological characters which can be fairly easily assessed on a glasshouse or small-plot scale as a substitute for large field trials. It is already possible to determine vigour of growth in row plots. It should also be possible to develop tests which give an adequate screening for disease tolerance, and even some which replace the laborious use of artifical wear machines.

In the collation of information and development of new routines, there is a need for the closest possible collaboration among workers in this country, and between them and those in other countries dealing with the same species—particularly those within easy reach in Europe. There seems no reason why there should not be a sharing of data already obtained, of techniques, and even of responsibilities for some aspects of future investigations. This suggestion not only applies to agricultural research workers in the UK, and those at official institutes and stations, but might apply also to the trial work of the seed trade—some of whose members have already in the past offered such collaboration—and to workers in other countries.

There has perhaps in the past been too great an emphasis on the need for numerous trials. One lesson from the first complete set of multi-centre trials of *Lolium perenne* under contract with NERC (Laycock & Shildrick, 1979) is that effects of centres are difficult to establish, generally predictable already from other data, and—when not predicted—of small importance when set against the total cost of the trials. Obviously, the more trials, the more data, and there is always the possibility of unexpected important results with other species. Nevertheless, cost-effectiveness must be considered.

The main variations attributable to location appear so far to be associated with winter effects—e.g. in *Lolium perenne* there was winterkill at Aberdeen and some discoloration of leaves at Aberdeen and Bingley (Laycock & Shildrick, 1979). The other main site effects—due to drought in east and south-east England in 1976—are interesting, but of less practical importance because of the abnormality of the 1976 summer.

In UK agriculture, with at least ten separate trials centres (six in England and Wales, three in Scotland, and one in Northern Ireland), the regional differences in results and recommendations are almost all associated with winter effects which generally become more severe as one moves north and east. There is also sound evidence from Norway of differences in the performance of *Festuca rubra* cultivars and *Poa pratensis* ecotypes according to location, in a country which extends in latitude from 58 °N to 71 °N, a greater range than that of the UK mainland (50 °N to 58 °N). But, even in Norway, it is only thought necessary to give recommendations for *F. rubra* for three separate zones—north, central, and south (Håbjørg, 1976*a,b*). On this basis, it would probably be unnecessary to divide the UK into more than two areas for recommendations of a comparable degree of detail.

Thus, while it is clear that differences between locations and areas can be important, and that some of them need to be taken into account in forming recommendations for the UK, this should not discourage attempts at synthesis. It would be unreasonable to say that no recommendations can be made for any region of the UK until full local trials of all cultivars and species have been made in it. The current trials should serve to show the features most likely to be affected by location, and it should then be possible to make some use of relevant external data (e.g. from agriculture on winterkill, or from other countries on disease) to make appropriate modifications of the general pattern of cultivar ranking.

The present need is clearly for as much pooling and consolidation of information as possible; plenty is available, if it can be brought together. Problems and uncertainties will still be left, that may be enough to justify further investigation. But there should be a strong effort made to pause and take stock, both nationally and internationally.

The need for financially-based information

Users of turfgrass are obviously interested in the merits of the various cultivars, but also—perhaps to a greater extent than in agriculture—they are concerned with the price of seed. This is particularly so when large purchases are made by local authorities and public bodies. The past lack of clearly defined criteria for merit comparisons, and the lack of primary data, have led to this state of affairs. If there is no available technical guidance on choosing one cultivar rather than another, price is clearly the only basis for choice. This situation will change as more information on cultivar merit becomes available and users pay more attention to it, but users would still be justified in wanting to see merit translated into financial benefit. This applies to the large-scale spenders of public money in particular. In agriculture, improvements in quality and quantity of fodder are fairly easily assessed and, once determined, produce self-evident benefits for the farmer, so that there is seldom any need to justify such slight extra seed cost as may be necessary in buying new cultivars. For amenity purposes, however, it is only reasonable for the user to ask what benefit he will get in return for buying seed that may cost more than traditional types. It is not enough just to say that a new cultivar is more persistent, or is more disease-resistant. These statements must be justified in financial or other equally definite ways. Persistence and wear tolerance must be shown to be translatable into more cover on a pitch throughout the playing season, and at the end of the season when renovation seed has to be bought. Similarly, low growth-rate must be translatable into reduced mowing costs. Other features such as freedom from disease, good winter colour, and so on, must also be able to be defined in terms of value to the user, using some scale of value judgements even if not hard cash. It can be argued that many sportsmen, and perhaps some lawn owners and other amenity users, will always be in the market for the best, regardless of cost. So long as improvement can be demonstrated, there will be a market for novelties. Nevertheless, this is neither a sensible basis for an industry, nor an adequate justification for a structure of cultivar breeding and assessment, in which expenditure must be related to measurable gains of some sort, and a watch must be kept for the point at which returns diminish below an acceptable level.

Some definition of cultivar differences probably has to precede the calculation of financial benefits. Certainly in the UK turfgrass industry there is at present more information on cultivar differences than there is convincing financial argument. Theoretical calculations can be made, based on known differences in wear tolerance or height of growth. It can be calculated that, other things being equal and satisfactory, a 25 per cent improvement in wear tolerance will allow x per cent more games before reaching a certain state of wear on a football pitch, or reduce the proportion of pitch requiring renovation by y per cent. It can be shown that one cultivar may be shorter, or slower in growth, than another by 25 per cent and this may allow a reduction of z per cent in the number of cuts per year. A few calculations of this sort have been published (Shildrick, 1977b). But there is a great need for practical examples rather than theoretical calculations. The users themselves must do their sums, and say what they find, if there is to be a sound justification for continued merit testing and the laborious work of preparing descriptive lists and Recommended Lists. Here, therefore, there is a need, not for research, but for consumer response. Can management regimes be adapted to take advantage of 25 per cent less growth? Must the figure be 50 or 100 per cent? What is a worthwhile gain in wear tolerance? 10, 25, or 50 per cent?

Choice of mixture

Here, some preliminary definition of terms is needed. Seed of any single cultivar starts the certification procedure in separate lots. During this procedure or afterwards, several seed lots of the same cultivar may be deliberately mixed. Under the Seeds Regulations this is called 'blending'. Any area sown with seed of a single cultivar is a 'monoculture'. If seed of two or more cultivars is mixed in some standard proportion for use, alone or in more complex mixtures, this is also sometimes called a blend or cultivar blend, although the correct term to be used here is 'cultivar mixture' (or mixture of cultivars). When two or more species are combined, they constitute a 'species mixture'. This use of the word 'mixture' both for two or more cultivars and for two or more species, corresponds to that given under the Seeds Regulations. Strictly speaking, the turf grown from a mixture of cultivars, even though within a single species, should not be described as a monoculture, although in practice it is sometimes so called.

The rest of this section deals with mixtures of species, but it must be borne in mind that mixtures of cultivars within species may be needed in many cases, particularly where there is heavy reliance on one species. The mixture of cultivars restores some of the adaptability which was previously obtained by diversity in species and gives insurance against weakness in seasonal colour, disease tolerance, and sward texture. The suggestions for further investigation imply the examination of mixtures of cultivars as much as mixtures of species and sub-species. Two or more cultivars of a species are frequently included in species mixtures, but generally for economic reasons or on rather elementary technical arguments. With increasing information, more refined and effective mixing of cultivars will be possible.

It could be claimed that mixtures would not be sown if users were confident enough about monocultures, or at least that two or more species would not be sown if users were confident enough about a single species. This is true for most artificial intensive uses, even if not for the restoration of natural grassland where diversity of species is part of the intention. *Lolium perenne* for turf receiving heavy wear (e.g. winter games), and one of the

Agrostis species for fine turf, would meet most UK requirements for sports turf, helped by unsown *Poa annua*. The lower-growing cultivars of *Festuca rubra* ssp. *commutata* Gaud. or ssp. *litoralis* (Meyer) Auquier would make very acceptable easily-mown ornamental areas and lawns.

There is even more substance in this claim now than there was a few years ago because new cultivars of *Lolium perenne* are coming on the market which seem to offer a broader spectrum of desirable features (persistence under close mowing and wear, and short growth) than conventional cultivars such as 'Aberystwyth S.23'. Thus *L. perenne* may be satisfactory in a wider range of uses than hitherto, perhaps even suitable by itself for some ornamental areas and lawns.

There are basically five types of mixture, as indicated in Table 4.8: three for intensively managed turf and two for turf less intensively managed. Of these, three are based respectively on *Agrostis* spp., *L. perenne*, and *Festuca rubra*. For the other two, the main species is not so obvious. The percentage proportions of seed weights are not shown, partly to avoid excessive detail and partly because proportions generally do not matter within quite wide limits. Also, the final composition of different turf areas all sown with the same mixture can vary greatly according to numerous factors of climate, soil, management, etc.

Table 4.8 Simplified summary of UK turfgrass uses and mixture components, showing the most important species (**×**) and subsidiary species of greater or lesser importance (× and (×)). For common names, see text

Species	Intensive use (relatively close frequent mowing; wear)			Non-intensive (low maintenance) use	
	Mown at 5–10 mm	Mown at 10–15 mm	Mown at 20 mm or more	Without *Lolium perenne*	With *Lolium perenne*
Agrostis castellana	**×**	×	(×)	(×)	×
A. tenuis, A. stolonifera, A. canina ssp. *canina*	**×**	×	—	(×)	—
Festuca tenuifolia, F. ovina	—	—	—	(×)	—
F. longifolia	(×)	—	—	×	—
F. rubra ssp. *commutata*	×	×	(×)	**×**	×
F. rubra ssp. *litoralis*, etc.	(×)	×	(×)	**×**	×
F. rubra ssp. *rubra*	—	(×)	(×)	**×**	×
Poa pratensis	—	×	×	×	(×)
Phleum pratense	—	(×)	×	—	—
Lolium perenne	—	—	**×**	—	×

Table 4.9   Recommended fine turf mixtures for lawns in some other European countries (per cent seed by weight). For common names, see text

	The Netherlands (RIVRO, 1978)			West Germany	
	Dry and normal soils		Moisture-retentive soils	Deutsche Rasengesellschaft (Boeker, 1977)	Skirde (1978)
	GZ1	GZ2	GZ5		
Agrostis tenuis	20	20	—		20†
A. stolonifera	—	—	—	0–10	
A. canina ssp.					
canina	—	—	20		
Festuca rubra ssp.					
commutata	80	40	40	40–60	40
F. rubra ssp.					
litoralis etc.‡	—	40	40	30–50	40

†Choice of *Agrostis* species according to required turf colour.
‡Designated slender creeping red fescue in the UK.

Intensive use: fine turf, mown at about 5 mm

For fine turf, the traditional mixture of an *Agrostis* sp. and *Festuca rubra* (approximately 20 and 80 per cent respectively by weight) is generally accepted (STRI, 1978). There is a need to examine the potentialities of the better cultivars of slender creeping red fescue (*F. rubra* ssp. *litoralis*, etc.) instead of, or added to, *F. rubra* ssp. *commutata*, particularly for greens and other fine turf areas built on sandy substrata or artificial constructions. A combination of these two types of *F. rubra*, in more or less equal parts, is widely recommended in the Netherlands and West Germany for fine turf, as Table 4.9 shows. Some investigation is also desirable on the potentialities for replacing *Agrostis castellana* Boiss. & Reut. either wholly or partly with other *Agrostis* species—*A. tenuis* (represented by the latest good cultivars), *A. stolonifera* (creeping bent) or *A. canina* ssp. *canina*. The scarcity and high price of seed of the three last species, however, give this a relatively low priority.

Intensive use: heavy duty turf, mown at about 20 mm or more

The standard UK mixtures for football pitches and playing fields are based on *Lolium perenne* (STRI, 1978) but there is work currently in progress by STRI under contract with the Natural Environment Research Council, to examine the role of the subsidiary species in mixtures of this sort. A first set of trials, at three sites, has been reviewed briefly in the context of UK turfgrass mixture practices by Shildrick (1977*c*), and reported in detail by Gore *et al.* (1979). A second set of three trials was started in 1978. The first set of trials showed that tolerance of an artificial wear treatment was strongly related to the proportion of *Lolium perenne* in the turf but in mixtures in which *L. perenne* was supplemented by *Poa pratensis* and *Phleum pratense* the two last provided substantial additional cover following wear treatment. Conversely, the higher the proportion of *Festuca rubra* and *Agrostis castellana* 'Highland', the poorer the wear tolerance, although mixtures based mainly on these two last-named species were consistently best for ground cover in the absence of wear (Shildrick, 1977*d*).

In these trials 'wear tolerance' was measured as live ground cover (first vertical hits with a point quadrat) soon after the artificial wear treatment with the DS 1 machine (described in Chapter 8 and by Canaway, 1976). It could be argued that other point quadrat methods, or assessment of above-ground biomass, would be better indications of wear tolerance. In an earlier trial of mixtures at STRI (Shildrick, 1975), the age of the turf when artificial wear treatments started and the treatments themselves (less realistic than that applied by the DS 1 machine) caused the worn sward to separate into three elements—live plant cover, dead leaf mat, and bare ground. The dead leaf mat represented biomass that reduced the area of bare, potentially slippery ground and would have provided 'grip' for players. Although it was eventually worn away, and with it the prospect of regeneration from crowns and shallow rhizomes, it was a significant element at one stage of wear, and clearly related to the content of *Festuca* and *Agrostis* spp. in the seeds mixture. So, there is need for caution both in judging the validity of the techniques used to assess the wear tolerance of mixtures, and in dismissing those subsidiary species in a mixture which by general agreement show the poorest durability in comparisons of species. These subsidiary species may have value in natural turf where above-ground biomass has become substantial. The second set of STRI trials under the NERC contract is, in fact, concerned partly with this possibility. It should however be borne in mind that the fine grasses, particularly *Agrostis* spp., are likely to dominate a playing field mixture if it is kept for a long period without wear (Vos & Scheijgrond, 1970; Gore *et al.*, 1979).

The broad conclusion of the first set of NERC contract trials was that for football pitches used heavily in winter, *Poa pratensis* and *Phleum pratense* are the most important subsidiary species to add to the basic *Lolium perenne*. This agrees broadly with current thinking in the Netherlands and West Germany (Table 4.10). Although some *Festuca rubra* is suggested (and even *Cynosurus cristatus* for some uses), there appears to be general agreement that *Agrostis* spp. are undesirable. It seems likely that, although *Phleum* spp. have given quite good results in UK trials, *Poa pratensis* has the greater potential for development in playing field mixtures, both in the range of its cultivars and

Table 4.10 Recommended playing field mixtures in some other European countries (per cent seed by weight). For common names, see text

	The Netherlands (RIVRO, 1978)				West Germany				
	Moisture-retentive soils			Dry soil	Deutsche Rasengesellschaft (Boeker 1977)	Skirde (1978)			
						Summer use		Year-round use	
	SV4	SV6†	SV7	SV5					
Festuca rubra	—	—	—	15‡	15–30	25	—	25	—
Cynosurus cristatus	—	—	—	—	—	10	15	—	—
Poa pratensis	60	95	25	50	40–60	60	70	50	70
Phleum pratense and/or *P. bertolonii*	10	5	—	—	0–3	5	10	—	—
Lolium perenne	30	—	75	35	25–30	—	—	25	30

†For hockey fields.
‡*Festuca rubra* cultivars with fine rhizomes, designated slender creeping red fescue in the UK.

in its durability (taking account of recovery from rhizomes). Improvements in durability are obviously important, but improvements in vigour of establishment might well prove even more important if they could be made. (This may partly be a matter of climatic adaptation: for example *Poa pratensis* currently appears to be more valuable in central Germany than in the Netherlands.)

Intensive use: intermediate mowing heights, about 10–15 mm

Between the two extremes of fine turf and winter football pitches there is a need in the UK for mixtures able to tolerate fairly close mowing (about 15 mm or less) and heavy wear. It has in the past generally been necessary to omit *Lolium perenne* from such mixtures, both because it could not be expected to persist at such heights of cut and because the relatively few surviving plants would look unkempt. These mixtures have, therefore, been based on *Festuca* and *Agrostis* spp. with *Poa pratensis, Phleum* spp., or *Cynosurus cristatus* added to improve the durability. However, trials at Bingley a few years ago, mown at 13 mm and given artifical wear (Shildrick, 1975), showed relatively little benefit from these latter species, and *Poa annua*, sown or unsown, was the only species which gave markedly more green cover and less bare ground after wear when added to *Festuca* and *Agrostis* spp. Nevertheless, *Poa pratensis* has generally been considered worth sowing to reinforce turf mown at 13 mm or so, at a height considered too low for *Lolium perenne* (STRI, 1978). The same reliance on *P. pratensis* in the absence of *L. perenne* is shown in Table 4.10, in the Dutch SV6 and Skirde's (1978) mixtures for summer use.

The development of new cultivars of *L. perenne*, however, requires new trials to examine their potential value even at such low heights. The picture may also have changed since 1975 because of improvements in *P. pratensis* and in slender creeping red fescue (*F. rubra* ssp. *litoralis* etc.), which seems to be the most useful type of *F. rubra* under wear.

Low maintenance use, without Lolium perenne

The combination of *P. pratensis* and *F. rubra* is suggested for the coarser types of lawns (GZ8) in the Netherlands and some types of general-purpose utility turf (*Gebrauchsrasen*) in West Germany, as shown in Table 4.11. This is also probably the main cool-season turfgrass mixture in North America. For UK turf uses in which there is a combination of fairly close mowing and quite heavy wear, i.e. heavy stresses on the grass, then—as already discussed above—this mixture is not completely suitable. With less stress, however, as under the higher mowing in other countries or in some UK domestic lawns, it can be quite satisfactory. In UK conditions *F. rubra* is likely to be

Table 4.11 Recommendations for mixtures for general purpose utility and recreation turf in some other European countries (per cent seed by weight). For common names, see text

| | The Netherlands (RIVRO, 1978) | | West Germany | | | | | | |
| | | | Deutsche Rasengesellschaft (Boeker, 1977) | | | Skirde (1978) | | | |
	GZ†	R1‡	A	B	C	1	2	3	4
Agrostis tenuis	—	10	—	—	—	5	—	—	—
Festuca tenuifolia, F. ovina	}15	}20	—	—	—	—	—	—	—
F. longifolia			—	—	—	20	20	20	—
F. rubra ssp. commutata	15	10	30–40	20–30	20–30	20	20	25	20
F. rubra ssp. litoralis, etc.	—	}20	30–40	20–30	10–20	20	20	—	—
F. rubra ssp. rubra	—		30–40	30–40	10–20	—	—	—	—
Poa pratensis	70	20	—	—	—	35	40	50	30
Phleum spp.	—	—	—	—	—	—	—	5	—
Lolium perenne	—	20	—	15–30	40–60	—	—	—	50

† For coarser lawns.
‡ For recreation areas.

dominant (as a result of poor establishment by the *P. pratensis*, and especially if fertility is relatively low). As Table 4.11 shows, the Dutch and Germans might use other *Festuca* spp. in such mixtures, but *Agrostis* spp. are not favoured abroad and *Agrostis* spp., particularly *A. castellana*, are also probably best omitted from UK mixtures to be mown with rotary mowers at about 18–25 mm, because of poor appearance and difficulties in cutting satisfactorily. On general-utility turf which is cut more closely, e.g. gang-mown public parks and local authority grassland, *Agrostis* spp. might be more appropriate.

Investigations on this type of mixture would be mainly concerned with ease of cutting, and appearance at various seasons.

Low-maintenance use, with Lolium perenne

If *L. perenne* is included at present in low-maintenance mixtures, it is probably for the sake of its vigorous establishment. Mixtures which include it are the same as, or very similar to, those used for heavy-duty on playing fields (as shown above), but there is probably more need for the fine turf element (*Agrostis* and *Festuca* spp.) and less need for *Poa pratensis* and *Phleum* spp. to give wear tolerance.

The main point to be investigated is the extent to which new cultivars of *L. perenne* can be used, providing the fineness and density hitherto given by *Festuca* spp. and perhaps being used in some of the areas where hitherto *L. perenne* would have been ruled out because of its growth rate.

Mixtures for special situations

The five types of mixture in Table 4.8, which have been reviewed one by one, are fairly generalized and adaptable mixtures. By definition, therefore, they may be less suitable for special situations than mixtures designed specially for those situations—shade, soil contamination, very high or very low pH, etc. Nevertheless, even when prescribing a mixture for a 'special' area, one of the basic mixtures may often be a good foundation and, indeed, may adapt quite satisfactorily to the special conditions, particularly if helped a little by appropriate management (e.g. lenient mowing in shade, occasional liming on very acid soils). The stresses of frequent defoliation and heavy wear may be more important than the special local circumstances, and it might be more sensible to sow species known to withstand these stresses (and ameliorate the special local circumstances for their benefit) than to choose species occurring naturally in the locality which seem appropriate at first but then prove unable to withstand the heavy stresses imposed on them.

94   *Amenity grassland: an ecological perspective*

References

Beard, J. B. (1973). *Turfgrass: Science and Culture*, Prentice-Hall, Englewood Cliffs, N.J.

Boeker, P. (1977). 'Qualitätszeichen für Rasenmischungen', *Rasen-Grünflächen-Begrünungen*, **8**, 133–5.

Bundessortenamt (1977). *Beschreibende Sortenliste für Rasengräser, 1977*, Alfred Strothe Verlag, Hanover.

Camlin, M. S. (1978). 'Perennial ryegrass—recommended varieties 1978–79', *Agriculture in Northern Ireland*, **53**, 5–11.

Canaway, P. M. (1976). 'A differential slip wear machine (D.S.1) for the artificial simulation of turfgrass wear', *Journal of the Sports Turf Research Institute*, **52**, 92–9.

Escritt, J. R. & Daniel, W. H. (1974). 'Recommendations for units of measure and uniform evaluation of turfgrasses', *Sub-committee Report, Second International Turfgrass Research Conference*, International Turfgrass Society, c/o V.P.I., Blacksburg, Va.

Gore, A. J. P., Cox, R. & Davies, T. M. (1979). 'Wear tolerance of turfgrass mixtures', *Journal of the Sports Turf Research Institute*, **55**, 45–68.

Håbjørg, A. (1976a). 'Sortsforsøk i *Festuca* spp. for Grøntanlegg', *Institutt for dendrologi og planteskoledrift, Norges landbrukshøgskole, Melding nr. 59.*

Håbjørg, A. (1976b). 'Effects of photoperiod and temperature on vegetative growth of different Norwegian ecotypes of *Poa pratensis*', *Institutt for dendrologi og planteskoledrift, Norges landbrukshøgskole, Melding nr. 61.*

Jensen, A. & Thuesen, A. (1978). 'Forsøg med sorter af almindelig rajgraes, rød svingel, lav timothe, almindelig hvene og engrapgraes til plaene 1974–77: Meddelelse 1418'. Statens Forsøgsvirksomhed i Plantekultur, Lyngby, Denmark.

Laycock, R. W. & Shildrick, J. P. (1979). 'Report on trials of cultivars of *Lolium perenne*, 1974–78', *Journal of the Sports Turf Research Institute*, **55**, 7–35.

NIAB (1978). *Recommended Varieties of Grasses, 1978/9, Farmers' Leaflet No, 16*, National Institute of Agricultural Botany, Cambridge.

RIVRO (1977). *Grassen voor Grasvelden, 1977: Rassenbericht Nr. 527*, Rijksinstituut voor het Rassenonderzoek van Cultuurgewassen, Wageningen, The Netherlands.

RIVRO (1978). *53e Beschrijvende Rassenlijst voor Landbouwgewassen, 1978*, Rijksinstituut voor het Rassenonderzoek van Cultuurgewassen. Leiter-Nypels, Maastricht, The Netherlands.

SAC (1978). *Classification of Grass and Clover Varieties for Scotland 1978*, Publication No. 36, The Scottish Agricultural Colleges, Edinburgh, Aberdeen, and Auchincruive.

Shildrick, J. P. (1975). 'Turfgrass mixtures under wear treatments', *Journal of the Sports Turf Research Institute*, **51**, 9–40.

Shildrick, J. P. (1976). 'Evaluation of red fescue cultivars, 1973–76: part III. Preliminary trial, with artificial wear', *Journal of the Sports Turf Research Institute*, **52** 38–51.

Shildrick, J. P. (1977a). 'What qualities are needed in turfgrasses?', *Journal of the Sports Turf Research Institute*, **53**, 109–10.

Shildrick, J. P. (1977b). 'Less work and more play—trends in turfgrasses', *Report of 17th Askham Bryan Horticultural Technical Course*, Askham Bryan College, York.

Shildrick, J. P. (1977c). 'Turfgrass mixtures in the United Kingdom', in *Proceedings of the Third International Turfgrass Research Conference*, American Society of Agronomy, Madison, Wisc.

Shildrick, J. P. (1977d). 'S.T.R.I. contract research on turfgrass: a summary of progress under the sub-contract with the Natural Environment Research Council, 1974–77', *Journal of the Sports Turf Research Institute*, **53**, 85–92.

Shildrick, J. P. (1978). 'Preliminary trials of cultivars of smooth-stalked meadow-grass, 1975–8: part II. Mown plots (Trial Y3)', *Journal of the Sports Turf Research Institute*, **54**, 79–96.

Skirde, W. (1978). *Vegetationstechnik—Rasen und Begrünungen*. Patzer Verlag, Berlin and Hanover.

STRI (1974). 'Cultivars of perennial ryegrass for turf use: descriptive notes', *Journal of the Sports Turf Research Institute*, **50**, 9–33.

STRI (1978). *Choosing Turfgrass Seed in 1978*, Sports Turf Research Institute, Bingley.

Vos, H. & Scheijgrond, W. (1970). 'Varieties and mixtures for sports turf and lawns in the Netherlands', in *Proceedings of the First International Turfgrass Research Conference*, Sports Turf Research Institute, Bingley.

Appendix 4.1

Notes on some current 'recommended lists' for turfgrasses and agricultural grasses

Information on turfgrass trials in the UK has been published from time to time in the *Journal of the Sports Turf Research Institute*, with regular articles in recent years, but only lately has the bulk of the information become such that a synthesis could be attempted. The first was in a set of descriptive notes on cultivars of perennial ryegrass (STRI, 1974): the next type of presentation, rather more successful, combined summaries of cultivar merit for all turfgrasses with information on availability and other more general notes (STRI, 1978).

In these two publications, considerable use was made of information from other countries, particularly in Western Europe. Notes on the principal cultivar publications of three important countries are given below:

(1) *Denmark*. Periodical bulletins report the trials of the Statens Forsøgsvirksomhed i Plantekultur (e.g. Jensen & Thuesen, 1978). The 'recognized' cultivars are marked with an S and trial results for them are summarized in numerical form (with data from one or two control cultivars for comparison). The cultivars are listed within trial reports according to score for general impression, but are arranged alphabetically within trial date groups in a recent summary (Jensen & Thuesen, 1978). Cultivars not qualifying for the S do not have data shown for them though they are listed as having been through trials.

(2) *The Netherlands*. The Rassenlijst (e.g. RIVRO, 1978) is published annually by RIVRO (Rijksinstituut voor het Rassenonderzoek van Cultuurgewassen). Sections on each turfgrass species list the recommended cultivars in order of merit with short notes on each cultivar and summary tables for the most important species, in which qualities are shown numerically on a 1–9 scale, 9 being best. There are different categories of recommendation, and not all the cultivars on the Dutch National Lists are mentioned in this part of the Rassenlijst.

Occasional cultivar information leaflets (e.g. RIVRO, 1977) give ratings on a 1–9 scale for a wider range of cultivars than those included in the Rassenlijst.

(3) *West Germany*. A descriptive list of turfgrass cultivars is published biennially by the Bundessortenamt (most recently, Bundessortenamt, 1977). Sections on each species give information on all those cultivars on the National Lists which have been tested for turf use; they are arranged alphabetically. The descriptions of cultivars and the summary tables in numerical form are much fuller and more difficult to weigh up than the Dutch information; there is no listing in order of merit, although the degree of suitability for each of four types of turf is shown.

These three publications illustrate slightly different approaches. The Danish arrangement indicates the cultivars worth considering, marked S, but then leaves the reader to weigh-up and compare results from different trials, and thus make his decision. The Germans provide ratings on many characters but still essentially leave it for the reader to make his decision, according to the characters he considers most important, among the cultivars shown as suitable for the type of turf in question. The Dutch provide a smaller range of choice, with cultivars discreetly arranged in order of merit, although enough numerical ratings are supplied to allow the reader to select features which he particularly needs.

In the UK, Farmers' Leaflet No. 16 of the National Institute of Agricultural Botany applies to England and Wales (e.g. NIAB, 1978); fairly detailed information is given for a limited number of recommended cultivars with yields expressed as percentages of controls and with ratings for characters such as winter hardiness and persistence. Arrangement is by heading date (a feature relevant to appropriate utilization) and the reader is left to make his own choice within quite small groups. There are four classes of recommendation:

G   recommended for general use,
P   provisional recommendation for a variety on which further trials are
    still in progress,
S   recommended for special use, and
O   becoming outclassed by other recommended varieties.

No variety is recommended on less than three years' trial.

The classification leaflet of the Scottish Colleges (e.g. SAC, 1978) does not give detailed trial data—yield percentages or ratings for particular qualities—but has six merit classes, defined as follows:

(1) recommended without reservation;
(2) recommended, but with reservation—satisfactory yields but may be
     less satisfactory in other respects;

(3) varieties with lower yields and poorer persistence, acceptable only when class (1) or (2) varieties are not available;
(4) varieties under test, but showing promise and likely to be in class (1) or (2);
(5) varieties under test, but not promising—likely to be in class (3) or (6);
(6) Poor varieties considered unsuitable.

Northern Ireland makes recommendations (e.g. Camlin, 1978) on broadly the same pattern as the NIAB, giving yield comparisons with controls and ratings for other important characters, and indicating quite small groups of recommended cultivars from which the reader can choose.

In each country, there must inevitably be differences in the number and quality of the available data, the degree of guidance given to the user by the recommendations of experts and committees, and the extent to which data are provided for the user to make his own choice. The brief review given here may help the UK turfgrass industry to decide what format will suit it best.

Part III
SOILS

Amenity Grassland: An Ecological Perspective
Edited by I. H. Rorison and R. Hunt
© 1980 John Wiley & Sons Ltd

5
Mineral nutrition

A. D. BRADSHAW *Department of Botany, University of Liverpool, Liverpool, England*

Introduction

Amenity grassland, whether designed for intensive or extensive use, is a community of cohabiting plant species which interact and compete with each other for light, water and nutrients. At the same time it is an integrated ecosystem, involving soil as well as plants. Particular nutrients pass from soil to plant and back to soil again in an endless cycle. The nutrient requirements of the plants are supplied by the soil, and the nutrient store of the soil is constantly replenished by the return of dead plant material. Even if artificial fertilizers are used to increase plant growth, this cycle remains critical to the performance of the grassland system.

Up to now there have been two main approaches to nutritional problems in grassland. Either the environment is accepted as it is, with species being chosen which have roughly the appropriate adaptations, and with the resulting community left to fend for itself, or the environment is improved by fertilizing or other treatment on an empirical basis to obtain improved performance, using either the species already present or those, such as *Lolium perenne* (perennial ryegrass) which are known to be responsive to high nutrient levels.

These approaches are well-established and are outlined in all the major textbooks. They have served us well. Yet if amenity grassland could be examined from the point of view of the complex, integrated ecosystem that it is, then we should be able to understand its nutrition more fully and be able to manage it more effectively, as is possible in other ecosystems (Lewis, 1969; Witkamp, 1971). In particular, we could look at the nature of the nutritional equilibrium of the ecosystem, for there are likely to be places where this can be altered so that species composition and performance, and therefore sward performance, can be manipulated.

Species differences

As a starting point we must appreciate that the plant species of amenity grassland exhibit major differences in soil preference. This can be seen from the comparison of the natural distribution of grassland species in the Sheffield district carried out by Grime & Lloyd (1973) (Figure 5.1). Since this work was done in a region of widely differing soil types and climatic conditions it provides first-class evidence for distinct preferences in a wide variety of species. The distributions are, however, the product of the growth of individual species in particular soil conditions and the competition encountered from other species. They do not give a clear picture of the nature of edaphic adaptation in individual species, which itself is made up of adaptation to several specific soil factors.

Species have very distinctive growth responses to nutrients (Bradshaw *et al.*, 1960, 1964) (Figure 5.2). These may be subtle and also may be dependent more on the balance between individual nutrients than on the absolute level of any one nutrient (Jefferies & Willis, 1964). The outcome in natural situations where competition is occurring may be still more complex. An inspection of Figure 5.2 suggests that *Lolium perenne* will, on the basis of its yield, always be the most successful species regardless of nutrient level. But this is not the case: under low-nutrient conditions it is replaced by species such as *Agrostis tenuis* (common bent-grass). The competitive mechanisms which may be occurring involve a number of different

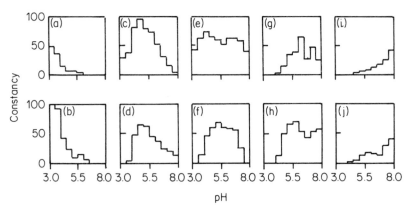

Figure 5.1 Contrasting distributions of ten grasses on grassland soils of varying surface pH in the Sheffield area. Constancy is the number of sites containing the species in each pH class, expressed as a percentage of all sites in that class. Species are: (a) *Nardus stricta*, (b) *Deschampsia flexuosa*, (c) *Agrostis tenuis*, (d) *Holcus lanatus*, (e) *Festuca ovina*, (f) *Anthoxanthum odoratum*, (g) *Trisetum flavescens*, (h) *Dactylis glomerata*, (i) *Zerna erecta*, (j) *Brachypodium pinnatum* (data from Grime & Lloyd, 1973)

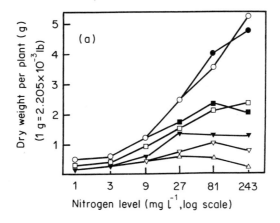

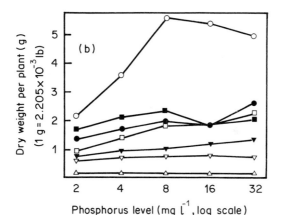

Figure 5.2 (a) Dry weight yields of seven grass species after 8 weeks' growth at varying levels of nitrogen: ○, *Lolium perenne*; ●, *Agrostis stolonifera*; □, *Agrostis tenuis*; ■, *Cynosurus cristatus*; ▼, *Agrostis canina*; ▽, *Festuca ovina*; △, *Nardus stricta* (from Bradshaw *et al.*, 1964). (b) as in (a), but with varying levels of phosphorus (from Bradshaw *et al.*, 1960)

attributes, not all of which are yet understood (van den Berg, 1969; Bradshaw, 1969).

But soil has other features besides nutrient level; in particular, there are features related to pH such as aluminium and manganese toxicity. We now have good evidence of considerable variation in tolerance to such toxicity (Grime & Hodgson, 1969) (Figure 5.3) as well as to the effects of high pH (Hutchinson, 1967).

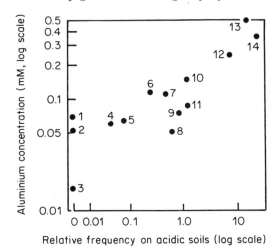

Figure 5.3   The relationship between the aluminium tolerance of various grassland species and their relative occurrence on soils of pH <4.5. The aluminium concentration is that required to produce 50 per cent inhibition of root growth. The relative frequency is the ratio of the occurrence of the species on soils of pH <4.5 to its occurrence on soils of pH >4.5; a constant 0.01 has been added to facilitate representation. 1, *Poterium sanguisorba* and *Leontodon hispidus*; 2, *Briza media*; 3, *Zerna erecta*; 4, *Plantago lanceolata*; 5, *Centaurea nigra*; 6, *Lathyrus montanus*; 7, *Anthoxanthum odoratum*; 8, *Holcus lanatus*; 9, *Rumex acetosa*; 10, *Festuca ovina*; 11, *Agrostis tenuis*; 12, *Holcus mollis*; 13, *Deschampsia flexuosa*; 14, *Nardus stricta* (from original data of Grime & Hodgson, 1969, adapted by Bannister, 1976)

In many situations we start with a sown sward consisting only of a few species. However, in most circumstances the normal processes of invasion and replacement occur. In the DoE/STRI extensive mixture trials, 7.5 per cent of alien grasses and 5.7 per cent of alien forbs appeared within 12 months (STRI, unpublished results). In time, species composition thus changes and slowly comes into equilibrium with soil, fertilizer use, and general management. Commonly, for instance, *Poa annua* (annual poa) invades amenity grassland on fertile soils and *Holcus lanatus* (Yorkshire fog) on poor, acidic soils, both lowering the 'quality' of the swards in terms of their original composition.

The way in which such invasion and replacement is controlled by soil nutrient conditions is very clear from long-term fertilizer experiments such as those conducted at Aberystwyth, Cockle Park, and Rothamsted (Bradshaw, 1963) (Table 5.1). It is also demonstrated in a very convincing manner by the flora to be found in old lime lines used to mark-out areas for football and tennis (Cocks *et al.*, 1980) (Figure 5.4 and Plate 5.1). The close limitation of a distinct flora to the region of the lime line shows the precise nature of the effects produced by the addition of lime.

Table 5.1 The long-term effects of fertilizer treatment on the per cent species composition of a hay meadow (Brenchley, in Bradshaw, 1963)

	Control		Ammonium sulphate		Ammonium sulphate and superphosphate		Ammonium sulphate and complete minerals	
		With lime		With lime		With lime		With lime
Agrostis tenuis	15.6	0.8	75.3	1.5	36.2	2.2	7.7	4.3
Alopecurus pratensis	7.9	6.2	0.1	2.5	0.7	24.3	0	38.1
Anthoxanthum odoratum	0.7	0.7	0.2	1.4	10.0	1.2	0.4	4.1
Arrhenatherum elatius	0.1	0.1	0	3.0	0	2.5	0.6	14.7
Dactylis glomerata	4.5	3.3	3.2	18.3	0	0.3	0	11.6
Festuca rubra	16.6	4.1	15.6	15.4	35.3	57.4	0.1	4.3
Holcus lanatus	4.3	2.5	0	5.8	17.5	0.1	90.6	2.5
Leguminosae	7.3	16.1	0	4.6	0	0	0	3.5
Other species (neither grasses nor legumes)	39.8	48.2	5.3	32.1	0.2	11.5	0.5	6.7

Some grass species omitted.

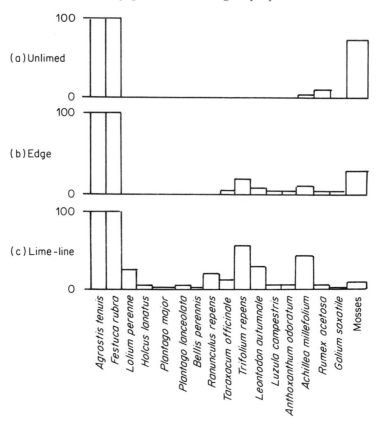

Figure 5.4   Percentage occurrence of various species on and around lime-lines on acidic park grassland in Liverpool (from Cocks *et al.*, 1980)

From such evidence, recommendations for the choice of particular species for use on particular soils have developed. At the same time, the use of particular fertilizer treatments to encourage particular species can be advocated. For example, the use of ammonium sulphate to encourage fine grasses such as *Agrostis tenuis*, *Festuca rubra* (red fescue), and *F. ovina* (sheep's fescue) by lowering soil pH is well established (Dawson, 1968). However, without understanding the total ecosystem such treatments can also bring deleterious effects.

Nutrient requirements

Despite individual differences, grass species have broadly similar patterns of nutrient uptake and requirements for growth (Fleming, 1973; Perkins *et al.*,

Plate 5.1 Heavily-worn tennis courts on acidic soil,
demonstrating the residual effects of lime-lines (Sefton Park,
Liverpool) (photograph by R. J. Cocks)

[*facing page 106*

Table 5.2 The nutrients removed by cutting hay (Russell, 1973) or amenity grass (Dawson, 1956), in kilograms per hectare per year[†]

		Yield	N	P	K	Ca	Mg	S	Na
Meadow hay		3160	55.0	6.1	47.5	25.7	9.8	6.4	7.6
Agrostis tenuis	Control	1345	38.6	4.7	25.5	8.2	(not done)		
	+ N	2354	97.6	8.8	47.1	9.3	(not done)		
Festuca rubra	Control	2063	60.5	7.4	34.7	10.4	(not done)		
	+ N	3363	128.7	11.0	50.5	12.7	(not done)		

[†] 1 kg ha^{-1} = 0.892 lb acre^{-1}.

1978), so nutrient requirements have often been assessed by determining the average content of nutrients in the above-ground crop (Dawson, 1968); Russell, 1973). The values given in Table 5.2 indicate the general magnitude of the amounts corresponding to a total dry matter yield of about 2500 kg ha^{-1} (2230 lb acre^{-1}). However, grassland yields can vary considerably (Hanley *et al.*, 1932) (Table 5.3). So the amount of nutrient being removed by mowing or grazing will differ in different situations and must be determined for specific sites if there is to be any equation between fertilizer application and nutrient loss.

But the quality of amenity grass depends on the quality of the plant material that remains after mowing or grazing. So we need to know the nutrient requirements of this capital element, or biomass, as well as the interest, or flux. A simple model of the system is given in Figure 5.5. We must be able to distinguish between B, the capital requirement of the grass biomass, and the fluxes F_3 and F_4, into material which is removed by

Table 5.3 The variation in yields of old pastures in England and Wales (Hanley *et al.*, 1932)

Grade	Site	Soil	1928	1929
1	Lincoln Marsh	Rich alluvium	5711	2712
1	Romney Marsh	Rich alluvium	4553	3696
2	Lledwigan, Anglesey	Rich calcareous drift	8909	6186
2	Reaseheath, Cheshire	Heavy marl	3577	2180
2	Norfolk	Loam	4782	3818
3	Dorset	Water meadow	3843	3811
3	Essex	Sandy loam	1597	1060
4	Shropshire	Sandy loam	1139	836
4	Yorkshire	Millstone grit	1650	1901
4	Wiltshire	Chalk down	419	210

Values are total of herbage cut to 25 mm (1 in) every 3 weeks, in kilograms of dry matter per hectare. (1 kg ha^{-1} = 0.892 lb acre^{-1}.)

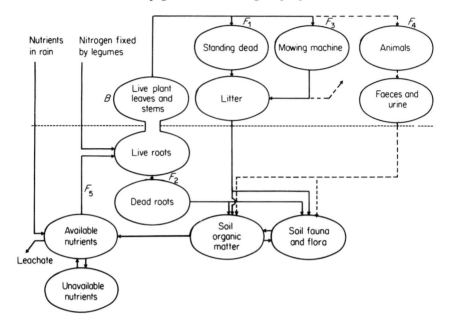

Figure 5.5   A simplified diagram showing nutrient movements in amenity grassland

mowing machine or animals or fluxes F_1 and F_2 into dead above-ground or below-ground material (representing what is required for replacement of that part of the biomass which has not been cropped). Unlike many other plant communities it is unlikely that the biomass will change significantly from year to year, so any increment component of the biomass can be disregarded. The total requirement of the turnover component of the biomass is then represented by the uptake flux F_5, which is the amount of nutrient which must become available to the plant in the soil during the growing season.

Unfortunately no attempt appears so far to have been made to determine even such simple values for amenity grassland. However, this approach is now well established for agricultural grassland (Wilkinson, 1973), and recently a detailed examination has been made of an upland, sheep-grazed grassland at Llyn Llydaw, North Wales, dominated by *Agrostis tenuis* and *Festuca ovina* (Perkins, 1978). Although at rather high altitude (488 m (1601 ft)) and with high rainfall (2930 mm (115 in)), the site has an underlying rock which leads to a base-rich brown earth and the plant community which this soil supports is equivalent to many in lowland grassland. At this site the total biomass is approximately 8200 kg ha^{-1} (7300 lb acre^{-1}), while the total production above and below ground is 8400 kg ha^{-1} year^{-1} (7500 lb acre^{-1} year^{-1}).

Table 5.4 Nutrients in capital and in production in an upland grassland at Llyn Llydaw, North Wales (Perkins, 1978), in kilograms per hectare per year†

Component	N	P	K	Ca	Mg
Capital total	98	7.7	28.3	15.5	43.3
Above ground	43	4.0	25.2	5.8	11.3
Below ground	54	3.7	3.1	9.7	32.0
Production above	132	13.9	72	24.6	52.1
Eaten	53	5.2	42	11.8	7.6
Left	79	8.7	30	12.8	44.5
Production below	30	2.1	1.7	5.4	17.9
Uptake	162	16.0	73.7	30.0	70.0

† 1 kg ha^{-1} = 0.892 lb acre^{-1}.

Since the biomass is not increasing, this means there is complete turnover of capital every year, consequently with high requirements for plant nutrients (Table 5.4). Thus, for example, the capital of nitrogen in the biomass is 98 kg ha^{-1} (87 lb acre^{-1}), while the above-ground production contains 132 kg ha^{-1} year^{-1} (118 lb acre^{-1} year^{-1}) of which 53 kg ha^{-1} (47 lb acre^{-1}) is removed by grazing, 79 kg ha^{-1} (71 lb acre^{-1}) is returned directly as litter, and the below-ground production is 30 kg ha^{-1} (27 lb acre^{-1}). The total annual requirement for nitrogen is therefore 162 kg ha^{-1} (145 lb acre^{-1}).

The same analysis is available for other major nutrient elements. In all cases, the amounts of nutrient contained in the total production are more than the amounts contained in the capital. In many cases they are nearly twice as much, despite the equivalence of biomass and production in terms of dry matter, because of higher concentration of nutrients in the latter. If the concentrations in young foliage are taken into account the amounts of nutrient in circulation are even higher. But a substantial proportion of this is returned directly to the plant by internal translocation or by leaching from the live matter and then immediate uptake by the roots: this has, therefore, not been presented in Table 5.4.

The amount of above-ground production removed by sheep in the Llyn Llydaw grassland ecosystem was approximately 2480 kg ha^{-1} year^{-1} (2212 lb acre^{-1} year^{-1}), of which 1990 kg ha^{-1} (1775 lb acre^{-1}) was living material. Although such values are lower than those obtained for intensively managed grasslands, whether grazed or mown (Table 5.2), they are comparable to those obtained for many old grasslands (Table 5.3). We can, therefore, presume that these Llyn Llydaw values can provide good guidance for temperate amenity grasslands of reasonable fertility, until other information becomes available. An independent check is provided by using the generally accepted concentrations of mineral nutrients in plant tissue (Epstein, 1972). If we assume a total dry matter yield of 5000 kg ha^{-1} year^{-1}

(4460 lb acre^{-1} year^{-1}), the amounts of nutrient would be

N   1.5 per cent, or 75 kg ha^{-1} year^{-1} (66.9 lb acre^{-1} year^{-1})
P   0.2 per cent, or 10 kg ha^{-1} year^{-1} (8.9)
K   1.0 per cent, or 50 kg ha^{-1} year^{-1} (44.6)
Ca 0.5 per cent, or 25 kg ha^{-1} year^{-1} (22.3)
Mg 0.2 per cent, or 10 kg ha^{-1} year^{-1} (8.9).

Values of this order can thus be taken as necessary for total of mown production in amenity grassland.

Nutrient supply

The major stores of nutrient in any soil/plant ecosystem are in the soil minerals, the soil organic matter, and on the soil exchange system. The nutrients available to plants are essentially contained only in the last two. The most important nutrient, nitrogen, is contained only in the organic matter. From its effect on controlling plant growth the second most important nutrient is phosphorus, a substantial proportion of which is also contained in organic matter. The decay of organic matter, whereby nitrogen and phosphorus are released in a form which the plant can utilize, is, therefore a very important process in the ecosystem. This has recently attracted considerable attention, although not in amenity grassland (Bartholomew & Clark, 1965; Dickinson & Pugh, 1974).

Differences in the rate at which organic matter decays in grassland soils can be investigated by measurements of soil respiration. We have already seen that the lime which is used for marking-out playing areas has a distinct effect on the vegetation. Equally, it has a very marked effect on soil respiration (Table 5.5). The effect on release of mineral nitrogen can be assessed by a nitrogen mineralization test (Bremner, 1965), in which the soil,

Table 5.5   Soil respiration and nitrogen mineralization in limed and unlimed areas of an acidic park grassland in Liverpool (Cocks *et al.*, 1980)

	Depth (mm)	Limed	Unlimed
Soil respiration (μl CO_2 h^{-1} g dry soil^{-1})	20–40	12.6	3.5
	60–80	6.5	1.2
	100–120	3.1	0.5
Nitrogen mineralization (increase in soluble N after 14 days at 30 °C in μg g^{-1})†	20–40	113.3	54.3
	60–80	83.5	28.3
	120–140	47.0	20.0

†1 μg g^{-1} = 1 ppm.

after drying, is rewetted and incubated for 14 or 21 days at 30 °C, during which time the increase in soluble nitrogen is measured. This demonstrates the substantial effect of liming on nitrogen mineralization, as might be expected from agricultural experience (Harmsen & van Schreven, 1955).

Other differences develop between the limed and unlimed areas, particularly those involving the soil fauna. Earthworms commonly occur on the limed areas but are absent from the unlimed. Earthworms have a major effect on aeration and on drainage and can bury as much as 300 kg ha^{-1} year^{-1} (268 lb acre^{-1} year^{-1}) of leaf matter (Satchell, 1967; Lofty, 1974). The result is soil with an entirely different potential for plant growth, The estimated above-ground production on the lime lines is 3260 kg ha^{-1} year^{-1} (2908 lb acre^{-1} year^{-1}) and on the surrounding areas 1240 kg ha^{-1} year^{-1} (1106 lb acre^{-1} year^{-1}). While production itself is not an asset in any amenity grassland it gives greater resistance to, and recovery from, wear (Chapter 8). This is very noticeable in areas receiving heavy wear: the lime lines may retain a vegetative cover when surrounding areas lose theirs completely. They are also considerably greener in autumn and winter (Cocks *et al.*, 1980), suggesting that normal seasonal fluctuations in nitrogen supply (Davy & Taylor, 1974) are less pronounced.

This indicates that a proper manipulation of soil conditions to allow organic matter breakdown is important in amenity grassland. The addition of lime to grassland in parks on acidic substrata can cause substantial improvements to growth, often equivalent to that obtained by addition of N, P, and K (Vick & Handley, 1975) (Figure 5.6). However, it muse be remembered that organic matter breakdown is also substantially increased by additions of N and P when these are deficient. Much of the problem of thatch and surface mat accumulation must be due to failure of the decomposition processes to operate effectively. Almost certainly this, in turn, is due to low pH. Thatch and mat are not found on lime lines or in agricultural pastures where the surface pH is above 6.0.

Another important factor affecting nutrient supply is grazing. A grazing animal returns more than 90 per cent of the nutrients it consumes, as dung and urine (Wilkinson, 1973; Perkins, 1978). The nutrients in urine (N. K. and Mg) are immediately available to plants; those in dung are less so but they are considerably more available than those contained in standing dead or litter material because of the decomposition processes occurring within the animal. Grazing, therefore, enhances the cycling process considerably: at Llyn Llydaw it involved 40 per cent of the total production. There is, however, some localization of deposition even with sheep (for example, that associated with night camping-grounds) which ultimately causes lack of uniformity, since this flux is large compared with other factors causing loss (Perkins, 1978; Table 5.6).

Mowing by machine, in which the cuttings are returned to the ground

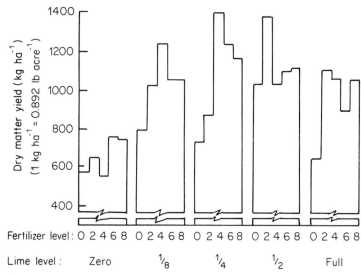

Figure 5.6   The interaction of fertilizer and liming levels on grass
yield in an acidic park grassland in Liverpool. The fertilizer levels of
0, 2, 4, 6, and 8 respectively represent 0, 20, 40, 60, and 80 kg ha^{-1} (0,
18, 36, 54, and 71 lb acre^{-1}) of nitrogen applied in an NPK fertilizer
(from Vick & Handley, 1975)

(Chapters 9 and 11), will have some effect in increasing the rate of nutrient
cycling since the decay of cut herbage is more rapid than that of standing
dead material. But soil conditions will exert an over-riding influence and, if
surface organic matter accumulation is to be avoided, such conditions must
be adjusted to give rapid decomposition.

Table 5.6   Nutrient inputs and outputs in an upland grassland at Llyn Llydaw, North
Wales (Perkins, 1978) in kilograms per hectare per year†

	Component				
	N	P	K	Ca	Mg
Precipitation	18.4	1.7	3.0	26.0	11.3
Fixation	nd	0	0	0	0
Leaching	nd	1.5	8.2	40.5	23.4
Sheep production	3.2	0.8	0.2	− 1.4	0.1
Net	0?	−0.6	− 5.4	−15.9	−12.2
(Grazing)	(54)	(5.2)	(42)	(25)	(7.6)

Grazing represents potential removal only.
†1 kg ha^{-1} = 0.892 lb acre^{-1}.

Maintenance of nutrient levels

In any ecosystem the capital of nutrients must obviously be maintained. A natural grassland ecosystem, such as at Llyn Llydaw, has good nutrient-retaining properties, presumably because of the active conservative action of an extensive root system (Table 5.6). There is also a significant input from rain and relatively little is removed in the sheep 'crop'. Nevertheless there are losses, particularly of the more mobile calcium and magnesium. Losses of calcium, and other bases, are considerable in urban areas where there is high SO_2 pollution (Vick & Handley, 1975) (Figure 5.7). At Llyn Llydaw these losses are made good by weathering of the underlying, soft, base-rich, pumice turf. Elsewhere, this may not be possible and the losses will have to be made good by artificial means. In moist, temperate climates they are equivalent to 2.5 kg $CaCO_3$ ha^{-1} mm^{-1} of rain (56.6 lb acre^{-1} in^{-1}) (Russell, 1973). So, in Britain an application of $CaCO_3$ equivalent to 500 kg ha^{-1} year^{-1} (446 lb acre^{-1} year^{-1}) is needed. Since leaching losses are related to climate, in more arid regions such losses of calcium do not occur and there may be accumulation, even, of very soluble ions such as those of sodium and magnesium.

Inorganic nitrogen compounds are very soluble and are readily leached. Unfortunately, leaching rates were not determined at Llyn Llydaw. However, elsewhere in moist, temperate, lowland grassland 20 kg ha^{-1} year^{-1} (17.8 lb acre^{-1} year^{-1}) has been found, but less in stable, low-nutrient situations (Allison, 1955; Russell, 1973). This degree of loss is readily replaced by nitrogen contained in rainfall (up to 30 kg ha^{-1} year^{-1} (26.8 lb acre^{-1} year^{-1}) is deposited in urban areas) and by fixation by legumes when these are present in the plant community.

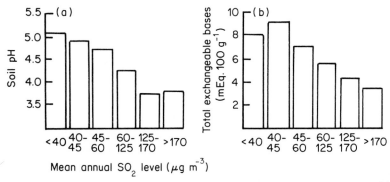

Figure 5.7 The effects of atmospheric SO_2 pollution on (a) pH and (b) total exchangeable bases in park grassland soils in the Merseyside region (Vick & Handley, 1975)

Where mowing occurs and the cuttings are removed (Chapter 11) there will be considerable losses of nutrients which must be replaced if the ecosystem is not to be depleted (Chapter 9): the amounts must be similar to those in Table 5.2. The result of not replacing the nutrients removed by cutting can be seen in the grounds of most Victorian houses—a depauperate vegetation cover consisting largely of mosses. Despite the fact that the replacement of the lost nutrients is extremely easy, using standard mineral fertilizers and lime (Escritt & Lidgate, 1964; Cooke, 1967), it is remarkable how many lawns in old housing areas are lacking in nutrients and are extremely acidic.

Replacement of Ca, P, and K using lime or mineral fertilizers presents no problems since either they are in an insoluble form or they are rapidly absorbed onto cation exchange sites and are retained. Nitrogen replacement is more difficult since it is needed in large amounts by plants and is normally available only in the form of very soluble ammonium salts or nitrates. Slow-release forms (Chapter 7), such as ureaform and isobutylidene-diurea, are available, but these are very expensive and may break down too slowly (Fuller & Clark, 1947; Musser *et al.*, 1951). Sulphur-coated urea appeared to have the opposite problem (Davis, 1973; Dancer *et al.*, 1979). As a result, there is a view that a series of small dressings of ammonium or nitrate nitrogen remains the most effective and economical method of applying this element (Robinson *et al.*, 1977).

However, in many amenity situations there is a very obvious alternative—the use of *Trifolium repens* (white clover) or a similar legume. Commonly-available pasture legumes can fix reasonable amounts of nitrogen even under difficult conditions providing they have been given adequate time and phosphorus (Dancer *et al.*, 1977a,b). Nitrogen accumulation rates of the order of 100–200 kg ha^{-1} year^{-1} (90–180 lb acre^{-1} year^{-1}) can occur in normal pastures. *T. repens* had a mean cover of 8 per cent at Llyn Llydaw and must have been contributing substantially to the ecosystem's total nitrogen level although unfortunately this was not measured as a separate component.

An accumulation in a sward of 100 kg N ha^{-1} year^{-1} (90 lb acre^{-1} year^{-1}) needs an application of fertilizer providing about 400–600 kg of ammonium nitrate or urea per hectare (357–535 lb acre^{-1}) when allowance is made for leaching losses. The economic value of legumes such as clover is, therefore, very clear. It is traditional to exclude them from fine turf because of their tendency to patchiness. But in an extensive amenity grassland, clover should be included as a matter of course, particularly in newly created areas where the quality of the soil must nearly always be suspect (Bloomfield *et al.*, 1980). The natural improvement of many newly sown amenity grass areas can be correlated with natural invasion by clover. Under close mowing, dwarf cultivars of white clover will not grow patchily if sown at the outset rather than left to appear by random colonization. Clovers can achieve a long-term balance with the grass and will disappear only when sufficient nitrogen has accumulated to change the competitive balance in favour of the grasses. In many situations the value of legumes is now understood. It is a component of the British standard seed mixture for roadside verges. In North America, seed mixtures effectively dominated by legumes such as *Coronilla varia* (crown vetch) and *Lespedeza sericea* (lespedeza) are widely used (Hanson & Juska, 1969).

Conclusions

We cannot escape the fact that amenity grassland is an ecosystem involving soil and plants interacting together continuously.

From this it follows that to achieve proper nutrition of the grass we have to pay attention to the functioning of the whole system and should not rely upon occasional inputs of fertilizer to improve grass growth in an *ad hoc* manner. Any wise greenkeeper or sports ground manager appreciates this already. But it is easy to get so involved in one particular aspect of grass management that the problems presented by the functioning of the whole ecosystem are not appreciated (Chapter 12).

It is, therefore, high time that the ecosystem approach was applied to amenity grass, whether the grass is to be used intensively or extensively. There appear to be two areas where this approach is likely to be most valuable:

(1) Studies of the balance between input and output of nutrients and of changes in nutrient capital, to understand the nutrient status and well-being of the whole system. These would involve detailed analysis of inputs and outputs in the manner recently carried out for agricultural ecosystems (Frissel, 1977). But this technique may be difficult when errors in measurement of input and output are large. In these cases it may be better to examine changes in capital with time, as has been done for natural and artifical communities (Crocker & Major, 1955; Dancer *et al.*, 1977*a*).

(2) Studies on the rate of internal cycling, to understand the extent to which nutrients are being made available to plants in amounts adequate for their proper growth. This can involve studies of certain fluxes only, but in the end a proper appreciation of what is going on will only be obtained by an assessment of all the different fluxes, as at Llyn Llydaw (Perkins, 1978) and elsewhere (van Dyne, 1969).

All this will require a great deal of detailed work, and will involve a wide variety of approaches and skills. But it will eventually be the only way by which we will obtain a full understanding of the nutrition of amenity grassland and so be able to achieve its most effective management.

References

Allison, F. E. (1955). 'The enigma of soil nitrogen balance sheets', *Advances in Agronomy*, **7**, 213–50.

Bannister, P. (1976). *Introduction to Plant Physiological Ecology*, Blackwell Scientific Publications, Oxford.

Bartholomew, W. V. & Clark, F. E. (eds) (1965). *Soil Nitrogen, Agronomy 10*, American Society of Agronomy, Madison, Wisc.

Berg, J. P. van den (1969). 'Distribution of pasture plants in relation to chemical properties of the soil', in *Ecological Aspects of the Mineral Nutrition of Plants* (I. H. Rorison, ed.), Blackwell Scientific Publications, Oxford, pp. 11–23.

Bloomfield, H., Handley, J. F. & Bradshaw, A. D. (1980). 'The quality of topsoil', in preparation.

Bradshaw, A. D. (1963). 'Turf grass species and soil fertility', *Journal of the Sports Turf Research Institute*, **10**, 1–13.

Bradshaw, A. D. (1969). 'An ecologist's view point', in *Ecological Aspects of the Mineral Nutrition of Plants* (I. H. Rorison, ed.), Blackwell Scientific Publications, Oxford, pp. 415–27.

Bradshaw, A. D., Chadwick, M. J., Jowett, D., Lodge, R. W. & Snaydon, R. W. (1960). 'Experimental investigations into the mineral nutrition of several grass species. III. Phosphate level', *Journal of Ecology*, **48**, 621–37.

Bradshaw, A. D., Chadwick, M. J., Jowett, D. & Snaydon, R. W. (1964). 'Experimental investigations into the mineral nutrition of several grass species. IV. Nitrogen level', *Journal of Ecology*, **52**, 665–76.

Bremner, J. M. (1965). 'Nitrogen availability indexes', in *Methods of Soil Analysis* (C. A. Black, ed.), American Society of Agronomy, Madison, Wisc.; part 2, pp. 1324–45.

Cocks, R. J., Gilham, C. & Bradshaw, A. D. (1980). 'The soils and vegetation of lime lines in amenity grassland', in preparation.

Cooke, G. W. (1967). *The Control of Soil Fertility*, Crosby Lockwood, London.

Crocker, R. W. & Major, J. (1955). 'Soil development in relation to vegetation and surface age at Glacier Bay, Alaska', *Journal of Ecology*, **43**, 427–48.

Dancer, W. S., Handley, J. F. & Bradshaw, A. D. (1977a). 'Nitrogen accumulation in kaolin mining wastes in Cornwall. I. Natural plant communities', *Plant and Soil*, **48**, 153–67.

Dancer, W. S., Handley, J. F. & Bradshaw, A. D. (1977b). 'Nitrogen accumulation in kaolin wastes in Cornwall. II. Forage legumes', *Plant and Soil*, **48**, 303–14.

Dancer, W. S., Handley, J. F. & Bradshaw, A. D. (1979). 'Nitrogen accumulation in kaolin wastes in Cornwall. III. Nitrogenous fertilizers', *Plant and Soil*, **51**, 471–84.

Davis, L. H. (1973). 'Two grass field trials with a sulphur-coated urea to examine its potential as a slow release nitrogen fertilizer in the U.K.', *Journal of the Science of Food and Agriculture*, **24**, 63–7.

Davy, A. J. & Taylor, K. (1974). 'Seasonal patterns of nitrogen availability in contrasting soils in the Chiltern Hills', *Journal of Ecology*, **62**, 793–807.

Dawson, R. B. (1968). *Practical Lawn Craft*, 6th ed., Crosby Lockwood, London.

Dickinson, C. H. & Pugh, G. J. F. (eds) (1974). *Biology of Plant Litter Decomposition*, Academic Press, London.

Dyne, G. M. van (ed.) (1969). *The Ecosystem Concept in Natural Resource Management*, Academic Press, New York.

Epstein, E. (1972). *Mineral Nutrition of Plants. Principles and Perspectives*, Wiley, New York.

Escritt, J. R. & Lidgate, H. J. (1964). 'Report on fertiliser trials', *Journal of the Sports Turf Research Institute*, **40**, 7–42.

Fleming, G. A. (1973). 'Mineral composition of herbage', in *Chemistry and Biochemistry of Herbage* (G. W. Butler & R. W. Bailey, eds), Academic Press, New York, pp. 529–66.

Frissel, M. J. (ed.) (1977). 'Cycling of mineral nutrients in agricultural ecosystems', *Agro-Ecosystems*, **4**, 1–354.

Fuller, W. H. & Clark, K. G. (1947). 'Microbiological studies on urea–formaldehyde preparation', *Soil Science Society of America, Proceedings*, **12**, 198–202.

Grime, J. P. & Hodgson, J. G. (1969). 'An investigation of the ecological significance of lime chlorosis by means of large-scale experiments', in *Ecological Aspects of the Mineral Nutrition of Plants* (I. H. Rorison, ed.), Blackwell Scientific Publications, Oxford, pp. 67–99.

Grime, J. P. & Lloyd, P. S. (1973). *An Ecological Atlas of Grassland Plants*, Edward Arnold, London.

Hanley, J. A., Godden, W., Heddle, R. G., Morr, J. B., Stapledon, R. G. & Woodman, H. E. (1932). 'Improvement of pastures', *Journal of the Ministry of Agriculture*, **39**, 24–36.

Hanson, A. A. & Juska, F. V. (eds) (1969). *Turfgrass Science*, American Society for Agronomy, Madison, Wisc.

Harmsen, G. W. & Schreven, D. A. van (1955). 'Mineralization of organic nitrogen in the soil', *Advances in Agronomy*, **7**, 299–398.

Hutchinson, T. C. (1967). 'Lime chlorosis as a factor in seedling establishment on calcareous soils. I. A comparative study of species from acid and calcareous soils in their susceptibility to lime-chlorosis', *New Phytologist*, **66**, 697–705.

Jefferies, R. L. & Willis, A. J. (1964). 'Studies of the calcicole-calcifuge habit. II. The influence of calcium on the growth and establishment in soil and sand culture', *Journal of Ecology*, **52**, 691–707.

Lewis, J. K. (1969). 'Range management viewed in the ecosystem framework', in *The Ecosystem Concept in Natural Resource Management* (G. M. van Dyne, ed.), Academic Press, New York, pp. 97–187.

Lofty, J. E. (1974). 'Oligochaetes', in *Biology of Plant Litter Decomposition* (C. H. Dickinson & G. J. F. Pugh, eds), Academic Press, London, vol. 2, pp. 467–88.

Musser, H. B., Watson, J. R., Stanford, J. P. & Harper, J. C. (1951). 'Urea-formaldehyde and other nitrogenous fertilizers for use on turf', *Pennsylvania Agricultural Experimental Station Bulletin*, *1951*, 542.

Perkins, D. F. (1978). :The distribution and transfer of energy and nutrients in the *Agrostis-Festuca* grassland ecosystem', in *Production Ecology of British Moors and Montane Grasslands* (O. W. Heal & D. F. Perkins, eds), Springer, Berlin, pp. 375–96.

Perkins, D. F., Jones, V., Millar, R. O. & Neep, P. (1978). 'Primary production, mineral nutrients and litter decomposition in the grassland ecosystem', in *Production Ecology of British Moors and Montane Grasslands* (O. W. Heal & D. F. Perkins, eds), Springer, Berlin, pp. 304–31.

Robinson, G. S., Moore, K. K. & Murphy, J. (1977). 'Effect of a number of standard and slow-release nitrogenous fertilizers on the quality of fine turf', *Journal of the Sports Turf Research Institute*, **53**, 74–84.

Russell, E. W. (1973). *Soil Conditions and Plant Growth*, 10th ed., Longman, London.

Satchell, J. E. (1967). 'Lumbricidae', in *Soil Biology* (A. Burges & F. Raw, eds), Academic Press, London, pp. 259–322.

Vick, C. M. & Handley, J. F. (1975). 'Lime and fertilizer use in the maintenance of turf in urban parks and open spaces', *Journal of the Institute of Park and Recreation Administration*, **40**, 39–48.

Wilkinson, S. R. (1973). 'Cycling of mineral nutrients in pasture ecosystems', in *Chemistry and Biochemistry of Herbage* (G. W. Butler & R. W. Bailey, eds), Academic Press, New York, pp. 247–315.

Witkamp, M. (1971). 'Soils as components of ecosystems', *Annual Review of Ecology and Systematics*, **2**, 85–110.

Amenity Grassland: An Ecological Perspective
Edited by I. H. Rorison and R. Hunt
© 1980 John Wiley & Sons Ltd

6

Soil drainage and soil moisture

V. I. STEWART *Soil Science Unit, University College of Wales, Aberystwyth, Wales*

Introduction

Soil consists of particles structured by physical and biological processes into the pore system that constitutes the space available below ground for air, water, and living organisms. The extent to which this delicate structure can be used for amenity grassland without adverse effect varies with climate, soil, and form of use.

Significant variation in climate

In Britain the annual rainfall is of the order of 750 mm (29.5 in) and no more than 500 mm (19.7 in) of this can be returned direct to the atmosphere by evaporation and transpiration. However, whereas our rainfall varies little throughout the year, potential evaporation can vary tenfold between mid-summer and mid-winter. As a result, our free-draining soils are liable to hover around or above field capacity from autumn to spring, and develop significant deficits only in summer. Adverse effects of waterlogging on wear are most likely to show up, therefore, either in the off-season for growth, when the vegetation is least able to contribute to its own repair or, in spring and autumn, when soil temperatures are adequate to promote biological activity but excess soil moisture may inhibit healthy growth because of inadequate aeration.

The extent to which soil moisture excess is likely to limit the safe use of even well-drained land is indicated by agricultural meteorological data used to define the grazing season, i.e. the season when soil temperatures can be expected to be adequate for grass growth and the soil dry enough to avoid being poached (MAFF, 1976). Thus, in Dyfed and Lancashire even freely-drained soils can be expected to be at risk from poaching for over 8 months in the year—early September to mid-May—whereas in Norfolk and Hampshire the period of risk is only 4–5 months—November/December to early April. Spring and autumn growth is liable to be at risk from the adverse effects of temporary waterlogging for a total of 110 days in Dyfed, 84 days in Lancashire, 53 days in Hampshire, and only 3 days in Norfolk. This could well have a bearing on the variable performance, in Britain, of 'continental' species such as *Poa pratensis* (smooth-stalked meadow-grass). Meteorological data have also been used to estimate, for different climatic regions, the number of days when the soil is likely to be too dry for grass growth—48 for Norfolk, 35 for Hampshire, and 5 or less for Dyfed and Lancashire. For those with amenity grass to look after the indications from meteorological data are that the major problem in the east and south of the UK is likely to be summer drought, and in the west and north, waterlogging.

Though, for good agricultural land, field capacity is likely to represent a soil adequately aerated for healthy root growth, this need not necessarily be so. Field capacity, as such, tells us nothing about the balance of air-filled and water-filled pores in a soil, merely that loss of water by drainage has virtually ceased. A compact soil entirely made up of small pores could be completely waterlogged at field capacity and, as such, might be capable of shunting water off the surface to a soakaway but incapable of emptying to admit air once surface water had been cleared. From the evidence of gley features, indicating micro-organisms turning to alternatives to oxygen for respiration, Stewart & Adams (1968) have suggested that adequate aeration is a feature of soil layers in which at least 30 per cent of the pore space drains to admit air at field capacity.

Significant variation in soil

Sands, clays, and loams differ in the means by which they can be modified to provide the ideal blend of free-draining macroporespace and water storing microporespace. Sands cannot do other than provide macroporespace and, if they are to retain water for plant growth, must be perched over a layer of gravel acting as an airlock or, in a normal field situation, must be heterogeneously packed with less than 30 per cent silt plus clay, or a similar volume of organic matter. Sandy soils, modified in these ways, are particularly valuable where compaction has to be accepted (Adams *et al.*, 1971).

Clay particles, though smaller even than silt, are unique amongst soil mineral particles in being very platey in shape and in carrying an electro-chemical charge. Soils comprising over 40 per cent clay can become strongly bound, even when moist, and become structured by the frag-menting effect of repeated cycles of swelling and shrinking. The resulting fine, angular, blocky fragments are micropore in character within and macropore in character between (Plate 6.1).

However, soils sufficiently sandy to be independent of structure for

Plate 6.1 Profile of a strong clay soil showing a
well-developed fracture structure. This has developed by
fragmentation rather than by aggregation (photograph by
V. I. Stewart)

Plate 6.2 A worm-worked loam, showing an abundance of worm runs and a granular surface structure, both advantageous to efficient drainage (photograph by V. I. Stewart)

Plate 6.3 Soil with the surface organic mat and compact mineral layers typical of an acidic pasture devoid of earthworms (photograph by V. I. Stewart)

Plate 6.4 On this sports field the cinder layer intended to aid surface drainage has discouraged earthworm activity, with the result that drainage through the topsoil has been impeded (photograph by V. I. Stewart)

drainage, and clays sufficiently strong to be capable of continual restructuring are exceptional soils in Britain. The great majority of British soils are loams, that is, they are fairly even mixtures of sand, silt, and clay. Such soils, when compacted, are likely to be entirely micropore in character. They are too low in sand for the macropore system between the sand particles to avoid being filled by silt and clay, and they have insufficient clay to achieve a fine fragmental structure by cracking. These are the soils for which nature has had to evolve a special structuring mechanism strong enough to resist collapse under the impact of raindrops. This natural mechanism would seem to be initiated be earthworm casting (Guild, 1955) and reinforced by roots (Stewart, 1975; Salih, 1978). The microporespace, within the granules, provides a reservoir for water and nutrients and the macrospore system, between granules, makes provision for drainage, aeration and root penetration (Plate 6.2).

If the key organisms involved in soil granulation are burrowing earthworms it would be as well to be aware of some at least of their known sensitivities: acidity, prolonged waterlogging, the litter of certain plants, some fertilizers, and certain extensively-used systemic fungicides (Edwards & Lofty, 1977). The active presence of earthworms in soil should not, therefore, always be taken for granted.

However, their habit of throwing casts up on the surface of the soil encourages weed invasion, affects the appearance of a close-mown sward, and may interfere with the reactions of a ball played over the surface. Not surprisingly, there is a market for 'wormicides'.

Earthworms or not? A fundamental dichotomy

There are both naturally and artificially maintained soils in which burrowing earthworms may, or may not, be present. This distinction is responsible for the contrasting trends in soil development which pedologists use to distinguish brown earths from podsols; foresters, mull from mor; farmers, mat from non-mat; greenkeepers, thatch from non-thatch; and ecologists, habitats typical of calcicole or calcifuge plants.

The ecological significance of this pedological dichotomy lies in a range of soil characteristics in respect of which these divergent systems are differentiated:

(1) incorporated or surface-segregated organic matter (Plate 6.3);
(2) mineral matter aggregated into a free-draining, well-aerated, granular soil structure, or soil with drainage impeded by the compact structure of the mineral surface;
(3) patterns of deposition of iron reflecting the distribution of organic matter and consequent distinctions in aeration;
(4) deep rooting, leading to vegetation not subject to extremes of moisture

stress, or shallow rooting, leading to vegetation necessarily adapted to cope with periodic, temporary waterlogging and periodic drought;

(5) calcicole plants not subject to, and not tolerant of, high concentrations of soluble iron and aluminium, or calcifuge plants adapted and, to varying degrees, now conditioned to require high concentrations of iron and to tolerate high concentrations of aluminium;

(6) plants to various extents dependent on mycorrhizal associations to exploit their substrate.

When constructing, planting, maintaining, or breeding for amenity areas it would be as well to recognize that a great deal can flow from the decision to foster or eliminate the earthworm population. Only on small areas of fine turf such as that used for ornamentation, for bowls or for golf, must the elimination of earthworms be sought. Elsewhere, this elimination can only be justified for aesthetic, environmental reasons, or where regular liming to counteract acidity is practically impossible.

Soil management and surface waterlogging

Though any feature of management can be considered essential, in that its neglect can lead to a sward unfit for its purpose, the most common problem on trodden turf is that of surface waterlogging brought about by the collapse of surface structure. This is frequently initiated by soil disturbance and perpetuated by inappropriate management or lack of discretion in use. Topsoil deteriorates in storage because, while biological activity continues, at depth aeration is impeded. Microbial populations with anomalous modes of respiration are favoured, using nitrate nitrogen, ferric iron, sulphur, and even carbon dioxide as alternatives to oxygen, producing as end-products nitrogen gas, ferrous iron, hydrogen sulphide, and methane (Turner & Patrick, 1968). Little wonder that the earthworm population virtually disappears and structure deteriorates.

Even on undisturbed sites the earthworm population may be adversely affected, unwittingly, as a side effect of normal management. This is most likely to happen as a consequence of the long-term use of acidifying fertilizers such as sulphate of ammonia but could also happen as a result of the indiscriminate use of some modern fungicides and pesticides. In either case the end result, on loam soils, is bound to be a slow drift to surface impedance (Plate 6.4).

However, even a well-granulated, worm-worked soil is too soft to avoid tearing and surface poaching if used intensively under wet conditions. A farmer accepts this in a field of kale used for winter feed because he can put things right by ploughing in the spring, but this practice cannot be followed on amenity sites.

The winter use of grass swards is an exercise in survival. A groundsman can usually identify which game, played under particularly adverse conditions, initiated the break-up of his sward. Once the surface cover and root reinforcement has gone the soil cannot cope alone and damaged areas are bound to extend until the summer lay-off period provides opportunities for repair.

A studded boot is designed to help players achieve the traction required to move effectively on turf. It is designed to achieve limited penetration of the surface—footballers speak of a good surface as 'taking a stud'—but once within the soil a studded boot is a very effective implement for testing the shear resistance of the sward. Many soils that will just about 'take a stud' at field capacity, under the weight of an adult, will not necessarily do likewise under the weight of a juvenile. It is not surprising, therefore, that pitches used only by juveniles require much less maintenance, a point worth keeping in mind when there is pressure for dual use of school playing fields.

It is a common fallacy to approach soil drainage as if all problems originate in the behaviour of a ground water table welling up from below to influence the surface adversely. This may be an important factor on receiving sites where it is usually best dealt with by appropriately sited peripheral ditches but, even when extraneous water has been intercepted, there still remains the need to deal with incident rainfall. Temporary surface ponding is a common manifestation of moisture excess but, where the soil surface has been poached or compacted by use, this is most likely to be a result of incident rainfall failing to enter the soil at the rate required to avoid surface run-off and, for this reason, any treatment aimed at improving the drainage of intensively-used sports turf must extend right through to the surface.

The crushed-rock, gravelly surfaces of hard, porous pitches can usually in-filter rainfall up to about 3 mm h^{-1} (0.12 in h^{-1}), but above this rate surface run-off can lead to ponding in dished areas. Even these pitches, therefore, though often erroneously called 'all-weather', are best crowned or uniformly sloped to provide for efficient surface run-off to the periphery. For example, dished areas, 5 m across and 30 mm deep (19.7 ft × 1.18 in.) at the centre, can clear themselves by surface run-off on a slope of 1 : 80.

Practical conclusions

On the majority of British soils, problems associated with poor surface drainage are bound to arise following disturbance or indiscriminate use (Stewart, 1976). To date, experience suggests that preventive and rehabilitation techniques must involve some combination of the following:

(1) surface grading to avoid enclosed hollows and promote a useful amount of surface run-off;

(2) installation of ditches and interceptor drains to control spring water and surface run-off;
(3) pattern drainage (down-slope) linked to subsoiling (across-slope) to improve the soil moisture regime, plus liming and return of organic residues, to promote the development of a biologically-stabilized structure;
(4) building a new surface, either predominantly made up of sand, or with sand and gravel confined to a close system of vertical drainage channels maintained open to the surface, both systems linked below ground to an appropriately designed soakaway or pipe drainage system (see Chapter 7).

(1), (2), and (3) are currently the subject of a land restoration research programme financed by the National Coal Board, and carried out on an area of 120 ha (300 acres) at a former opencast, coal-mining site in South Wales. (4) has been the subject of a research project sponsored by the Sports Council (Thornton, 1978). Both projects have been supervised by the author.

It is at present uncertain whether academic research or trial and error will be the main means by which the full range of these techniques will be developed. Meantime, it is my view that the greatest need is for close monitoring of the effectiveness of work already carried out and an extensive re-education programme to up-grade the knowledge of those already involved both in education and in the field.

References

Adams, W. A., Stewart, V. I. & Thornton, D. J. (1971). 'The assessment of sands suitable for use in sportsfields', *Journal of the Sports Turf Research Institute*, **47**, 77–85.
Edwards, C. A. & Lofty, J. R. (1977). *Biology of Earthworms*, 2nd ed., Chapman and Hall, London.
Guild, W. J. McL. (1955). 'Earthworms and soil structure', in *Soil Zoology* (D. K. McE. Kevan, ed.), Butterworth, London, pp. 83–98.
MAFF (1976). *The Agricultural Climate of England and Wales*, Ministry of Agriculture, Fisheries and Food, HMSO, London.
Salih, R. O. (1978). 'The assessment of soil structure and the influence of soil treatment on this property', PhD thesis, University College of Wales, Aberystwyth.
Stewart, V. I. (1975). 'Soil structure', *Soil Association Quarterly Review*, **1** (3).
Stewart, V. I. (1976). 'Wallowing in mud?', *Journal of Parks and Recreation*, **41**, 38–51.
Stewart, V. I. & Adams, W. A. (1968). 'The quantitative description of soil moisture states in natural habitats with special reference to moist soils', in *The Measurement of Environmental Factors in Terrestrial Ecology* (R. M. Wadsworth, ed.), Blackwell Scientific Publications, Oxford, pp. 161–73.
Thornton, D. J. (1978). 'The construction and drainage of some specialized sportsfield playing surfaces', PhD thesis, University College of Wales, Aberystwyth.
Turner, F. T. & Patrick, W. H. (1968). 'Chemical changes in waterlogged soils as a result of oxygen depletion', *Transactions of the 9th International Congress on Soil Science*, **4**, 53–65.

Amenity Grassland: An Ecological Perspective
Edited by I. H. Rorison and R. Hunt
© 1980 John Wiley & Sons Ltd

7
Construction and maintenance of sports turf

J. R. ESCRITT *Sports Turf Research Institute, Bingley, West Yorkshire, England*

Introduction

This chapter concerns sports grounds of the local authority type rather than first-class professional facilities on the one hand or extensive amenity areas subject to low maintenance levels on the other. But many of the points made have some significance for all types of amenity turf since grass growing in soil (ameliorated or otherwise) will be their basis for many years to come.

It is necessary to emphasize the importance of using the knowledge and expertise currently available; in this respect there is a definite need for education. Grass pitches result from a combination of biology and engineering and when constructing new grounds it is necessary to reconcile the two disciplines. Failure to take either into proper account, or to organize a proper balance between them, usually leads to very poor results. Constructional projects should be organized in the light of current biological knowledge and of facts of life such as site conditions, the capabilities of contractors and of their labour forces, economics, and, of course, the current objectives.

Sometimes odd things are allowed to happen. A new golf course recently constructed on light sandy soil had its greens built on an undrained stone layer, with the grass established in about 300 mm (12 in) of heavy roadworks loam, inadequately ameliorated with sand. It is now necessary to reconstruct the greens, at considerable cost, this time using the excellent native soil. Possibly £50 000 has been wasted—and this by a commercial concern! Further large sums will be needed for reconstruction. To avoid mistakes such as this requires careful attention to a number of vital processes.

The consultant's brief

When creating a new playing field or sports ground the organizer or consultant-in-charge needs to be given some basic information:

(1) the number and size of pitches required;

(2) guidance on the use they are intended to receive (kind and number of games, type of player);
(3) the standard or quality required.

The last is likely to cause difficulty, since customers vary in what they are willing to provide—some are quite content to have an area of ground which can be called a pitch, even though it is too wet to use in January or February. Research work is required to provide some kind of quantitative testing procedure for assessment of 'pitch quality'. This would facilitate the levelling-up of standards and perhaps result in more public money being allocated for the construction of sports grounds on, say, clay soil in an area with an annual rainfall of 1500 mm (60 in), than for grounds on a sandy loam in an area with 500 mm (20 in) of rain.

The aim is normally a suitable playing surface of maximum durability. For this, the type of sward is possibly less important than the soil and its drainage properties. The work reported by Canaway (1978) could be helpful by making it possible to quantify durability. It should not be too difficult to quantify drainage properties but it will certainly be difficult to get agreement on what constitutes a proper degree of durability or a proper degree of drainage relative to rainfall. Van Wijk & Beuving (1975) suggested that suitable criteria for 'playability' and 'dependability' might be obtained through penetrometer readings over a long period.

Timing

The bulk of the construction work on a new sports ground should best be done in the months April to August inclusive. In order that this can be accomplished, tenders need to go out in, say, the previous December to allow for lengthy committee procedures. This, in turn, means that the preparation of the contract documents needs to be done not later than November. Prior to this a site survey showing, for example, existing levels and possible drainage outfalls, is usually essential and there may be permits to obtain from bodies such as the planning authority and the water authority. In all, a whole year can easily elapse between making the first decision and starting construction. After construction is completed, a further year is usually required before the new turf is put into use (Figure 7.1).

It will be appreciated that when a new school is being built, the construction of its playing field may need to be started before the building itself if the field is to be available for use when the school opens. Here we see a need for the education of committee members who spend large amounts of public money. All too frequently, decisions to get work done are made in December, with the money to be spent in the financial year ending on the following 31 March. I know of no successful practical outcome to this kind of approach.

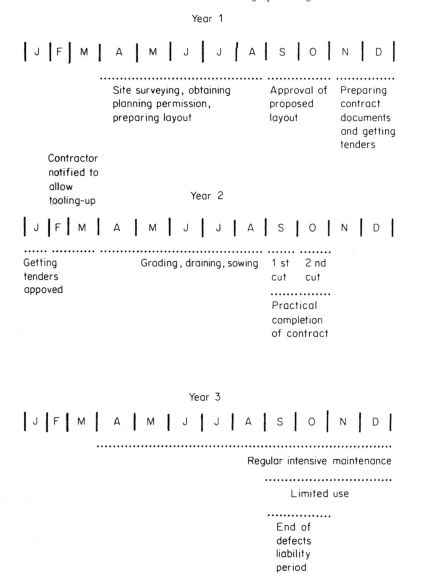

Figure 7.1 A calendar of events in the construction of a new sports field

The contract

Those organizing contracts for the production of new sports grounds tend principally to be persons experienced in organizing contracts. There are very few such people who are also expert on sports ground construction. Those who do not have the necessary biological knowledge should obviously take the advice of specialist consultants. It is important that the contract documents be adequate in covering contract conditions, specifications of work required, suitable drawings for drainage, etc., and bills of quantities. Some guidance is given by Gooch & Escritt (1975) but in view of variation in circumstances it is considered that at this stage to proceed to a British Standard similar to the German Deutsche Industrie-Norm (DIN) 18035/4 would be of doubtful value.

The practical work

Grading

The majority of sports ground sites seem to receive major grading, but in considering new projects it should be borne in mind that grading is expensive and detrimental to drainage; it should not be embarked upon without adequate justification. It is also undesirable to lay down hard-and-fast rules regarding gradients. Playing fields do not need to be completely level, nor need they necessarily have a through bone (a continuous, uniform gradient). Indeed, a slight slope helps drainage, although it is not advisable to leave ungraded slopes which are steeper than 1 in 30. Where major grading is carried out the aim might reasonably be 1 in 60 across a pitch and 1 in 100 along the length of a pitch. Certainly, the maximum slopes should not exceed 1 in 40 across a pitch or 1 in 80 along the line of play if undue fatigue is to be avoided. The subsoil formation should be finished in accordance with the levels and gradients prescribed, and should be smooth so that when topsoil is replaced it is of uniform depth. The whole of the topsoil should be returned in uncontaminated condition, preferably to a final depth of at least 150 mm (6 in). Whereas quite close tolerances in level are imposed for special areas such as grass tennis courts, e.g. 13 mm (0.5 in) when tested with a 3 m (10 ft) straight edge, it has, so far, been found sufficient to prescribe for general playing fields finished levels with no 'noticeable' ruts or depressions.

Major grading involves the use of heavy equipment with consequent detriment to the structure of both topsoil and subsoil. These can be much reduced by ensuring that the work is carried out only when ground conditions are suitable. Major grading also involves the temporary storage of topsoil in heaps, which inevitably leads to some deterioration in physical structure. Since the soil is usually stacked for no more than a few weeks marked deterioration from storage (as opposed to damage during handling) is probably not of great consequence. But storage for any greater length of time can be more serious (Hunter & Currie, 1956).

Subsoil cultivation

As a result of grading and topsoiling, the subsoil becomes highly compacted even in the best of circumstances. Some means of alleviating this to provide suitable conditions for drainage is essential unless a drainage layer and emptying drains are also being installed. Subsoil cultivation is done (after topsoil replacement and before installing the drains) by means of suitable subsoil cultivators, commonly working to a depth of 450 mm (18 in) and at spacings of not more than 600 mm (2 ft). Efficient shattering of the subsoil by subsoil cultivators needs dry conditions and, whilst it is usually possible in an English summer to get topsoil conditions sufficiently dry for satisfactory work, it can be extremely difficult to get conditions right for efficient subsoil cultivation. There is evidence that multi-shank subsoilers are more efficient than single-shank models but the whole subject merits some investigation in the sports ground context since impervious subsoils lead to serious drainage problems which are not necessarily removed by pipe drainage. Efficient shattering can increase hydraulic conductivity by a factor of 10 000 or more. Subsoil cultivation is commonly done after installation of drains as well as before, although this time to a rather shallower depth so as to avoid damaging the drains. If subsoil cultivation of existing turf areas is undertaken there is a risk of severe disruption.

Drainage

There are still people who do not appreciate the need for adequate drainage—one can find those who say a site is adequately drained because it has never been seen under water! In fact, on playing fields, good drainage (artificial or natural) in the fullest sense is essential to maintain a stable system able to withstand the amount of wear imposed.

There are very few new sports turf facilities which do not require artificial drainage. This usually involves the installation of pipe drains within the site and, sometimes, around, or partially around, it to intercept water from outside areas. Many quite reasonable playing areas have been made which are dependent upon conventional pipe drainage systems (e.g. systems with lateral drains at 5.5 m (18 ft) centres at a depth of 600 mm (2 ft)) and covered with porous fill to within 150 mm (6 in) of the surface. These need to be supplemented only by regular mechanical aeration to assist the water away from the surface.

Because problems in usage normally arise from surface water rather than from a high water table, developments beyond this basic approach often include the following:

(1) The amelioration of topsoil by cultivating-in massive amounts of sand. The amount required to ameliorate the whole of the topsoil is

quite considerable and so is not often economically feasible; but amelioration of the surface inch or two has proved quite useful in some cases. Of course, for sites lacking in topsoil, sand may also be easier and cheaper to buy than soil.

(2) The use of suitable slit drainage which allows surface water to travel to the drains rapidly without having to go through the topsoil. For existing areas slit drainage has to be organized to suit existing drains but for new fields an integrated slit drainage/pipe drainage scheme can be arranged.

(3) The construction of pitches to specifications which are luxurious by everyday standards although the cost of which is acceptable to organizations such as first-division soccer clubs. These specifications involve drains to empty a 150 mm (6 in) permeable mattress of gravel blinded with 50 mm (2 in) of coarse sand and surmounted by a specially-prepared rooting layer of suitable thickness which consists mainly of sand and is pre-mixed off-site (Plate 7.3).

Present-day (1978) costs of drainage can be frightening, e.g.:

Installation of pipe drains at 5.5 m (18 ft) centres	about £6250 ha^{-1} (£2500 acre^{-1})
Installation of 50 mm (2 in) slit drains at 600 mm (2 ft) centres	about £8750 ha^{-1} (£3500 acre^{-1})
Installation of 13 mm (0.5 in) sand injection slits at 300 mm (1 ft) centres	about £5000 ha^{-1} (£2000 acre^{-1})
Construction of a whole pitch to the luxury standard mentioned above	£60 000 per pitch

At STRI we have always emphasized the outstanding importance of soil moisture control at both ends of the range. Current trials (Daniells, 1977) are underlining the importance of this factor. Here, drainage carpets are proving of considerable help but this is at the expense of drought resistance. The trials are also confirming the desirability of the rooting medium providing a balance between the rapid removal of surface water and the retention of available water and nutrients. Whatever the nature of the medium, the infiltration rate is very much conditioned by the state of the immediate surface, which is in turn dependent on good management, including the prevention of accumulation of excess fibre and other organic material.

'Special' systems of drainage include not only those used already at the famous football grounds in this country but also patented systems such as the Mulqueen Prunty sand carpet system (Mulqueen, 1976) and those systems such as the Cellsystem (UK patent 1 158 434), the Purr–Wick system (Daniel, 1969) and the PAT system (US patent 3 461 675), all of which involve a completely artificial structure, isolated from its surroundings by polythene sheeting. In these three, irrigation, nutrition, and under-drainage are all provided by the one set of perforated pipes while the rooting medium/bearing course consists almost entirely of suitable sand.

V. I. Stewart and W. A. Adams at Aberystwyth have done a great deal of research on the effects on sports ground drainage of particle size distribution of soils and sands (Adams *et al.*, 1971a,b; Adams, 1976) and on integrated slit drainage/pipe drain systems for sports grounds (Stewart, 1973, 1976). Considerable progress has also been made in other countries and the time seems right to take stock of the position reached and to assess what further research (if any) is needed. A review might attempt to cover the following:

(1) Cost benefits of good drainage.
(2) Factors relevant to the choice of a complete drainage system:

(a) Best targets for water removal rate (is it necessary to aim at 25 mm (1 in) per hour or more?) and the relationship of drainage systems to proposed usage with attention to strength of surface, year round vigour of the turf and the amount of use which can be imposed.
(b) Numerous technical points relating to soil and subsoil (including amelioration of either) which affect choice of drainage system, and testing procedures for both laboratory and field.

(3) Evaluation of different ways of reaching the desired objective including the production of special systems of various kinds and use of the various forms of combined slit and pipe drainage.

In the latter connection the practical know-how of firms such as Chipman Ltd and Cambridge Soil Services should not be overlooked. The latter have devised a wide range of approaches to slit drainage, although experience with the whole range is of necessity limited at this stage. They have machines to give *sand grooving*, i.e. the production of slits 13 mm (0.5 in) wide and 100 mm (4 in) deep at perhaps 200 mm (8 in) centres; *sand injection* (Plate 7.1) which gives slits 16 mm (0.6 in) wide and 230 mm (9 in) deep; *surface banding* which gives slits 25–50 mm (1–2 in) wide and up to 300 mm (12 in) deep and intended for use at, say 1 m (1.1 yd) spacing; and what they call *ordinary slitting* (Plate 7.2), when slits 50–150 mm (2–6 in) wide and up to 355 mm (14 in) deep are made at suitable intervals.

Topsoil cultivation

Even in the apparently simple subject of topsoil cultivation there is an educational requirement, because efficient ploughing or harrowing can be relied upon from only a handful of those contractors who specialize in sports ground construction. NERC (1977) lists several problems in this connection, though none is believed to be as important as drainage. An independent assessment of suitable cultivating machinery might still be worth while. Final smoothing to ensure a level surface is obtained from a form of 'blade grading' where skilled judgement is required to achieve an acceptable degree of smoothness and a good seed bed, without the excessive compaction that a blade grader is liable to leave.

In theory a period of fallowing is desirable to deplete the seedbank of weeds but, in practice, time and weather considerations limit what can be done in this respect. Research on economically feasible measures of ensuring a clean seed bed is worth considering.

Lime and fertilizer treatment

Chemical treatments are commonly governed by the results of soil tests but it should be borne in mind that, during construction, additives can be mixed into the full depth of soil whereas, after the area has been sown, materials can be put on top only. Lime is often applied (as carbonate of lime) in sufficient quantity to bring the top 150 mm (6 in) of soil to pH 6. There appears to be little consistency in pre-seeding fertilizer practice but, for normal soils and subject to modification in the light of soil tests, a pre-treatment which gives satisfactory results on new sports grounds is granular fertilizer containing 10 per cent N, 15 per cent P_2O_5, and 10 per cent K_2O applied at 750 kg ha^{-1} (6 cwt acre^{-1}). This fairly generous treatment helps good early growth despite any loss in availability of nutrients through storage (or even loss) of topsoil. The cost is negligible when compared with total costs of sports ground construction.

For fine turf areas, where recycling of mineral nutrients through return of cuttings does not occur, the fertilizer applied to the seed bed often takes the form of a powdered material containing some relatively slow-releasing organic materials.

Sowing grass seed

The choice of seeds mixture to provide a wear-resistant sward, suitable for the purpose intended and amenable to renovation but without excessive demands for maintenance, is an important one. For many years there has been little change in the accepted mixtures for each of the different sports turf purposes, except for the introduction of improved cultivars. Mixtures for local authority sports grounds and playing fields are usually on the lines of 40 per cent *Lolium perenne* (perennial ryegrass), 20 per cent *Poa pratensis* (smooth-stalked meadow-grass), 35 per cent *Festuca rubra* ssp. *commutata*

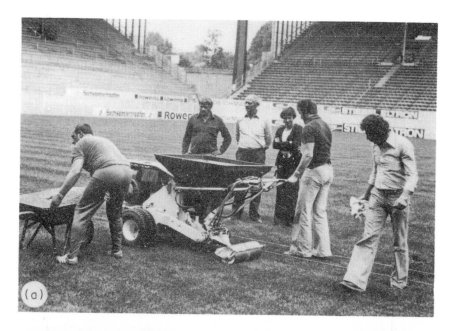

Plate 7.1　(a) Slit drainage by sand injection, producing 16 mm (0.6 in) wide slits; (b) a close-up view of the turf after passage of the machine (photographs by J. R. Escritt)

Plate 7.2   Slit drainage machinery in operation, producing slits 50 mm (2 in) wide
(photograph by J. R. Escritt)

Plate 7.3 Off-site mixing of sand, soil, and peat to create a topsoil for reconstruction of a soccer pitch (photograph by J. R. Escritt)

(chewings fescue) (or a mixture of chewings fescue and ssp. *rubra*, creeping red fescue), and 5 per cent *Agrostis tenuis* (common bent-grass). Such mixtures are commonly sown at 188 kg ha^{-1} (1.5 cwt acre^{-1}) and, of course, for each of the species good, persistent cultivars should be chosen. Seeds mixtures like the above for playing fields and other sports turf areas are based partly on experience, partly on trials by seeds firms but mainly on many years of trials such as those reported upon in the *Journal of the Sports Turf Research Institute*. Further information on seeds mixtures is given in Chapter 4.

Until quite recently, trials were carried out without the imposition of a wear factor, assessments being related mainly to persistence under mowing at appropriate heights. Tolerance of regular mowing is definitely a critical factor but more studies including a wear factor are considered necessary, such as those being pursued under NERC/STRI contracts to investigate properties both of cultivars and of mixtures (see Chapter 8). For informal amenity areas we need to study grass species, and suitable forbs, other than those commonly used. Indeed, such studies might well help sports turf development, since in New Zealand, for example, there are many first-class bowling greens which use hard-wearing *Cotula* species in place of grass.

It is a matter of observation that whilst grass seed can be sown throughout most of the period from April to August, the most reliable results on sports grounds are obtained from late summer sowings, especially at the end of August. Sowings outside the above period are likely to meet cold and wet conditions and may be affected by damping-off. Even in the absence of disease, conditions may well affect the balance of species in favour of *Lolium perenne*, which is better able to germinate and establish at lower temperatures. Seed rates used in sports turf establishment are heavy compared with those used in agriculture (see Chapter 10) but reduced rates seem to be satisfactory only when all conditions are optimal.

Initial maintenance

Often there are inadequate money, men, materials, and equipment for initial maintenance after construction has finished. This initial period in the life of an amenity turf is of the utmost importance; ensuring a dense cover of the sown species quickly is a useful insurance against many troubles. Stone picking, mowing, and feeding, possibly with a simple nitrogenous fertilizer, e.g. sulphate of ammonia at 188 kg ha^{-1} (1.5 cwt acre^{-1}), may have to be carried out within a short period of the contractor leaving the site.

Maintenance in the development period

Experience indicates that the first full year in the life of new sports turf should be regarded as the main development period and emphasizes the importance of regular maintenance. Sufficient nitrogen to help the new sward to thicken-out is important, not only to get a sward ready for use as soon as possible, but also to get a good cover of the sown grasses as opposed to 'invaders'. The amounts of fertilizer to be used are considered a matter of judgement—the need might be for two or three dressings of granular fertilizer, containing 20 per cent N, 10 per cent P_2O_5, and 10 per cent K_2O at 250–375 kg ha^{-1} (2–3 cwt acre^{-1}).

Routine maintenance

Maintenance standards are extremely variable. For many purposes it would be useful to have quantitative recommendations for minimum acceptable standards, e.g. frequency of cutting, fertilizer treatment, and aeration requirements. This, in turn, will involve the need for some quantitative measurements of performance, as discussed earlier.

The first requirement is regular mowing to contain growth and encourage tillering. NERC (1977) lists a number of difficulties related to mowing which are very costly and there is still great reliance on the older-established vandal-proof mowing machines. Some of the research needs listed are more applicable to extensive grasslands than to sports turf but many merit attention—keeping herbage short by an appropriate grazing regime would, for example, seem to call for investigation in some situations.

Over-compaction and destruction of surface-soil structure, leading to poor drainage, provide the greatest problems of sports ground maintenance. They are important in other public areas, too. Over-use and the passage of heavy equipment, particularly under wet conditions, are the causes. An important effect is a much-reduced infiltration rate and so damage is increasingly incurred—'mud breeds mud' is an oft-repeated saying.

Remedial slit drainage has become a new possibility, but the procedures are very costly and there is still great reliance on the older-established methods of coping with the situation. Repeated 'aeration' of some kind can be remarkably successful. It has been known for pitches established on clay to be under water in the morning but quite playable in the afternoon as a result of mechanical spiking. Where slit drains have been installed it is necessary to keep them effective by top dressing with sand and/or by adding further sand slits (possibly of a cheaper nature and of a relatively shallow depth). But the former procedure can result in a shallow-rooted turf which chips-off readily.

An important factor in the maintenance of a robust cover of vegetation on sports grounds is the wise use of lime and fertilizer. Lime is used to correct soil acidity and fertilizer application replaces nutrient losses resulting from leaching and immobilization. Each year a dressing of granular fertilizer containing 20 per cent N, 10 per cent P_2O_5, and 10 per cent K_2O may be given at, say, 250 kg ha^{-1} (2 cwt acre^{-1}). Existing practice in the UK is based partly upon experience and partly upon research. Further research would be valuable in the interests of economy and efficiency, and would clarify the situation regarding the wisdom or otherwise of the popular autumn/winter fertilizer treatments given to some kinds of turf. Really good, synthetic, gradual-release, nitrogenous fertilizers would be very useful for some situations but, of those marketed and so far tested at STRI (Woolhouse, 1973, 1974) only one has shown much promise.

Weed control for sports turf is not merely cosmetic. Weediness affects playing quality and durability; it may even affect drainage. There are few problems from weeds in sports turf which cannot be dealt with by commercial selective weedkillers but elimination of unwanted flora in larger areas must depend upon ecologically-sound management (see Chapters 2, 10, and 11).

Usage

Over-use in the wrong conditions is extremely detrimental to the soil and to the cover of vegetation. When the latter is worn off the protection it gives the soil is lost and in some situations the original cover is irreplaceable. For these reasons attempts to maintain the cover are essential. On sports grounds, keeping up with repairs and renovation between seasons is an important factor in maintaining good playing conditions. NERC (1977) mentions a need for research on renovation procedures. This seems to be a very real need for extensive amenity areas but in the context of sports turf there is probably a bigger need for the education and training of users in well-established procedures.

References

Adams, W. A. (1976). 'The effect of fine soil fractions on the hydraulic conductivity of compacted sand/soil mixes used for sportsturf rootzones', *Rasen-Turf-Gazon*, **7**, 92–4.

Adams, W. A., Stewart, V. I. & Thornton, D. J. (1971*a*). 'The assessment of sands suitable for use in sportsfields', *Journal of the Sports Turf Research Institute*, **47**, 77–85.

Adams, W. A., Stewart, V. I. & Thornton, D. J. (1971*b*). 'The construction and drainage of sportsfields for winter games in Britain', in *Welsh Soils Discussion Group Report no. 12*, 85–95.

Canaway, P. M. (1978). 'Trials of turfgrass wear tolerance and associated factors. A summary of progress 1975–1977', *Journal of the Sports Turf Research Institute*, **54**, 7–14.

Daniel, W. H. (1969). 'The Purr–Wick rootzone system for compacted turf areas', *Proceedings of the First International Turfgrass Research Conference*, Sports Turf Research Institute, Bingley, pp. 323–5.

Daniells, I. G. (1977). 'Drainage of sports turf used in winter: a comparison of some rooting media with and without a gravel drainage layer', *Journal of the Sports Turf Research Institute*, **53**, 56–72.

Gooch, R. B. & Escritt, J. R. (1975). *Sports Ground Construction: Specifications*, 2nd ed., National Playing Fields Association, London.

Hunter, F. & Currie, J. A. (1956). 'Structural changes during bulk soil storage', *Journal of Soil Science*, **7**, 175–80.

Mulqueen, J. (1976). 'Aspects of the construction of sportsfields and recreation grounds in Ireland', in *The Next Decade in Amenity Grassland* (C. E. Wright, ed.), Queen's University Press, Belfast, pp. 40–65.

NERC (1977). *Amenity Grasslands—the Needs for Research*, Natural Environment Research Council, Publications Series 'C', No. 19, London.

Stewart, V. I. (1973). 'Sportsfield drainage', *Playing Fields*, **34**, 70–4.

Stewart, V. I. (1976). 'Wallowing in mud?', *Journal of Parks and Recreation*, **41**, 38–51.

van Wijk, A. L. M. & Beuving, J. (1975). 'Relation between playability and some soil physical aspects of the top layer of grass sports fields', *Rasen-Turf-Gazon*, **3**, 77–83.

Woolhouse, A. R. (1973). 'An assessment of the effectiveness of a slow release nitrogen fertilizer on sports turf', *Journal of the Sports Turf Research Institute*, **49**, 8–20.

Woolhouse, A. R. (1974). 'Further assessment of the effectiveness of a slow release nitrogen fertilizer on sports turf', *Journal of the Sports Turf Research Institute*, **50**, 34–46.

Amenity Grassland: An Ecological Perspective
Edited by I. H. Rorison and R. Hunt

8
Wear

P. M. CANAWAY *Sports Turf Research Institute, Bingley, West Yorkshire, England*

Introduction

Wear was considered by NERC (1977) as 'the outstanding management problem on amenity grassland. A proper understanding of all the influencing factors and the processes involved could immediately allow better utilization of existing amenity turf and the production of more durable new turf ...'. When authorities responsible for large areas of amenity grassland (e.g. county and district councils, airport authorities, and the DoE Property Services Agency) were questioned, only the problems concerned with mowing and labour were felt to be more important than those related to wear. In terms of research priorities, managers of amenity grassland suggested that in their view mowing and wear were of the highest priority for research (NERC, 1977).

Definition of wear is made difficult by the wide use of the word in the English language and also by the wide range of situations in which it occurs. 'To wear' can mean to damage or to change by use, or to suffer damage or change; 'wear' can also mean the result of such action (Canaway, 1975a). Because of the great variety in amenity grassland it is impossible to specify all the causes of wear. In general, wear is caused by: human trampling (formal sports and informal recreation); vehicles (including maintenance operations); ancillary equipment to sports, e.g. golf clubs, hockey sticks; and animals such as horses. The nature of wear resulting from any given type of use depends upon the type of grassland under consideration, the frequency and intensity of use and whether there are constraints on use leading to a concentration of wear in specific places, e.g., tracks, footpaths, golf tees, goal mouths, or at specific times, e.g. at week-ends or according to seasonal tradition within the sport.

The effects of human trampling on semi-natural vegetation have recently been reviewed by Liddle (1975a) and earlier by the same author (Liddle, 1973) and also by Leney (1974) in her work on the effects of public pressures on picnic sites. Turf wear, with emphasis on intensively managed grassland, was also recently reviewed by Canaway (1975*a*). Hence at present a further complete review would be inappropriate. This chapter, therefore, seeks to update existing information where necessary and to outline the general principles involved in the study of wear occurring on amenity grasslands.

The mechanics of wear

Wear occurs as a result of the forces applied during use. These are applied at various angles but can be resolved into horizontal forces acting parallel to the ground and vertical forces acting perpendicularly to the ground (Figure 8.1(a)). Horizontal forces can further be sub-divided into those acting in the line of travel and those acting at right angles to the line of travel. Also, torque is applied as a result of the twisting action of the foot while it is in contact with the ground (Figure 8.1(b)). The use of force platforms has permitted accurate measurement of the forces involved in various activities, beginning with the well-known work of Harper *et al.* (1961) on the forces applied by the foot in walking. In walking, the vertical force is slightly greater than the body weight and the horizontal force in, and opposite to, the direction of travel may rise to 25 per cent of the body weight. The value for torque in straight walking is about 8 N m (see Appendix I for information on units and symbols) and for turning a right-angled corner about 15 N m. In sporting activities, where movements are more violent, the forces are usually much larger (A. H. Payne, personal communication). In a flat-out run the vertical force may reach 3.7 times the body weight for about 0.1 s and at, or soon after, a sprint start the horizontal force may reach 87 per cent of the body weight for about 0.3 s.

With vertical forces an important consideration is the contact area through which they act. Studded, spiked, or cleated footwear or partial foot contact, e.g. the heel, all reduce contact area and hence increase the local pressure caused by the foot on the ground. In walking, typical values are of the order of 70 kPa for much of the time although much greater momentary pressures can be produced as the heel makes contact with the ground (Harper *et al.*, 1961). Football studs could in theory produce even greater pressures (3000–4000 kPa) during a flat-out run but with such large values complete stud penetration would occur and some of the force would be borne by the sole. For comparison the average pressure beneath a lugged, agricultural tractor-tyre has been estimated as 60–140 kPa (Soane, 1970), but these values are averages based on the total area of contact and in practice the pressure beneath the individual lugs would be much greater.

The effects of linear horizontal forces depend greatly upon the type of footwear used. Studded or spiked footwear causes tearing and disruption of the sward and in vigorous sports the surface soil may be smeared out. Long,

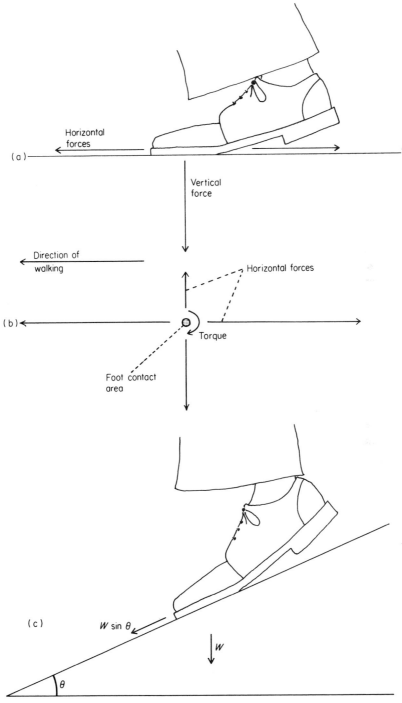

Figure 8.1 (a) Vertical and horizontal forces applied in walking. (b) Plan view of (a), to show horizontal forces and torque applied by the foot in walking. (c) Effect of walking on a slope

smeared tears with a terminal divot are frequently seen on pitches in winter. With non-studded footwear such as street shoes, training shoes, etc., the horizontal forces cause friction between the sole and the turf and consequent abrasion of the grass, In walking, the linear horizontal forces are generally too small for abrasive effects to occur and it is generally held that abrasion of floor finishes and shoe-soles is caused by the twisting action of the foot, i.e. torque (Harper *et al.*, 1961; P. D. Perkins, personal communication). Recent measurements on the friction coefficients of turfgrass species Canaway (1979) suggest that torque may also be responsible for turf abrasion caused by walking.

Although consideration of the forces involved in different activities is useful both for the purpose of comparison between these activities and in providing a basis for realistic simulation of wear (see below) these forces are of very short duration and follow complex and varying patterns in time. Because of these difficulties it might be more fruitful to study other ways of quantifying activity in relation to wear. Cavagna *et al.* (1963, 1964) have studied the mechanical work involved in walking and running. This work (or energy expenditure) can be divided into two components: 'external' work and 'internal' work. External work is that work done by the body on the turf in sustaining locomotion, as distinct from internal work which is used up in joint, limb and muscle movements. It is the external work which can be considered as responsible for causing wear. In the study of Cavagna *et al.* (1963, 1964) it was shown that in running the external work performed per kilometre (and per kilogram of body weight) is independent of speed, amounting to $1.05 \text{ kJ kg}^{-1} \text{ km}^{-1}$. In walking the external work is not as independent of speed as in running but remains in the range of 0.38–$0.42 \text{ kJ kg}^{-1} \text{ km}^{-1}$ between speeds of 3 and 6.5 km h^{-1}. Thus, under prescribed conditions, only the distance travelled and the body weight of the subjects are required in order to provide an estimate of the external work performed in causing wear in walking or running. An obvious application would be the study of wear on running tracks where, naturally, the distance travelled is known precisely. In sports such as soccer, approaches similar to that of Müller & Axtmann (1976) could be used. These workers used video equipment to monitor the 'wear events' occurring in $2 \text{ m} \times 2 \text{ m}$ areas of several German Federal League soccer pitches during a number of matches and it was shown that walking and running were the most frequent wear events to occur. An extension of this method would be firstly to monitor the activities occurring per unit area of the pitch, secondly to calculate the external work performed in these activities, and thirdly to record the occurrence of wear on the pitch over a number of matches. This would provide a quantitative relationship between the external work performed in activity and the resulting wear.

Clearly the problem is not as simple as outlined here in that, in addition, it would be necessary to consider the effects of site factors (e.g. soil moisture content), human factors (e.g. level of skill), and environmental factors (e.g. weather conditions) on the external work performed. For example, on a heavy soil subjective experience suggests that much more work is performed under wet conditions than when the ground is dry, which in itself could account for the greater amount of wear occurring under wet conditions. This raises an important point since it is often assumed that increased wear occurring under wet conditions is due only to the reduced wear tolerance of the turf. But an important additional consideration is the influence of site factors (in this example soil moisture) on the external energy expenditure of the players. In the example given (a heavy soil under wet conditions) additional exertion on a weakened turf will inevitably lead to severe wear. This conclusion alone is perhaps adequate justification for the recommendation of the use of free-draining sand or sandy soils in sports field construction.

On footpaths a similar argument could be put forward for the effects of ground conditions on energy expenditure but perhaps more important is the effect of slope. It is a common observation that wear of footpaths is often worse on sloping ground (Plate 1.5). Weaver & Dale (1978) studied the effects of motorcycles, horses, and walkers on grassland and forest ground flora. In all three types of activity vegetation cover was lost more rapidly on a sloping site than on the flat. This effect can also be predicted from first principles as follows. On a slope of gradient θ degrees an individual of weight W experiences a force of $W \sin \Theta$ tending to pull him down the slope (Figure 8.1c). In ascending the slope this force must be overcome by an expenditure of energy in addition to that required for normal progress. In descending, a braking force must be applied to prevent runaway acceleration. For example, on a slope of 15° (that studied by Weaver & Dale, 1978) the additional external work required to overcome this force alone amounts to 2.54 kJ kg^{-1} km^{-1}, about six times the total external work required for walking on the flat. Therefore, it is not surprising to find severe wear on sloping footpaths.

It is clear that there is a need to forge a link between mechanical and/or physiological studies of physical activity and studies of wear resulting from these activities under a wide range of conditions. This would permit a greater understanding of wear, the comparison of wear studies on the same basis (i.e in terms of external work or energy expended in causing wear) and a direct comparison with artificial wear (see below).

Effects of wear on the amenity grassland system

Implicit in the use of the word 'system' to describe amenity grassland is the concept of wholeness. Sub-systems, or parts, which make up this whole are mutually interacting and interdependent. The two major components of grassland are the plants and the soil; considering only these two and the way they interact, one can obtain a reasonable understanding of the effects of wear. There are of course other components such as soil fauna, e.g. earthworms, burrowing and grazing mammals, and soil microflora, but the simple model outlined above is sufficient as a starting point for studies of wear. More complex models are possible, for example, Liddle (1975a) gave a 'logical model' for the ecological effects of trampling on footpaths. Indeed modelling, already widely used in studies of agricultural grassland, might be an avenue for further research on amenity grasslands.

Effect of wear on the grass

A general term 'the grass' is used in preference to more specific terms such as the sward, the population, or the plants for two reasons. The first is that some properties of grass are relevant at the sward level but not at the plant level, e.g. the property of resilience is a function of the sward as a whole whereas the resilience of an individual plant is not meaningful. Conversely, anatomical, morphological, and physiological properties generally relate to the individual plant, although these, when expressed at the sward level, can also contribute to sward properties, e.g. a certain morphology may be expressed as 'sward resilience'. The second reason for choosing the term rather than 'the plants' is the problem of individuality of grass plants. In grasses, tillering may lead initially to a many-tillered plant and later to many 'plants' of identical genotype. Some would argue that the individual is still the collection of tillers of identical genotype even though now physically separated. Thus population ecologists use the term 'genet' and 'ramet' to overcome this problem, the genet being the genetic unit and the ramet being the vegetative unit or tiller (Kays & Harper, 1974).

The detailed effects of wear on the grass depend upon the type and intensity of use but, in general, the grass is either scuffed, crushed, or bruised. Leaves, shoots, roots, and rhizomes may be broken and plant material may be removed in divots, or by abrasion. Biomass and ground cover are reduced by moderate or heavy use but very light wear may stimulate growth of some grass species, e.g., along path margins (Liddle, 1975b). This latter observation could be explained by: increased soil moisture availability, improved lateral lighting in the case of path margins, or direct response to damage or change in species composition (Liddle, 1975b). Height is markedly reduced by wear (Liddle, 1975a) and species composition may change in favour of more wear-tolerant species (Pietsch, 1968; Liddle, 1975a).

At a given level of usage the resulting wear is affected by a large number of factors; intrinsic factors, environmental, management, and edaphic factors. Intrinsic factors include the wear tolerance of the species and cultivars present and the age and vigour of the sward. Wear tolerance is discussed further in a separate section below. Related to usage of the sward is the accumulation of leaf litter and other fibrous material at the soil surface which may produce a cushioning effect absorbing some of the mechanical energy (Beard, 1973).

Environmental and management factors which enhance wear tolerance are generally those which provide optimum conditions for the maintenance of a healthy, vigorous sward. Any deviation from the optimum conditions reduces wear tolerance. Shade due to overhanging trees around golf greens or large stands around sports fields is known to reduce wear tolerance (Beard, 1973; Dahlsson, 1973). Frosted turf is very easily damaged as is turf wilted due to drought or where there is excess moisture (Beard, 1973; Dahlsson, 1973; Adams *et al.*, 1971). Close mowing is known to reduce wear tolerance (Youngner, 1961; Madison, 1971; Beard, 1973; Dahlsson, 1973) and Dahlsson (1973) suggests raising the height of cut when other adverse conditions prevail. Close mowing reduces root growth which is also known to influence wear tolerance (Gandert, 1973). Moderate amounts of fertilizer increase wear tolerance but high levels of nitrogen tend to produce a succulent growth easily damaged by use (Beard, 1973).

Effects of wear on the soil and the plant/soil interactions

Wear causes damage to the soil, locally through soil smearing and more generally through soil compaction. Soil smearing occurs where there are large horizontal forces. This commonly occurs in vigorous sports such as football and as a result of the passage of vehicles.

Soil compaction may not be so obvious to the user in the early stages as is wear of the grass but it is, if anything, more troublesome in the long run and more difficult to alleviate. It reduces the overall growth and vigour of the sward and makes further damage more likely as a result. Soil compaction is a more general phenomenon than soil smearing, occurring in most situations where wear occurs. It takes place when the application of a force results in an increase in soil bulk density. The degree of compaction which occurs depends upon the characteristics of both the applied force, e.g., a vehicle or a walker, and the soil characteristics. The soil and force characteristics influencing the degree of compaction and the properties of soil altered by compaction have been discussed by Soane (1970) and Canaway (1975a). The factors thought to be responsible for determining the plant response to soil compaction have been reviewed by Rosenberg (1964) and Canaway (1975a). Therefore these topics are not discussed in great detail but for the sake of completeness the main points are summarized in Table 8.1. Under many circumstances the effects of compaction are detrimental to the growth of a healthy sward, for example in the extreme case waterlogging and anaerobic soil conditions may be produced. However, on very sandy soils compaction

Table 8.1   Summary table showing the force characteristics and soil characteristics influencing the degree of soil compaction, the effects of soil compaction on soil properties and the consequences of these effects for plant growth

Force characteristics (Soane, 1970)	Soil characteristics (Soane, 1970)	Soil properties changed by compaction (Soane, 1970; Canaway, 1975a)	Important effects of soil compaction on plant growth conditions (Rosenberg, 1964)
Shape and size of object applying force	Particle size distribution	Bulk density	Mechanical impedance to root penetration
Average pressure produced	Moisture content	Total pore space	Root aeration reduced
Distribution of pressure	Soil strength	Air-filled porosity	Moisture availability altered
Rate of application of force	Organic matter content	Hydraulic conductivity	Mass flow of nutrients impeded
Duration of force	Aggregate size distribution	Soil aeration	Root zone temperature gradients altered
Impact effects		Water retention	
Presence of shear forces		Thermal conductivity	
Vibrational effects		Structure	

may be beneficial in increasing moisture availability and reducing leaching of nutrients. Whether soil compaction hinders or improves plant growth depends upon whether the soil is looser than, at, or more compact than, the optimal bulk density for the sward under the prevailing conditions. In sports turf, soil bulk density is likely to be greater than the optimum for much of the time. Therefore, during construction the topsoil may be ameliorated with large amounts of sand, or in some cases sand alone may be used for the surface layer. The aim is to produce a rooting medium which will remain free-draining even when compacted so as to avoid the problems of waterlogging and the development of anaerobic conditions (Escritt & Daniells, 1977).

Wear tolerance of amenity grass species

The term 'wear tolerance' is defined as the ability to withstand wear (Beard, 1973; Canaway, 1975*a*). It must be stressed, however, that evaluation of wear tolerance is an arbitrary process depending both on the method of assessment used and on the type and intensity of wear applied. The principle used in most wear trials is to produce a ranking of the species, cultivars or mixtures being studied rather than to attempt to provide absolute values as in, for example, agricultural work on crop yields. Also it is recognized that during the period of wear some short-term recovery of the grass, which contributes to its overall wear tolerance, may take place. This again emphasizes the arbitrary nature of wear tolerance. In practice, one is often concerned with the end results of wear tolerance and recovery over several cycles of wear and recovery which may be termed 'durability' (Canaway, 1975*a*).

Some of the most recent information on the wear tolerance of the main turfgrass species is summarized in Table 8.2 in which species rankings from four European sources are compared. These rankings are, in general, based on continuing appraisal of the species in trials at research stations in the UK, the Netherlands, and France. The data of Canaway (1978) are taken from more detailed work on a small number of the more wear-tolerant species only (hence the rankings in the range 5–10). The data from other sources were already comparable. RIVRO (1978) uses a 1–10 scale and the values of Bourgoin (1974) were readily convertible to a 1–9 scale from very good = 9 to bad = 1. In addition an approximate score for *Cynosurus cristatus* (crested dog's-tail) has been added on the basis of Bourgoin (1974). The data of STRI (1978) were originally expressed on a 1–5 scale; therefore the values appearing in Table 8.2 are given as twice these scores. In general, there is a good agreement among the rankings of different species, but *Poa pratensis* (smooth-stalked meadow-grass) appears to perform less well in France and *Cynosurus cristatus* and *Poa trivialis* (rough-stalked meadow-grass)

Table 8.2 Comparison of wear tolerance rankings of the main turfgrass species. (1–10 scale; 10 = most wear tolerant). See also Tables 4.4, 4.6, and 4.8

Species	UK (STRI, 1978)	UK (Canaway, 1978)	Netherlands (RIVRO, 1978)	France (Bourgoin, personal communication)	Tolerance
Lolium perenne	10	8	9	7	Very tolerant
Poa annua	6–10	10	—	—	
Poa pratensis	8	8	8	5	Tolerant
Phleum pratense	8	8	7	—	
Phleum bertolonii	8	—	7	7	
Festuca rubra					
ssp. *litoralis*	6	—	6	6	Intermediate
ssp. *commutata*	6	5	5	6	
F. longifolia	6	—	5	6	
Cynosurus cristatus	4	—	7	(4–5)	
Agrostis tenuis (incl. 'Highland', *A. castellana*)	4	5	5	5	
Festuca rubra					
ssp. *rubra*	4	—	5	2	Intolerant
F. tenuifolia	4	—	5	2	
A. stolonifera	4	—	4	4	
A. canina					
ssp. *canina*	4	—	4	2	
Poa trivialis	2	—	6	2	

appear to perform better in the Netherlands than elsewhere. A wide range of values is given for *Poa annua* (annual poa) in the data of STRI (1978) to allow for the variation among different ecotypes of *P. annua*. These range from the lax, upright, agricultural types to dense, prostrate, turf types which are exceedingly wear-tolerant. One of the latter types was used in the trials reported by Canaway (1978). Comparison with rankings obtained in the USA is less easy because of differing conditions and methods of assessing wear tolerance but the values obtained by Shearman & Beard (1975*a*) for simulated wheel wear are broadly similar to those in Table 8.2 for *Lolium perenne* (perennial ryegrass), *Poa pratensis*, *Festuca rubra* (red fescue), and *Poa trivialis*. In the USA *Festuca arundinacea* (tall fescue) also performs well, being comparable with *Poa pratensis* in tolerance of wheel wear (Shearman & Beard, 1975*a*).

It is natural to enquire why these species differ in their wear tolerance. Recently, experiments have been carried out in which attempts have been made to correlate the observed wear tolerance of different species with various attributes measured before wear. In the work of Shearman & Beard (1975*b*) wear tolerance was significantly correlated with the fibre content (neutral detergent fibre) expressed as grams of the species studied per square metre. Canaway (1978) found that, in one experiment, fibre (acid detergent fibre) as a percentage of dry weight showed a significant correlation with wear tolerance and that, in a second experiment, biomass and fibre as grams per square metre were correlated with wear tolerance in partial agreement with Shearman & Beard (1975*b*). However in the second experiment the two correlations were weak, and furthermore, when the data were re-analysed omitting *Poa annua* the correlations disappeared. Hence the evidence is rather tentative and further work is required.

Considering trampled areas in general, Frenkel (1970), reporting on a study of 223 trampled stands in Germany carried out by Haessler (1954), lists a number of properties as being characteristic of trampling-tolerant vegetation. Some of these include: small plant size, growth close to the ground, small leaves anatomically and physiologically tolerant of trampling, rapid nutrient uptake leading to quick recovery, the ability to bend without breaking, short life-cycles under unfavourable conditions, ability to reproduce vegetatively, small self-fertile flowers, short root-to-flower distance, small seeds with the ability to germinate rapidly at shallow depths, and growth-forms leading to protection of meristems.

There is always a tendency to isolate a single factor to account for wear tolerance or trampling tolerance of plant communities. Liddle (1975*c*) compared the trampling tolerance and primary productivity of an extremely wide range of communities ranging from very unproductive stone-stripe and snow-bank vegetation, through *Calluna* (heather) moorland, to more productive dune pasture. He was able to demonstrate a relationship between trampling tolerance and primary productivity over this wide range of habitats.

Little is known about the physiology of wear tolerance; Smith (1978) found that wear increased shoot relative growth rate (RGR) but reduced root RGR in damaged plants. It seems likely that mechanical damage causes mobilization of stored assimilates which, if the wear is prolonged, may eventually be exhausted, especially if conditions are unfavourable as, for example, on winter pitches.

Simulation of wear

In theory, the best method of studying wear is to study it where it occurs in practice. However, this raises a number of problems such as: obtaining personnel in the case of sports studies; applying 'real' wear in a uniform manner—commonly *patterns* of wear develop, e.g. on soccer pitches wear is more severe around goal mouths and in the centre than on the wings; and the need for randomization in trials of different species, cultivars, or mixtures. For these and other reasons, methods of simulating wear have been devised which fall into two categories, small-scale and large-scale. Small-scale techniques are useful for detailed experimental work on plots or very small areas in the field, e.g., the methods of Bayfield (1971), Leney (1974), and Canaway (1975b). Large-scale methods are most useful for field trials where the area may be considerable, e.g. where many cultivars or mixtures are being compared.

Small-scale techniques are often in the form of 'falling weight' compaction machines where a tamp is allowed to fall repeatedly onto the test material. Such machines have been used by Bayfield (1971), Leney (1974), and Smith (1978). Canaway (1975b) also devised a small-scale wear simulator which could be used in this manner but its main purpose was to permit the experimental application of known horizontal and vertical forces to turf. Further developments of small-scale techniques (Canaway, 1979) have made it possible to quantify abrasion treatments in terms of the energy dissipated.

Large-scale methods of simulating wear are mostly confined to research on intensively managed sports turf although they are occasionally used in semi-natural situations, e.g. Cieslinski & Wagar (1970). Since wear is one of the most important considerations in sports turf research, many different machines, termed 'wear machines', have been devised. The earliest was described by Perry (1958) and Youngner (1961). This was a self-propelled machine rotating about a central axis. It contained two types of 'wear element', one consisting of four corrugated feet which sucessively struck the turf and then were dragged across it, the other 'wear element' carrying two golf-spike rollers. A number of other methods has been described by

Plate 8.1   A differential-slip wear machine, model DS 2 (photograph by STRI)

Plate 8.2   Close-up of the wear machine with belt guard removed to show drive to front and rear rotors by means of pulleys of unequal size causing differential slip (photograph by STRI)

Canaway (1975*a*). The commonest method of simulating wear due to winter games has been the studded roller (Shildrick, 1971; Vos, 1972; Dahlsson, 1973; Versteeg, 1973). Studded rollers are usually fitted with studs similar to those on football boots and are towed behind a heavy-duty mower or tractor. There are, however, two main drawbacks to the use of studded rollers, the first being related to the forces produced in real wear and the second due to the effects of the towing unit. In sports, horizontal forces produced by the players can be large. The studded roller, by contrast, produces only small horizontal forces with consequently very little of the tearing effect seen in real wear. Suggestions have been made of ways to overcome this problem. For example Riem Vis (1977) describes a machine where two rollers are coupled together with non-parallel axles to produce additional drag. The second drawback of the studded roller is that under the conditions in which wear trials are carried out, i.e. in winter when ground conditions are often wet, the damaging effects of the towing unit cannot be disregarded. A heavy mower or tractor itself produces soil compaction and thus the actual wear treatment consists of the effects of the studded roller and in addition the effects of the power unit under winter conditions. If steps are taken to increase drag, e.g. Riem Vis (1977), the wear produced by the power unit will also increase since it must produce greater traction to tow the 'dragging' rollers.

In view of the disadvantages of studded rollers, a new machine has been recently developed (Canaway, 1976). The differential-slip wear machine (see Plate 8.1) is about the size of a large mower and is self-propelled, overcoming the problems associated with towing. Vertical forces are produced by virtue of the weight of the machine, which is 158 kg (348 lb). This can be increased to 218 kg (481 lb) using ballast. Pressure exerted by the machine is difficult to calculate accurately because of the dependence of contact area on ground conditions but theoretical values of pressure beneath the studs are estimated at about 600 kPa (average) and 1200 kPa (maximum). These are of the same order as those which could be produced by a footballer in walking but not as great as those which might occur in running. Horizontal forces are produced as a result of differential slip between the front and rear sets of studded rotors. This is achieved by coupling the front and rear rotors by means of drive pulleys of unequal size (see Plate 8.2) which causes the front rotors to slip and the rear rotors to skid, resulting in the application of horizontal forces to the ground. The severity of the wear treatment can readily be varied by changing the speed-ratio between the drive pulleys. The type of wear treatment can be changed by removing the studded rotors and fitting different rotors of the desired type. Work is now in progress on further development of the machine for simulation of wear caused by walking. Although these wear treatments will initially be used on trials of *Festuca* spp. in connection with the type of wear occurring on golf greens from spiked footwear and on bowling greens, tennis courts, etc., from rubber soles, they are clearly of wider relevance to other kinds of amenity grassland.

At present there are eight differential slip wear machines operating at different trial centres in the UK and France. Six of these are in use on trials conducted by STRI, and one machine is in use at the Welsh Plant Breeding Station at Aberystwyth. A further machine is based at the Institut National de la Recherche Agronomique at Lusignan in France. When the same type of machine is used by different workers at different locations the possibilities of collaboration and standardization of wear treatments are greatly increased.

Future developments on techniques for simulation of wear must be considered in terms of the needs for research on amenity grasslands. At a fundamental level there is a need for further quantification of the processes of real and artificial wear so that these can be understood on a common basis. More important at present is the use of existing techniques or refinements of them to fill some of the numerous gaps in our knowledge of the factors, mentioned above, which influence the durability of amenity grasslands.

Acknowledgement

All the author's work referred to in this article was carried out under contract from the UK Department of the Environment, sub-contracted by the Natural Environmental Research Council. This continuing support of research into wear is gratefully acknowledged.

References

Adams, W. A., Stewart, V. I., & Thornton, D. J. (1971). 'Drainage', *Welsh Soils Discussion Group Report No. 12.*

Bayfield, N. G. (1971). 'Some effects of walking and skiing on vegetation at Cairngorm', in *The Scientific Management of Animal and Plant Communities for Conservation* (E. A. G. Duffey and A. S. Watt, eds), Blackwell Scientific Publications, Oxford, pp. 469–85.

Beard, J. B. (1973). *Turfgrass: Science and Culture*, Prentice-Hall, Englewood Cliffs, N.J.

Bourgoin, B. (1974). 'The behaviour of the principal turfgrasses under French climatic conditions', *Journal of the Sports Turf Research Institute*, **50**, 65–80.

Canaway, P. M. (1975a). 'Turf wear: a literature review', *Journal of the Sports Turf Research Institute*, **51**, 92–103.

Canaway, P. M. (1975b). 'Fundamental techniques in the study of turfgrass wear: an advance report on research', *Journal of the Sports Turf Research Institute*, **51**, 104–15.

Canaway, P. M. (1976). 'A differential slip wear machine (D.S.1) for the artificial simulation of turfgrass wear', *Journal of the Sports Turf Research Institute,* **52**, 92–9.

Canaway, P. M. (1978). 'Trials of turfgrass wear tolerance and associated factors—a summary of progress 1975–1977', *Journal of the Sports Turf Research Institute,* **54**, 7–14.

Canaway, P. M. (1979). 'Studies on turfgrass abrasion', *Journal of the Sports Turf Research Institute*, **55**, 107–20.

Cavagna, G. A., Saibene, F. P., & Margaria, R. (1963). 'External work in walking', *Journal of Applied Physiology*, **18**, 1–9.

Cavagna, G. A., Saibene, F. P., & Margaria, R. (1964). 'Mechanical work in running', *Journal of Applied Physiology*, **19**, 249–56.

Cieslinski, T. J., & Wagar, J. A. (1970). 'Predicting the durability of forest recreation sites in Northern Utah—preliminary results', *USDA Forest Service Research Note INT-117*.

Dahlsson, S. (1973). 'Gräsytans klipphöjd och slitstyrka (Cutting height and wear tolerance of turf)', *Weibulls Gräs-tips*, Dec. 1973, 23–30.

Escritt, J. R., & Daniells, I. G. (1977). 'Getting the water through to the drains', *Journal of the Sports Turf Research Institute*, **53**, 98.

Frenkel, R. E. (1970). 'Temperate and tropical treading vegetation', *Proceedings of the Oregon Academy of Science*, **6**, 46–53.

Gandert, K. D. (1973). 'Zur Bewertung der Gebrauchseigenschaften von Sportrasenflächen', *Rasen-Turf-Gazon*, **4**, 53–56.

Haessler, K. (1954). 'Zur Ökologie der Trittpflanzen', PhD thesis, Technische Hochschule, Stuttgart.

Harper, F. C., Warlow, W. J., & Clarke, B. L. (1961). 'The forces applied to the floor by the foot in walking', *National Building Studies Research Paper 32*, HMSO, London.

Kays, S., & Harper, J. L. (1974). 'The regulation of plant and tiller density in a grass sward', *Journal of Ecology*, **62**, 97–106.

Leney, F. M. (1974). 'The ecological effects of public pressure on picnic sites', PhD thesis, University of Aberdeen.

Liddle, M. J. (1973). 'The effects of trampling and vehicles on natural vegetation', PhD thesis, University of Wales.

Liddle, M. J. (1975a). 'A selective review of the ecological effects of human trampling on natural ecosystems', *Biological Conservation*, **7**, 17–36.

Liddle, M. J. (1975b). 'A survey of tracks and paths in a sand dune ecosystem II. Vegetation', *Journal of Applied Ecology*, **12**, 909–30.

Liddle, M. J. (1975c). 'A theoretical relationship between the primary productivity of vegetation and its ability to tolerate trampling', *Biological Conservation*, **8**, 251–5.

Madison, J. H. (1971). *Practical Turfgrass Management*, Van Nostrand Reinhold, New York.

Müller, K. G., & Axtmann, K. W. (1976). 'Spielnahe Belastung von Sportrasenversuchen', *Rasen-Turf-Gazon*, **7**, 106–9.

NERC (1977). *Amenity Grasslands the Needs for Research*, Natural Environment Research Council, Publications Series 'C', No. 19, London.

Perry, R. L. (1958). 'Standardized wear index for turfgrasses', *Southern California Turfgrass Culture*, **8**, 30–1.

Pietsch, R. (1968). 'Der Künstliche Standort und der Pflanzenbestand der Fussballplätze im Bundesgebiet', in *Pflanzensoziologie und Landschaftsökologie* (R. Tüxen, ed.), W. Junk, The Hague, pp. 336–47.

Riem Vis, F. (1977). 'Eine effective Stollenwalze', *Rasen-Turf-Gazon*, **8**, 64.

RIVRO (1978). *53e Beschrijvende Rassenlijst voor Landbouwgewassen 1978* (53rd descriptive list of varieties of field crops 1978), Leiter Nypels, Maastricht, The Netherlands.

Rosenberg, N. J. (1964). 'The response of plants to the physical effects of soil compaction', *Advances in Agronomy*, **16**, 181–96.

Shearman, R. C., & Beard, J. B. (1975*a*). 'Turfgrass wear tolerance mechanisms: I. Wear tolerance of seven turfgrass species and quantitative methods of determining turfgrass wear injury', *Agronomy Journal*, **67**, 208–11.

Shearman, R. C., & Beard, J. B. (1975*b*). 'Turfgrass wear tolerance mechanisms: II. Effects of cell wall constituents on turfgrass wear tolerance', *Agronomy Journal*, **67**, 211–5.

Shildrick, J. P. (1971). 'Grass variety trials, 1971', *Journal of the Sports Turf Research Institute*, **47**, 86–126.

Smith, P. E. (1978). 'The functional response of plants to trampling pressure', PhD thesis, University of Keele.

Soane, B. D. (1970). 'The effects of traffic and implements on soil compaction', *Journal and Proceedings of the Institution of Agricultural Engineers*, **25**, 115–26.

STRI (1978). *Choosing Turfgrass Seed in 1978*, Sports Turf Research Institute, Bingley.

Versteeg, W. (1973). 'Die eiserne Mannschaft—Stollenwalze als Pflegerät für Rasensportplätze', *Rasen-Turf-Gazon*, **4**, 12–13.

Vos, H. (1972). 'Zuchtziele für Rasengräser im maritimen Klimabereich', *Rasen-Turf-Gazon*, **3**, 74–7.

Weaver, T., & Dale, D. (1978). 'Trampling effects of hikers, motorcycles and horses in meadows and forests', *Journal of Applied Ecology*, **15**, 451–7.

Youngner, V. B. (1961). 'Accelerated wear tests on turfgrasses', *Agronomy Journal*, **53**, 217–8.

Appendix I

Units and symbols used

Commonly-used units (such as metres and kilograms) are not defined here, but many readers may be unfamiliar with the following:

Physical quantity	Name of unit	Symbol for unit	Definition of unit
Force	Newton	N	$kg\ m\ s^{-2}$
Work or energy	Joule	J	$kg\ m^2\ s^{-2}$
Pressure	Pascal	Pa	$N\ m^{-2}$
Torque	Newton-metre	—	$N\ m$

Conversion factors: $1\ N = 0.2248$ lbf; $1\ J = 0.2388$ cal $= 0.7375$ ft lbf; $1\ Pa = 0.01$ bar $= 7.5 \times 10^{-3}$ torr; $1.N\ m = 0.7375$ lbf ft.

Part IV
Usage and Maintenance

Amenity Grassland: An Ecological Perspective
Edited by I. H. Rorison and R. Hunt
© 1980 John Wiley & Sons Ltd

9
Management of extensive amenity grasslands by mowing

B . H . G R E E N *Countryside Planning Unit, School of Rural Economics and Related Studies, Wye College, nr Ashford, Kent, England*

Introduction

It has been estimated (NERC, 1977) that perhaps three-quarters of UK amenity grassland consists of extensively managed grassland, in nature reserves, country and urban parks, commons, public open spaces, roadside and railway verges, airfields, golf course rough, and domestic lawns. Presently its management by mowing is based on principles and practices derived largely from the intensive management of sports turf and agricultural grassland (see for example, Chapter 12). But it is argued here that the management requirements of much extensive amenity grassland are quite different from those for these other kinds of grassland and that, in consequence, quite different management systems, both in terms of machinery and personnel, would perhaps be both more economic and produce more suitable swards for extensive amenity use.

Much of the extensive amenity grassland with which we are concerned was created, and once maintained, as part of the agricultural economy. Open-range, pastoral husbandry of sheep and other stock on marginal land maintained attractive short-sward grasslands. Their amenity value was a by-product of their main usage, which was the rearing of livestock for meat. In lowland areas, where hill-farming subsidies do not apply, this kind of agriculture is no longer economic and is now rarely practised. Large areas of grassland have either been ploughed for cropland or abandoned. Rabbits, also, contributed to the management 'task' until their populations were cut back by myxomatosis (Chapter 11). They now contribute little, though at least one nature reserve is managed by rabbits grazing inside rabbit-proof fences. Only in very few lowland areas, of which the New Forest is perhaps the best example, does agriculture still maintain grasslands which are incidentally of high amenity value. Some amenity grassland in nature reserves, country parks, golf courses, airfields, and other amenity areas is still grazed, often under licence, but with the management of the sward being the primary objective or at least ranking equally with the rearing of stock (Lowday & Wells, 1977). In many situations such grazing is undoubtedly the best way of maintaining attractive amenity grasslands. But there can be many problems, such as the provision and maintenance of fencing and water, stock worrying by dogs, litter, and the need to have primary concern for the well-being of the stock rather than the state of the sward (Green, 1973).

Management objectives and principles

In these circumstances the cutting of amenity swards by various kinds of mowing machines offers a more readily controllable alternative management. Considerable areas have long been treated in this way. Mowing accounts for by far the greatest of the various costs involved in managing all kinds of amenity grassland and also creates the problems of most concern to amenity grassland managers. The basis of all mowing difficulties lies in some fundamental dilemmas in management objectives for amenity grasslands. There are generally two main objectives in the mind of the amenity grassland manager; first (and usually overriding), to minimize management costs by cutting as infrequently as possible; second, to produce tough swards which will sustain and repair the heavy wear required for many amenity uses. In nature reserves and country parks there may frequently be a third objective, namely the maintenance of high species diversity in the sward. In them it may have priority; in other amenity grasslands it may also be regarded as an important, if not primary, objective.

These objectives are difficult to reconcile with one another for the reasons already made clear in Chapters 2 and 5. Wear-resistant swards are mostly composed of fast-growing, vigorous, and nutrient-demanding species which can rapidly repair trampling and other damage. They thus need frequent cutting. They are also poor in species because those such as *Lolium perenne* (perennial ryegrass) and *Dactylis glomerata* (cock's-foot), which have a competitive strategy (Chapter 2) are, under fertile conditions, easily able to exclude the vast majority of slower-growing and less competitive species. Species-rich swards occur only where these vigorous species are differentially penalized by frequent defoliation or by low fertility. Whilst, inevitably, the objective of wear resistance cannot be completely reconciled with the need to minimize management, the maintenance of high-diversity swards can. Wear resistance, or the high productivity which confers it must be a primary objective of the management of playing surfaces and agricultural grassland. But there is no need for it in most extensive amenity grasslands. Traditionally-managed permanent pastures and meadows can contain 40 or 50 species of flowering plants and numerous species of insect, maybe as many as 24 species of butterfly. Modern leys commonly contain only one or two grasses and no butterflies at all. Why should road verges, airfields, golf rough, or even domestic lawns look like leys or bowling greens? Managing them for diversity would reduce their intensity of management and would create more interesting swards which would help to compensate for the losses of species and amenity in farmed grasslands.

The application of fertilizer, the removal of nutrients in cuttings (or by other means), the frequency of cutting, and the type and height of cut produced by the machine are all of significance in determining the nature of the sward produced and the amount of management required. In addition, since plants flower, set seed, and germinate at different times, the season of cutting can also influence the composition of the sward. There is a vast fund of practical experience in the heads of managers as to how these factors affect the sward. Its collation, and further studies of these problems, are amongst the main priorities of amenity grassland research. This paper describes some studies of this kind and the practical implications arising from them.

The effects of nutrients

If lowland grassland is not grazed, nor cut, nor burnt then succession to coarse grass, scrub, and ultimately, woodland occurs. This succession involves a build-up of nutrients in the ecosystem. Any attempt to reclaim short-sward grassland from these seral stages must remove these accumulated nutrients if slow-growing and diverse grassland is required. If they are not removed then the recolonizing sward will consist mainly of a few vigorous and nutrient-demanding species and will be difficult to convert to a more diverse and less productive sward. Trials at Lullington Heath National Nature Reserve (Gay et al., 1968; Green, 1972), showed that the gorse, about 12 years old, which had colonized openchalk heath sward contained about 500 kg N ha^{-1} (446 lb acre^{-1}). When this was cleared with a flail mower and left in a comminuted state where it lay, the recolonizing sward bore little resemblance to the original species-rich chalk heath grassland. It was weedy, with abundant *Dactylis glomerata*, *Holcus lanatus* (Yorkshire fog), *Agrostis stolonifera* (fiorin), and other known nitrophiles like *Chamaenerion angustifolium* (rose-bay willow-herb). If the cut gorse and its nutrient load were removed, however, swards much more like the original chalk heath were obtained (Plate 9.1).

Many colonizing shrubs fix nitrogen even if they are not, like gorse, legumes. *Hippophaë rhamnoides* (sea buckthorn) is an example. Nettle beds often develop when it is cleared from sand dune grassland. Some eutrophication also can take place under shrubs which do not fix nitrogen and there is evidence that there might be an immobilization of nitrogen under grassland which shrub colonization then releases (Malone, 1970).

In the Lullington trials, subsequent management of the swards reclaimed by leaving or abstracting the gorse nutrients involved annual mowing. Here, the grass cuttings were themselves left and collected respectively. It was shown that the cuttings provided more than 20 kg N ha^{-1} (17 lb acre^{-1}) year^{-1} but, unfortunately, because of the large differences between swards generated by the much larger nutrient load in the initial gorse cover, any effects of removing annual cuttings were undetectable. Since cuttings can contain as much as 60 kg N ha^{-1} (54 lb acre^{-1}) and grass growth requires the uptake of some 100 kg N ha^{-1} (89 lb acre^{-1}) (see Chapter 5) it has long been appreciated by grassland managers that removing cuttings greatly impoverishes productive systems and increases the fertilizer requirements necessary to maintain vigorous growth (Adams, 1977).

Trials on chalk grassland (Duffey *et al.*, 1976) have, however, shown no differences in species composition between swards where cuttings were left and removed (see Chapter 11); perhaps because under these conditions fertility is already so low as to have maximized diversity. In more fertile sites, such as the Lullington scrubland, their removal may be more important if diversity is desired for there is little leaching from grass swards and, in the absence of the extraction of nutrients by burning or as 'crops' of grazing animals, it is one of the few practical ways of impoverishing the ecosystem. Furthermore, if nutrient accumulation is, as would seem possible, a continuous process which drives the succession, removal of cuttings and their nutrient load may be necessary not so much as a means of lowering fertility, as of arresting the succession by balancing gains from mineralization, rain, and biological fixation. On poor soils, any concentration of disposed cuttings certainly leads to loss of diversity and causes changes in the sward of sites used for tipping very like those caused by addition of fertilizer.

The timing, frequency, and height of cut

At Lullington, the trials also included different times of cutting (spring and autumn), different frequencies of cutting (once or twice a year) and different machines (rotary swipe and reciprocating haymower). No marked differences could be detected between these treatments apart from a better suppression of gorse regeneration from two cuts a year. A trial set up at Wye and Crundale Downs National Nature Reserve pursued the effects of these factors in more detail (Williams & Duffield, 1978). Here the main management problem was the invasion of chalk grassland by *Brachypodium pinnatum* (tor grass) which, through its coarse growth and thick litter, suppresses all but a very few of the characteristics and numerous species of the short-sward community. (Another trial had, incidentally, shown this species to be the worst in this respect of the three grasses commonly assuming dominance on

Plate 9.1 A silage mower and trailer collecting clippings during the Lullington Heath trials (photograph by B. H. Green)

Plate 9.2   Mown plots at Wye and Crundale Downs NNR. Control (unmown) plots with luxuriant growth of grass and scrub are in the foreground (photograph by B. H. Green)

Plate 9.3 Spring burning into the wind at Wye and Crundale Downs NNR. This treatment 'opens up' vegetation dominated by *Brachypodium pinnatum* (photograph by B. H. Green)

abandoned downland grazings: *Zerna erecta* (upright brome) accumulates less thatch; *Festuca rubra* (red fescue) much less). The *Brachypodium pinnatum* trial was started in February 1964 in a field of chalk grassland heavily infested with this species. The area was first cleared by cutting with an Allen scythe and the litter was removed (Plate 9.2). Plots were then treated under one of nine different mowing regimes, each replicated three times. The mowing regimes were designed to simulate sheep grazing seasons:

(1) control; no mowing;
(2) deep-winter cutting (October–March);
(3) long-winter cutting (September–May);
(4) summer cutting (April–September);
(5) all-year cutting.

Each mowing treatment was duplicated, one cut being made at a sward height of 25 mm (1 in) and one at 75 mm (3 in). The plots were mown with a rotary hand mower and the cuttings were removed. Within the mowing seasons the plots were not cut at set dates or frequencies, but when the growth was adjudged by the warden to be such that a farmer would put sheep on the sward. In practice, this has meant that the deep-winter plots have been cut once a year, the long-winter plots twice, the summer plots two or three times and the all-year plots three times.

The results show that removal of the cuttings by mowing can maintain species-rich chalk grassland swards. The mown plots all have a reduced frequency and cover of *Brachypodium pinnatum* and 30–40 species in their swards compared to the half-dozen which are able to survive alongside the luxuriant growth of *Brachypodium pinnatum* in the control plots. There are no substantial differences in species composition between the mowing treatments, though the greatest numbers of species occur on the deep-winter plots. Since these are cut only once a year, mowing at 75 mm (3 in) during this season would seem to be the most economical means of managing chalk grassland for species diversity. The winter-cut plots perhaps contain most species because cutting at this time interferes least with flowering and setting of seed. The summer-cut plots show fewest species, but although the differences in species number are not statistically significant, the amount of flowering and conspicuousness of some species which are important wildlife and amenity assets is notably less on these plots. Thus, the timing of the cut in relation to the phenology of species can appreciably alter the appearance of a sward. All cuttings were removed in this trial; whether leaving them would have in any way reduced the diversity of the swards so obtained cannot be assessed. It is perhaps worth noting that the greatest yield of cut grass was removed by the single cut of the deep-winter plots which also had the greatest number of species. Furthermore, the soils of all cut plots contained less soil potassium (but not nitrogen or phosphorus) than the controls. The plots were not fenced against rabbits, which were absent (following myxomatosis) when the trial was started. Latterly, rabbits have grazed all plots but their effect is undetermined. Observation suggests, however, that they graze equally on all plots and are unlikely to have influenced the conclusions stated above.

Other means of growth control

Burning has been very much a part of the traditional grazing management of marginal grasslands in many parts of the country (Plate 9.3). It is still used widely for heathland and moorland management and for maintaining railway embankments. It both defoliates and removes nutrients and trials show that rotational winter burns every 2 or 3 years can 'open up' *Brachypodium pinnatum* swards and increase their diversity. Controlled burns within the statutory burning season (1 November to 31 March) are perhaps of most importance as a safety measure. By removing dead grass and litter they greatly reduce the risk of accidental burns in the summer which are far more destructive to wildlife, person, and property. Fire is also a useful tool for clearing areas of coarse grass prior to introducing a mowing or grazing regime. Herbicides like dalapon and maleic hydrazide can also be effective in maintaining short-sward grassland, but their high cost is prohibitive for the management of very extensive areas (see Chapter 10).

In conclusion

Theory, and the experimental results quoted above, suggest that diverse grassland swards suitable for many extensive amenity uses should be easy to achieve. On some soils diversity is, of course, unlikely ever to approach that of calcareous soils, but even on very acid podsols an impoverishing system of management would still give a more representative selection of the typical flora than uniform swards of the common, mesotrophic, pasture grasses as produced by standard management techniques.

Acknowledgement

The mowing trials at Lullington Heath and Wye and Crundale Downs National Nature Reserves were originally set up by Dr P. A. Gay. I am grateful for his permission to describe them.

References

Adams, W. A. (1977). 'Fertilizer use on sports turf', *Parks and Sports Grounds*, **43**, 62–70.

Duffey, E. A. G., Morris, M. G., Sheail, J., Ward, L. K., Wells, D. A., & Wells, T. C. (1976). *Grassland Ecology and Wildlife Management*, Chapman & Hall, London.

Gay, P. A., Green, B. H., & Labern, M. V. (1968). 'The experimental management of chalk heath at Lullington Heath National Nature Reserve, Sussex', *Journal of Ecology*, **56**, 24–5P.

Green, B. H. (1972). 'The relevance of seral eutrophication and plant competition to the management of successional communities', *Biological Conservation*, **4**, 378–84.

Green, B. H. (1973). 'Practical aspects of chalk grassland management in the Nature Conservancy's South East Region', in *Chalk Grassland, Studies on its Conservation and Management in South East England* (A. C. Jermy & P. A. Stott, eds), Kent Trust for Nature Conservation, Maidstone.

Lowday, J. E. & Wells, T. C. E. (1977). *The Management of Grassland and Heathland in Country Parks*, Countryside Commission, Cheltenham.

Malone, C. R. (1970). 'Short-term effects of chemical and mechanical cover management on decomposition processes in a grassland soil', *Journal of Applied Ecology*, **7**, 591–601.

NERC (1977). *Amenity Grasslands—the Needs for Research*, Natural Environment Research Council, Publications Series 'C', No. 19, London.

Williams, G. & Duffield, J. (1978). *The Effect on the Flora of Mowing a* Brachypodium pinnatum *Community*, unpublished report, Nature Conservancy Council, S.E. Region, Wye, Kent.

Amenity Grassland: An Ecological Perspective
Edited by I. H. Rorison and R. Hunt
© 1980 John Wiley & Sons Ltd

10
Weed control and vegetation management by herbicides

R . J . H A G G A R *ARC Weed Research Organization, Yarnton, Oxford, England*

Introduction

Weed control in both amenity and agricultural grassland is intended to promote long-term 'crop' ascendancy by preventing the ingress of unwanted species. Thus, 'sward wear' and 'sward persistence' have been identified as common research objectives (Smith, 1977). But, whereas yield improvement is a primary aim of weed control in agricultural grassland, low productivity is often desirable in amenity areas. Moreover, in extensive amenity grassland, low sward maintenance assumes even greater importance, whilst an additional aim is often the achievement of a highly diverse sward composition. Thus, at first sight, interests in weed control of intensively-used grassland on the one hand, and vegetation management in more extensive grassland on the other, appear to be diametrically opposed.

However, it must be realized that herbicides are negative management tools, being used to suppress one species in order to promote another. Hence, in agricultural grassland, selective herbicides have been used to control broad-leaved weeds as a means of increasing grass output. Similarly, other selective herbicides (and possibly growth retardants) could be applied to amenity grassland to increase the abundance of dicotyledonous plants, simply by suppressing the more competitive grasses.

During the last 30 years considerable progress has been made in developing herbicides for use in agricultural grassland. Techniques are now available for the management both of single-species swards and of quite complex vegetation. This chapter aims to relate this knowledge to amenity grassland so that new management options can be worked out to meet the increased recreational needs, leisure pursuits and conservational demands of the future.

Weed control in turf grass

Plants may be considered as weeds if they: (a) are unsightly, (b) interfere with play, (c) harbour pests and diseases, or (d) crowd out the preferred species. In general, amenity grasses are slower to establish than agricultural grasses, so weed control is relatively more important.

Broad-leaved weeds are fairly easily controlled by a range of commercially available herbicides (Fryer & Makepeace, 1978) and, although in Britain their use accounts for several million pounds of the establishment and maintenance costs (NERC, 1977; see Table 1), this aspect of weed control is rarely mentioned as a problem by turf managers. But there are often several additional costs involved in the prevention of weed ingress. For instance, it can be necessary to kill off heavy weed infestations before construction work starts, to provide a clean seedbed (by fallowing, cultivation, or soil fumigation) and to use high quality, weed-free seed. Further, it could be claimed that the exceptionally high seed rates used, in comparison with those employed in agricultural grassland, probably have weed control as one of their justifications (see Chapter 7). Knowing that tiller density of established swards is largely independent of seed rate (Kays & Harper (1974) have shown that established tiller density was quite independent of a 30-fold range of seed densities), it is worth pondering whether the very large number of deaths that occurs during the thinning process results in the surviving populations departing significantly from the sown population, especially in terms of yield.

Weed grasses are more insidious than broad-leaved weeds in that they tend to persist longer, to be more competitive, and, certainly, to be more difficult to eradicate. *Poa annua* (annual poa) is a major contaminant of turf grass but there is some divergence of opinion on its weed status. In fine turf, it may often become dominant and, whatever its faults (e.g. susceptibility to *Fusarium* spp.), greenkeepers are reluctant to replace it without assurance of an equally robust replacement—which is a virtual impossibility! On the other hand, in turf subject to heavy wear, e.g. football pitches, *P. annua* is often considered to be extremely valuable, assisting grass ground-cover (although the shallow-rooted plants can often be kicked out). Thus, there has been only limited demand for elimination of this species. Moreover, the means of achieving selective control by herbicides has also been very limited. For instance, trials with bensulide at STRI (J. Shildrick, personal communication) have not been as successful as in America, while the effectiveness of arsenic compound and endothal depends greatly on the ecotype that is present, the truly annual form being more susceptible than the perennial.

There has recently been some clarification of the weed status of *P. annua* in agricultural grassland. Some evidence points to the positive contribution which this species can make to increased yield under grazing conditions (Wells & Haggar, 1974). On the other hand, under cutting conditions, the replacement of more than 30 per cent of *Lolium perenne* (perennial ryegrass) ground cover by *P. annua* usually results in losses of yield (Dibb &

Haggar, 1979). Recently, ethofumesate has been developed for the control of *Poa* spp. in ryegrass leys. Now, for the first time, the effects of selective removal of *P. annua* can be measured. Preliminary results emphasize the substantial damage that the weed can have on tillering of *L. perenne*, especially during the early stages of pasture establishment (Haggar & Passman, 1978); the failure of the crop to reach optimum tiller density per unit area soon after sowing reduces the productive life of the sward and so hastens the time for costly reseeding. The use of ethofumesate allows target levels of tiller numbers per unit area to be achieved in a more predictable manner.

In established swards, the presence of large numbers of seedlings of *P. annua* will restrict tiller production of the spot-bound *L. perenne*. So, where gaps are created in the sward, e.g. as happens through excessive wear, *L. perenne* is not likely to spread into these gaps unless they are kept free of *P. annua* for several weeks. This is where ethofumesate can play a useful role, especially as only low rates are needed to kill the sensitive seedlings of *P. annua* (Haggar & Bastian, 1976).

Holcus lanatus (Yorkshire fog) is another grass weed that has been identified as a problem in amenity grassland (NERC, 1977), forming unsightly patches in closely mown turf, especially on acidic, worm-free soil. Asulam applied in the autumn is showing considerable promise in controlling this species in swards based on *L. perenne* (Haggar & Squires, 1979).

A new approach to selective weed control in grassland has been the breeding of varieties of *L. perenne* that are tolerant to low doses either of paraquat (Faulkner, 1978*a*) or of dalapon (Faulkner, 1978*b*), both reasonably 'clover-safe' herbicides. Although neither herbicide is at present recommended for the selective control of undesirable species in amenity grass (Fisher, 1977), this is an area where the concept has considerable potential, since aesthetic appearance is of utmost importance and the constraint of high yield is removed.

Weeds of extensive amenity grassland

In the non-agricultural grassland characterized by roadside verges, railway embankments, canal and river banks, airfields, etc., the major management aims are to maintain complete vegetative cover to prevent erosion, at the same time as preventing vegetation from growing so tall as to restrict visibility and cause a hazard through fire risk, litter control, drainage impedance, etc. Certain plants occurring in these situations would commonly be referred to as weeds, especially tall-growing species such as *Anthriscus sylvestris* (cow parsley), *Heracleum sphondylium* (hogweed) and *Urtica dioica* (stinging nettle). Also included would be those species named in the Weeds Act 1959.

However, the dangers of these agricultural weeds spreading from roadsides to cause economic infestations of neighbouring land have frequently been over-emphasized (Way, 1970); in recent years, acute shortages of labour and increased costs have forced Highway Authorities to become much more lax in their control of these species.

In most other amenity grassland areas, the term 'weed control' scarcely applies and 'vegetation control' becomes a more appropriate term, with emphasis on selective suppression rather than eradication. What constitutes 'undesirable vegetation' really depends upon what the general public expects to find in a particular situation. For instance, on the common land of Port Meadow near Oxford, *Cirsium arvense* (creeping thistle) and *Ranunculus* spp. (buttercup) are accepted and there might well be a public outcry if they were sprayed out. But, eyebrows would be raised if these species were left to grow unhindered in the formal parks within the city. Nevertheless, even in extensive amenity grassland, certain species are clearly undesirable if present in substantial numbers, e.g., *Cirsium vulgare* (spear thistle) and *Urtica dioica* on picnic or camp sites. Similarly, invasion by *Rubus* spp. (brambles), *Prunus spinosa* (blackthorn) or *Ulex* spp. (gorses) would not be tolerated on public footpaths. Fortunately, recommended methods of controlling these species safely are available (Fryer & Makepeace, 1978), based mainly on 2,4,5-T and 2,4-D.

In extensive amenity grassland such as country parks and nature reserves, management is principally concerned with regulating vegetation height, to provide public access (or exclusion), to control scrub ingress, to establish and maintain species-rich communities, and to preserve rare or beautiful species. In general, trying to create and maintain a visually attractive landscape is fraught with difficulties. Firstly, little is known about people's vegetation preferences (see Chapter 13). For instance, it might be a myth to assume that forested landscapes are less attractive than more open countryside (Burton & Muir, 1978). Secondly, land managers, trying to achieve acceptable standards at least expense, need more precise guidelines based on ecological principles. Unfortunately, as pointed out by Harper (1971), as a consequence of our present ignorance of the ecological mechanisms controlling natural vegetation, attempts to manage it are bound for some time to be largely empirical. It is to be hoped that this volume will encourage ecologists to collect basic 'actuarial' data to explain species regulative mechanisms along the lines being pursued by Grime (1973), so that vegetation management can become a more predictive science.

Need for new management options

In the meantime, alternative methods of vegetation management are urgently needed. Country parks and picnic areas can serve their purpose only if the vegetation in them is maintained in an acceptable condition. Moreover, for the enjoyment, instruction, and interest of the public, it is desirable that the vegetation contains a diversity of wild plants and is not limited to grasses.

Once these leisure areas have been created, satisfactory maintenance is proving a major problem to local authorities. Frequent cutting is costly, often impracticable, and does not necessarily provide the desired sward composition. Grazing, too, is frequently out of the question. Many of the sites have, therefore, become semi-derelict with rank, coarse grasses and scrub. Planted trees are neglected and are in a permanent state of check from weed competition.

In the past, herbicides have not been used as a management option because they were considered, or suspected, to be expensive, to cause unsightly and deformed growth, to be dangerous to handle, to destroy rare flora and fauna, and to require too specialized knowledge and machinery. Consequently they were used only on pathways, as spot treatments to control noxious weeds, or on small areas where a particularly aggressive grass was threatening a species-rich plant community (Lowday & Wells, 1977). However, economic pressures, combined with greater awareness of the potential use of herbicides available in agriculture, are forcing a change in attitude towards their increased use. For instance, aerial spraying of asulam is now widely practised for controlling bracken which is invading heathland or acid grassland.

Herbicides as a new management option

Herbicides, by virtue of their much greater specificity in comparison with cutting or grazing (Harper, 1971), can effect rapid change in the botanical composition of swards. However, such change can revert quickly unless coupled with changes in defoliation or nutrient status. In an attempt to create change in any specific direction, an understanding of the successional stages involved is necessary, as exemplified in the classic work of Jones (1933) and others. It must be realized that grass swards are in a highly dynamic state and that grassland is a plagioclimax vegetation throughout lowland Britain.

The historical development of selective herbicides makes intriguing reading. After the discovery of MCPA and 2,4-D in the mid-1940s, their use for broad-leaved weed control in agricultural grassland was slow to gain acceptance, mainly because of their toxicity to clover and the lack of convincing data to demonstrate the benefits to animal production. Since then clover-safe herbicides have been developed, notably MCPB, dalapon and asulam, and the concept of using such herbicides to cause a gentle shift in species composition, rather than outright kill, is now an accepted aspect of practical grassland management. Using selective herbicides in this way to adjust the competitive balance between species in a sward can usually be achieved by low doses and therefore at small cost. Moreover, several herbicides can be applied in late autumn or winter without interference to grazing.

Research at WRO has demonstrated the many possibilities that now exist for regulating sward composition. For instance, *Agrostis* spp. (bents) can easily be suppressed in *Lolium perenne* swards by low-dose dalapon (Haggar & Oswald, 1976), *Holcus lanatus* by asulam (Watt, 1978) and *Poa* spp. by ethofumesate (Haggar & Passman, 1978). In addition, grass-suppressing herbicides such as paraquat, carbetamide, and propyzamide can be used on mixed swards in the winter to encourage spring growth of *Trifolium repens* (white clover) (Haggar, 1974). Plate 10.1 shows the effects of propyzamide on a ryegrass/clover sward. This diverse array of selective herbicides, mostly developed for other crop uses but found to have value in grassland, now means that swards can often be manipulated at will to meet varying requirements of different systems of utilization by people or livestock.

Selective herbicides can be effective only if there is a nucleus of desirable species both present and uniformly distributed. Thus, the tufted, non-stoloniferous habit of *Lolium perenne*, coupled with low reserves of seed in the soil, means that this species has only a limited ability to spread laterally into space made available by weed control. Hence, some form of seed introduction is often required. Simply broadcasting seed over the sprayed area can be a costly gamble. Moreover, since bare ground is seldom a feature of such herbicide-treated swards, some means of placing seed into contact with mineral soil, away from harmful root-mat and surface litter is required (Squires & Elliot, 1975). This is where a new slot-seeder machine that has been developed at WRO might prove most useful (Squires *et al.*, 1978; see Plate 10.2 and Figure 10.1). It is able to remove a narrow strip of

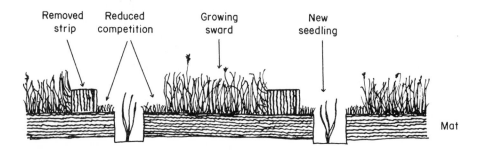

Figure 10.1   A schematic section through slot-seeded turf, taken across the line of the trenching

Plate 10.1 A ryegrass/white clover sward seen 5 months after spraying with propyzamide at 1.5 kg ha^{-1} (1.3 lb acre^{-1}). An unsprayed plot is on the left (photograph by the Weed Research Organization)

[facing page 168

Plate 10.2   (a) A rear view of the Weed Research Organization's slot-seeder unit. Turf-cutting discs and the seed coulter are shown, but not the adjacent band-spray (photograph by the Weed Research Organization)

(b) A close-up of the sward after one pass with the slot-seeder unit shown in (a). The trench has been sown with seed of *Lolium perenne*. See also Figure 10.1 (photograph by the Weed Research Organization)

Plate 10.3 (a) The 'natural' vegetation of the wide verge of a lane at Staveley, Derbyshire, July 1977. The average height of the rank vegetation exceeds 1 m (3.3 ft). Prominent in this 'control' area are *Prunus spinosa* and *Rubus fruticosus* and the Umbellifers *Heracleum sphondylium* and *Anthriscus sylvestris*. Grasses include *Arrhenatherum elatius* and *Agropyron repens*, but constitute only a relatively small proportion of the total vegetation (photograph by G. Woods)

(b) The vegetation of a sprayed plot at Staveley in July 1977 adjoining an untreated 'control' area. The scrub vegetation of this plot was cut in 1971 and stumps were locally treated with a herbicide containing 2,4,5-trichlorophenoxyacetic acid. From 1971 the plot was sprayed once a year with maleic hydrazide in spring. The sward shown is nearly pure *Festuca rubra* of average height 320 mm (12.6 in) but in other parts of the plot more dicotyledonous plants are present. When the mixed spray MH + 2,4-D is used, treated plots typically have the appearance illustrated here (research by A. J. Willis, photograph by G. Woods)

turf and has facilities for band-spraying to reduce competition from the surrounding vegetation, plus the provision of nutrients and protectants, all in a one-pass sowing operation. (Other machines are available, or are being developed elsewhere, the one based on the rotovating principle by Pascal & Sheppard (1977) being of particular use on deep, peaty soil.)

This two-stage approach to sward improvement, of slot-seeding and selective herbicides, means that the costly reseeding of deteriorated swards (Haggar, 1977) can be avoided, making the concept of managing productive grassland as a truly perennial 'crop' a reality.

Application to amenity grassland management

In productive grassland, there has been considerable debate recently between ecologists and agronomists over the significance of botanical composition of grass swards in terms of yield and animal output (Dibb & Haggar, 1979). Fortunately, productivity in amenity grassland is much less of an issue but aesthetic appearance is of major importance. Thus the question is, 'Can selective herbicides be used to enhance the visual attractiveness of swards, principally by encouraging species diversity, without endangering the survival of rare flora and fauna?'. Many naturalists would say 'No', claiming that modern grassland farming replaces plant-rich pastures with temporary leys containing only one or two species, lowers water tables, uses undesirable pesticides and generally creates a far poorer habitat for wildlife. However, simply removing all constraints of management and letting grassland 'go' generally leads to a reduction in species diversity, with litter-tolerant species often assuming a dominant position (Grime, 1973). Thus, a reduction in animal grazing has led to large areas of chalk grassland being invaded by *Brachypodium pinnatum* (tor grass) and acidic grassland by *Pteridium aquilinum* (bracken). Selective herbicides could be used to reverse this trend, e.g. by breaking up the initial infestations using dalapon and asulam, respectively (thus allowing improved public access and achieving increased benefits through treading).

Herbicides can often be used to trigger-off major flushes of growth by dicotyledonous species (Douglas, 1965; Harper, 1971). Similarly, certain growth retardants can reduce herbage biomass and lead to increased species diversity. For instance, Willis (1969), using a combination of the growth-retardant maleic hydrazide (which is non-toxic to animals) with 2,4-D, applied in a single application in spring, showed that it was possible to convert an unsightly roadside verge dominated by the tall tussock grasses *Arrhenatherum elatius* (oat-grass) and *Dactylis glomerata* (cock's-foot) to a short grassy sward of pleasant appearance in which fine-leaved, rhizomatous *Festuca rubra* (red fescue) and *Poa pratensis* (smooth-stalked meadow-grass) were prominent (see the poster demonstration by A. J. Willis, and Plate

10.3). This principle is now being applied on many roadside verges (D. Waterhouse, personal communication) and on the central reservation of motorways. It could also be considered as a complement to the use of mowing machines in reducing peaks of grass growth in May. Also, growth retardants might be used in country parks initially to create new pathways to encourage people away from over-populated areas.

The potential for using selective herbicides to control woody, herbaceous and aquatic weeds to improve public use of amenity areas, has long been known (Fryer, 1958). Even so, much work still remains to determine the inherent relative susceptibility of the major species of amenity grassland to existing herbicides, most of which have not been evaluated in this way, at the same time as checking the tolerance of any associated rare species. This will involve a considerable amount of preliminary screening in pots, with promising herbicides being tested under field conditions. The main variables would be dosage over a logarithmic range and timing of application. The effect of repeated treatments and the reversion of sprayed areas would also need to be studied.

Devising ways of increasing selectivities based on phenological differences between species should be possible, involving studies on timing of applications. Emphasis would need to be given to treatments applied during the period from late summer to early winter to reduce the risk of unsightly growth.

A new approach to selective weed control is being developed at WRO, using height as the basis of separation. Small quantities of translocated herbicides like glyphosate and dicamba can be stuck onto leaves of tall-growing plants, using a non-drip gel, without affecting the underlying species (A. K. Oswald, personal communication). The technique has considerable potential for controlling many troublesome, tall-growing and unsightly weeds of amenity grassland, e.g. *Urtica dioica*, *Brachypodium pinnatum* and *Pteridium aquilinum*, although further research is needed to determine the minimum leaf areas that need to be smeared with herbicide.

On sites where there is a dearth of dicotyledonous species, the selective removal of unwanted vegetation needs to be complemented by the sowing of seed of desirable species. This is where the WRO slot-seeder could play a role; a seed mixture supplied by the Nature Conservancy Council, containing a variety of grasses, *Poterium sanguisorba* (salad burnet) and *Onobrychis viciifolia* (sanfoin), has already been slot-seeded in Dorset into steep chalk banks dominated by *Festuca ovina* (sheep's fescue) (C. Dibb, personal communication). The future development of such work is likely to be delayed by a shortage of seed. Considerable efforts are, therefore, needed to build up supplies of seed of the main amenity species (see Chapter 3). This will involve growing stands of individual species free of weed contaminants.

The future

Herbicides have revolutionized approaches to plant production on agricultural land and the scope for their use in amenity grassland is equally great. But any new concept offering a radical change from traditional methods has to be challenged, tested and developed before being accepted. Herbicides are currently a controversial tool in many amenity grassland circles. However, there are signs of changing attitudes and it is our duty to see how the benefits that herbicides can bring can be used creatively and responsibly for man's enjoyment of the environment, bearing in mind that an increase in leisure time (if not unemployment) is likely to be a major feature of the next quarter-century. As anticipated by Robinson (1978), more people will want to establish a 'oneness with nature' but they will still want to have nature under their control.

Several advances in herbicide technology can be expected in the near future. For instance, the use of controlled-release formulations could be of considerable value in giving sustained and safe control of selected vegetation types. Indeed, safety for the environment is likely to be even more of a consideration in all future development work. New and safe ways of applying herbicides more efficiently are likely to be developed, along the lines of the height-selective applicator described above. Another example is the current development of controlled-droplet application (Cussans & Taylor, 1976), which greatly reduces the possibility of spray drift damage.

We hope that research workers and planners in amenity grassland will respond to the new thinking and opportunities that these chemicals offer. But if technical advances are to be implemented by amenity grass managers, then more advisers and commercial contractors will be needed, with the necessary specialist knowledge of the herbicides and machines that will be required.

References

Burton, R. &.Muir, K. (1978). 'Public preferences for forest landscapes', *Proceedings of the International of Union Forestry Research Organizations*, in press.

Cussans, G. W. & Taylor, W. A. (1976). 'A review of research on controlled drop application at the ARC Weed Research Organization', *Proceedings of the 1976 British Crop Protection Conference—Weeds*, **3**, 885–94.

Dibb, C. & Haggar, R. J. (1979). 'Evidence on effect of sward changes on yield', *Proceedings of British Grassland Society Occasional Symposium no. 10*, 11–20.

Douglas, G. (1965). 'The weed flora of chemically-renewed lowland swards', *Journal of the British Grassland Society*, **20**, 91–100.

Faulkner, J. S. (1978a). 'The use of paraquat for controlling weeds in seedling swards of paraquat resistant *Lolium perenne* L.', *Proceedings of the 1978 British Crop Protection Conference—Weeds*, **1**, 349–55.

Faulkner, J. S. (1978*b*). 'Dalapon tolerant varieties—a possible basis for pure swards of *Lolium perenne* L.', *Proceedings of the 1978 British Crop Protection Conference—Weeds*, **1**, 341–8.

Fisher, R. (1977). 'The selective control of undesirable grasses in amenity grassland', *Journal of the Sports Turf Research Institute*, **53**, 11–30.

Fryer, J. D. (1958). 'The potential value of herbicide in nature reserves', *Proceedings of the Linnaean Society*, **199**, 107–10.

Fryer, J. S. & Makepeace, R. M. (1977). 'Principles, including plant growth regulators', in *Weed Control Handbook*, Vol. 2, Blackwell Scientific Publications, Oxford.

Fryer, J. D. & Makepeace, R. M. (1978). 'Recommendations, including plant growth regulators', in *Weed Control Handbook*, Vol. 1, Blackwell Scientific Publications, Oxford.

Grime, J. P. (1973). 'Control of species diversity in herbaceous vegetation', *Journal of Environmental Management*, **1**, 151–67.

Haggar, R. J. (1974). 'Legumes and British grassland, new opportunities with herbicides', *Proceedings of the 12th British Weed Control Conference*, **1**, 771–7.

Haggar, R. J. (1977). 'Herbicides and low cost grassland establishment with special reference to clean seed-beds and one-pass seeding', in *Proceedings of the International Conference on Energy Conservation in Crop Production*, (C. J. Baker, ed.), Massey University, Auckland, pp. 31–8.

Haggar, R. J. & Bastian, C. J. (1976). 'Controlling weed grasses in ryegrass by ethofumesate with special reference to *Poa annua*', *Proceedings of the 1976 British Crop Protection Conference—Weeds*, **3**, 603–9.

Haggar, R. J. & Oswald, A. K. (1976). 'Improving ryegrass swards by a low dose of dalapon', *Weed Research Organization Technical Leaflet no. 1*, 1–2.

Haggar, R. J. & Passman, A. (1978). 'Some consequences of controlling *Poa annua* in newly sown ryegrass leys', *Proceedings of the 1978 British Crop Protection Conference—Weeds*, **1**, 301–8.

Haggar, R. J. & Squires, N. R. W. (1979). 'The scientific manipulation of sward constituents in grassland by herbicides and one-pass seeding', *Proceedings of British Grassland Society Occasional Symposium no. 10*, 223–34.

Harper, J. L. (1971). 'Grazing, fertilizers and pesticides in the management of grasslands', in *The Scientific Management of Animal and Plant Communities for Conservation* (E. A. G. Duffey & A. S. Watt, eds), Blackwell Scientific Publications, Oxford, pp. 15–31.

Jones, M. G. (1933). 'Grassland management and its influence on the sward', *Empire Journal of Experimental Agriculture*, **1**, 43–57.

Kays, S. & Harper, J. L. (1974). 'The regulation of plant and tiller density in a grass sward', *Journal of Ecology*, **62**, 97–105.

Lowday, J. E. & Wells, T. C. E. (1977). *The Management of Grassland and Heathland in Country Parks*, Countryside Commission, Cheltenham.

NERC (1977). *Amenity Grasslands—the Needs for Research*, Natural Environment Research Council, Publications series 'C', No. 19, London.

Pascal, J. A. & Sheppard, B. W. (1977). 'Development of a sod seeder for introduction of clover into hill pastures', *ARC Research Review*, **3**, 74–8.

Robinson, D. W. (1978). 'The challenge of the next generation of weed problems', *Proceedings of the 1978 British Crop Protection Conference—Weeds*, **3**, 800–21.

Smith, A. (1977). 'Persistence of perennial grasses: some objectives for research on agricultural and amenity grassland', *Journal of the Sports Turf Research Institute*, **53**, 102.

Squires, N. R. W. & Elliott, J. G. (1975). 'The establishment of grass and fodder crops after sward destruction by herbicides', *Journal of the British Grassland Society*, **30**, 31–40.

Squires, N. R. W., Haggar, R. J. & Elliott, J. G. (1978). 'A one-pass technique for establishing grasses and legumes in existing swards', *Weed Research Organization Technical Leaflet no. 2*, 1–4.

Watt, T. A. (1978). 'The biology of *Holcus lanatus* (Yorkshire fog) and its significance in grassland', *Herbage Abstracts*, **48**, 195–204.

Way, J. M. (1970). 'Further observations on the management of road verges for amenity and wildlife', in *Proceedings of a Symposium on Road Verges in Scotland*, Nature Conservancy (Scotland), Edinburgh, pp. 1–13.

Wells, J. G. & Haggar, R. J. (1974). 'Herbage yields of ryegrass swards invaded by *Poa* species', *Journal of the British Grassland Society*, **29**, 109–10.

Willis, A. J. (1969). 'Road verges—experiments on the chemical control of grass and weeds', in *Proceedings of a Symposium on Road Verges, Their Function and Management*, Monks Wood Experiment Station, Monks Wood, pp. 52–60.

Appendix 10.1

List of common names and chemical names used for herbicides and plant growth regulants mentioned in the text

Common name	Chemical name
Asulam	Methyl(4-aminobenzenesulphonyl) carbamate
Bensulide	N-[2-(O,O-di-isopropyldithiophosphoryl)ethyl]benzene sulphonamide
Carbetamide	D-N-Ethyl-2-(phenylcarbamoyloxy)propionamide
2,4-D	2,4-Dichlorophenoxyacetic acid
Dalapon	2,2-Dichloropropionic acid
Dicamba	3,6-Dichloro-2-methoxybenzoic acid
Endothal	7-Oxabicyclo-[2,2,1]-heptane-2,3-dicarboxylic acid
Ethofumesate	2-Ethoxy-2,3-dihydro-3,3-dimethylbenzofuran-5-yl-methyl sulphonate
Glyphosate	N-Phosphonomethyl glycine
Maleic hydrazide	1,2-Dihydropyridazine-3,6-dione
MCPA	4-Chloro-2-methylphenoxyacetic acid
MCPB	4-(4-Chloro-2-methylphenoxy)butyric acid
Paraquat	1,1'-Dimethyl-4,4'-bipyridylium-2A
Propyzamide	3,5-Dichloro-N-(1,1-dimethylpropynyl)benzamide
2,4,5-T	2,4,5-Trichlorophenoxyacetic acid

Amenity Grassland: An Ecological Perspective
Edited by I. H. Rorison and R. Hunt
© 1980 John Wiley & Sons Ltd

11
Management options for lowland grassland

T. C. E. WELLS *Institute of Terrestrial Ecology, Monks Wood Experimental Station, Abbots Ripton, Huntingdon, England*

Introduction

Our definition of amenity grassland as 'all grass with recreational, functional, or aesthetic value, and of which agricultural productivity is not the primary aim' embraces a great variety of different grasslands. These range from an intensively managed group, which may loosely be called 'sports turf' (e.g. bowling greens, cricket, football, hockey, and rugby pitches, school playing fields, and golf courses) to grasslands on commons and many public open spaces where deliberate management is infrequent or much less intensive. In between these two extremes, there are considerable areas of amenity grassland, for example on roadside verges and on nature reserves, which may be managed regularly, yet at low intensities.

It has been estimated that out of a total grass area of 49 163 km^2 (12.15 × 10^6 acres) in the United Kingdom, 8500 km^2 (2.1 × 10^6 acres) may be

Table 11.1 Composition, after 7 years, of chalk grassland plots cut once, twice, and three times annually, compared with uncut controls. Based on dry weights of individual species

| Component | Per cent composition (Dry weight basis) | | | |
	Control	Cut once	Cut twice	Cut three times
Grasses	19.1	73.1	74.7	70.4
Sedges	0.52	0.64	0.42	0.50
Forbs	6.14	6.22	9.69	17.30
Mosses	0.26	0.15	0.07	0.14
Unknown	—	0.10	0.24	—
Litter	73.7	19.8	14.8	11.0
No. of species	19	27	31	31
Mean yield (g m^{-2})†	621.5	192.5	187.5	149.7

†1 g m^{-2} = 0.205 × 10^{-3} lb ft^{-2}.

Plate 11.1 (a) Rabbit-grazed plagioclimax grassland at Kingley Vale NNR, West Sussex in 1954. Following the spread of myxomatosis, there was a progressive invasion of the site by scrub. Further photographs were taken (b) in 1956, (c) in 1961, and (d) in 1973. For full-colour versions of (a) and (d) see Frontispiece.
(Photographs by A. S. Thomas ((a) and (b)) and T. C. E. Wells ((c) and (d))

broadly classed as amenity grass (NERC, 1977). Of this total, roughly half $(4100 \text{ km}^2 \ (1.01 \times 10^6 \text{ acres}))$, may be classified as semi-natural grassland. Grassland on roadside verges, on National Trust land, on nature reserves and on commons (Table 1.1) accounts for at least three-quarters of this area. This review will be concerned mainly with the management of semi-natural grasslands and will not deal with the management of intensively managed grasslands about which much has already been published (e.g. Youngner and McKell, 1972; Beard, 1973; and other chapters in this volume). This restricted view of amenity grasslands is taken for the following reasons: (a) there seems little scope for changing the management of sports turf, although there is clearly room for improvement in some aspects such as soil drainage, which may in turn affect above ground management; (b) the concept of managing areas of semi-natural grassland outside the framework of agriculture and for different objectives is relatively new, and is still largely in an experimental stage.

The need for management

All grassland in lowland Britain is a plagioclimax vegetation largely created and maintained either by grazing animals, of which the principal kinds have been sheep, cattle, and rabbits, or by some other process such as mowing or burning, which removes the annual production of plant material. The main changes which occur in grassland when it is not managed are well known, and may have important consequences, not only for the plants and animals in the grassland, but also for people who want to use the area for recreation. In the absence of grazing or other management, grasses, which usually constitute more than 60 per cent of the total above-ground biomass, increase in leaf area and compete with the lower-growing species. Litter, formed principally from the grasses, accumulates at the base of the sward and eventually low-growing species are eliminated (Table 11.1). Aesthetically, the sward becomes dull and for many recreational pursuits unmanaged grassland is unacceptable. It is unpleasant to sit on, remains wet when shorter grassland would have dried out, and may become tussocky and difficult to walk across. At the same time as the structure of the grassland is changing, scrub may invade. While the early stages of scrub colonization may be beneficial, providing a 'screen' for people and nesting sites for birds, scrub eventually spreads and forms thickets which become impenetrable. The rate at which these changes occur depends on site conditions—in a period as short as 3 years unmanaged grassland may become structurally unacceptable for most amenity purposes, while in less than 25 years, short, floristically-rich turf on the chalk may change to incipient woodland (Frontispiece and Plate 11.1).

Objectives of management

It is essential that the objectives of management should be clearly defined before management begins. What these objectives should be and how to achieve them is the most difficult part of the whole exercise. The dilemma which faces all managers of land when there may be conflicting or different objectives was highlighted by Way (1973), who found that in regard to the management of road verges 'conservationists want them left alone, town dwellers want them kept as lawns, farmers want them cultivated and Highway Authorities want to save cash'.

Objectives of management may be very varied. They may be specific and detailed, aimed towards preventing erosion of the grassland or towards maintaining a grassland at a specific height. On the other hand, they may be much more general and have aims such as 'the perpetuation of a typically rich chalk grassland flora and fauna'. The more general the objectives, the more difficult it is to assess their achievement and, usually, the more resources and effort are needed to achieve them. What criteria are to be used to measure success, where there are many different objectives, especially where there are complex interactions between different parts of the system?

It has been suggested by Wells (1969) and Green (1973) that the most commonly stated objective of chalk grassland management, the maintenance of characteristic assemblages of plants and animals, can be achieved for plants by creating or maintaining a short sward. In the case of insect species, Morris (1971) has demonstrated the importance of tall components in chalk grassland for certain species, especially those which pass part of their life-cycle in the flowers or fruiting bodies of tall-growing herbs. Clearly, these different requirements for plants and animals cannot be achieved under the same management regimes unless some sort of rotational management programme is used, in which different phases are separated in time and in space.

It is useful to distinguish between reclamation management and maintenance management. Since most areas of semi-natural grasslands in lowland Britain are on land which the agriculturalist describes as marginal, these areas tend to be the first to be neglected and taken out of the agricultural system during periods of agricultural or economic depression. As a result, coarse grasses and scrub take over. When the land is later required for some form of amenity use, it has first to be reclaimed before regular, or maintenance, management can proceed. For example, on many public open spaces which had been neglected during the Second World War, a great deal of scrub removal and the burning of grass litter took place before the land was made available for amenity purposes. The same type of problem had to be faced when new country parks were created during the 1960s and 1970s in areas which included derelict ground or clay workings, or disused mine workings, e.g. Irchester Country Park (Northamptonshire) and Shipley Country Park (Derbyshire).

Ecological basis of grassland management

One of the main aims of ecological research is to understand the factors determining the local presence or absence of a particular species, or assemblages of species (Dempster, 1977). Ideally, the management of grassland for whatever objective should be based upon the results of sound research, since only then can it take into account the very different needs of different species. This 'ideal' will not be realized in the forseeable future and we have to base management proposals and predictions on some of the general characteristics of grassland plants which have been shown to be important. Detailed discussions of these characteristics have been published elsewhere (e.g. Wells, 1973; Duffey *et al.*, 1974; Lowday & Wells, 1977) and other aspects are covered in this volume in Chapter 2. Only the most important characteristics of grassland plants will be repeated here.

Life-forms

More than two-thirds of all grassland plants from temperate regions are hemicryptophytes, with their overwintering bud and growing point at or near the surface of the ground (Table 11.2). Geophytes form an important fraction of the total life-form spectrum, but annuals are of little importance. Most grassland plants are adapted by habit of growth and position of apical meristem to withstand grazing and cutting.

Perennial habit and longevity

Most grassland plants are perennials, and many are long-lived, although details of longevity, except for a few species, are unknown. Vegetative means of reproduction are widely used by grassland plants and the loss of flowers and seed production by grazing or cutting does not seem important. In any event, flower and seed production by perennials varies considerably, quantity and frequency being a characteristic of each species.

Table 11.2   Percentages of different life-forms found in samples of chalk grassland, dry acidic grassland, and meadow grassland. (Analysis based on 182, 53, and 300 taxa respectively)

Life form	Position of over-wintering bud	Chalk grassland	Acid grassland	Neutral grassland
Chamaephytes	Soil surface to 250 mm (9.8 in)	7.6	20.8	7.2
Hemicryptophytes	At soil surface	67.6	54.6	70.3
Geophytes	Below soil surface	16.5	5.6	13.5
Therophytes	As seed	8.2	18.8	8.6

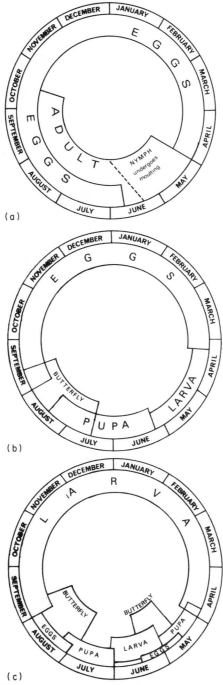

Figure 11.1   Phenology of three grassland
insects: (a) Common green grasshopper;
(b) Chalk hill blue butterfly; (c) Brown
argus butterfly

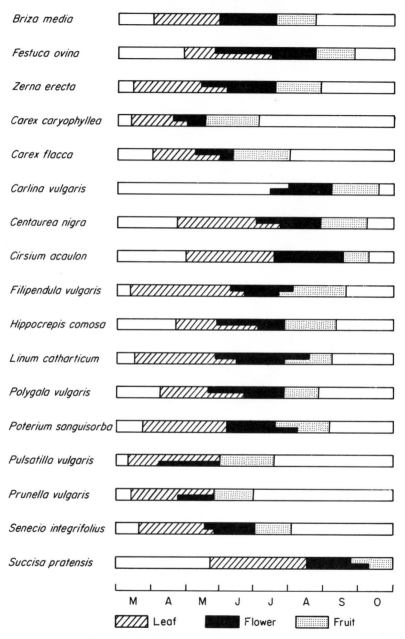

Figure 11.2   Phenology of 17 grassland plants

Phenology and growth curves

Phenology is the recording and study of periodic events such as biomass and leaf production, flowering, fruit formation, and fruit dispersal. A knowledge of the phenology of individual species is likely to be helpful in predicting the effect of cutting or grazing on the growth and reproduction of grassland plants. It may be particularly important in supporting insect life, some of which depends on aerial plant structures for passing part of the life-cycle.

Phenological charts (Figures 11.1 and 11.2) are available for some grassland plants and insects. They may be useful in helping to predict the effect of cutting or grazing on the growth and reproduction of grassland species. This type of information may be particularly useful on nature reserves, in country parks and similar areas which contain species of high wildlife interest, since management can then be prescribed which considers their conservation.

The pattern of growth of a wide range of pasture grasses has been shown to be bimodal with a major peak of production in spring, with a reduced growth rate during and after flowering, with a secondary lower peak in late summer. Detailed information of growth curves is available for only a few species, but such data may be particularly useful in identifying the most effective time for applying a particular cutting or grazing treatment.

There is little information available on the growth cycles of dicotyledonous pasture plants except for the recent studies of Al-Mufti *et al.* (1977) on shoot phenologies in 13 types of herbaceous vegetation. Many more studies of this type are needed if grassland management is to have a sound scientific base.

Management options

While management objectives will usually vary considerably in different types of amenity grassland, the practical means of achieving these objectives will usually depend upon grazing, cutting, or, less frequently, burning. At first sight, there seems little opportunity for choice or flexibility in management, but a closer look reveals that a wide range of possibilities exists, not only in types of grazing animal or cutting machine which may be used, but also in the frequency and intensity of these operations.

Grazing in general

Grazing is likely to be a preferred form of management on many types of grassland, especially in country parks, on nature reserves, on land managed by the National Trust, and on common land, but clearly it cannot be used on roadside verges. From the wildlife point of view, grazing is more satisfactory than cutting because it creates a series of plant micro-habitats within the sward which may provide niches for germination and growth which are not available in mown grassland. On economic grounds, grazing is likely to generate income while cutting may be costly, but many other factors such as size of area being managed have a bearing on the profitability of grazing, and more research is needed here. It has been argued that the presence of animals on land used for amenity helps to create a 'countryside atmosphere' which is certainly one of the primary objectives in country parks. Livestock not only add interest and perspective to the landscape, but also enable urban visitors to identify with the countryside.

The advantages and disadvantages of cattle, sheep, deer, and horse grazing are summarized in Table 11.3, together with suggestions for the kind of situation in which they might be used.

Cattle

Cattle tend to be less selective than sheep, and because of this, often create a grassland which consists of a mosaic of short grassland interspersed with taller patches. Little is known about the effect of different breeds of cattle on semi-natural grasslands, although anecdotal evidence supplemented by observation suggests that considerable differences do exist. For example, winter grazing by Ayrshire cows at low intensities on chalk grassland in Wiltshire appears to produce a uniform sward practically indistinguishable from that produced by sheep. On the other hand, Hereford × Friesian bullocks grazing all the year round on meadow grasslands tend to produce a tufted grassland, but much will depend on the grazing intensity. More research is needed here. There is surprisingly little information on food preferences of different breeds of cattle. In a study of the diet of Galloway cattle at Woodwalton Fen NNR, Williams *et al.* (1974) showed that grasses, particularly *Calamagrostis epigejos* (bushgrass), *Arrhenatherum elatius* (oat-grass) and *Agropyron repens* (couch) were strongly represented in the early winter diet, but that certain animals showed decided preferences for *Juncus effusus* (soft rush) and *Poa pratensis* (smooth-stalked meadow-grass). The effect of this positive selection of grasses during the winter months at Woodwalton Fen was to create an open grassland which benefited those species which made use of the spring and summer grazing period—in particular, there has been a large increase in the amount of *Dactylorchis incarnata* (marsh orchid) in one field, in addition to increases in other low-growing species such as *Viola canina* (heath violet), *Luzula compestris* (field woodrush) and *Prunella vulgaris* (self-heal). Experience gained at this site over the past 12 years has demonstrated the value of paddock grazing on a rotational basis for this type of coarse fen grassland—it has also demonstrated the value of a knowledge of the phenology and life-cycle of those species which may be special objectives for conservation. Common species, like *Juncus bufonius* (toad rush), *J. articulatus* (jointed rush), and *Lychnis flos-cuculi* (ragged Robin) have increased in fields grazed in summer by cattle. Similar increases in two nationally rare species, *Luzula pallescens* (pale woodrush) and *Viola stagnina* (fen violet) occurred, especially where trampling had been heavy.

At Heaton Park, in the centre of Manchester, the Recreational Services Department have used belted Galloways and Highland cattle for 14 years to manage 17 ha (42 acres) of land. The cattle have become established features of the park. Replacements for the herd are bred on a farm on the outskirts of the city, and the herds are often overwintered there. The stocking rate is 0.8 ha beast^{-1} (2 acre beast^{-1}). Details of the system are given by Lowday & Wells (1977).

Sheep

Sheep have been the traditional grazing animal on certain grassland types and are also used extensively on open moorland and heathland. In many parts of lowland England, for example on the chalk, they have been responsible for creating and maintaining the rich flora and fauna. The appearance and composition of grassland can be manipulated by varying the intensity of grazing and also by altering the time of year when grazing takes place. In experiments on chalk grassland at Aston Rowant NNR tall *Arrhenatherum elatius*/*Brachypodium sylvaticum* (slender false-brome) grassland was reduced after 2 years from 470 mm (18.5 in) to 70 mm (2.8 in) in height in plots grazed at 7.4 sheep ha^{-1} (3 sheep acre^{-1}) for 5 months of the year, whereas in plots grazed at 2.5 sheep ha^{-1} (1 sheep acre^{-1}) the vegetation was taller, around 150 mm (5.9 in). In the heavily grazed plots, accumulated litter was rapidly broken down as a result of treading, and the growth habit of *Arrhenatherum* was changed from coarse tussocks to scattered tufts in a shorter grassland. In the same experiment, annual species, such as *Euphrasia nemorosa* (eyebright), *Crepis capillaris* (smooth hawk's-beard), and *Linum catharticum* (purging flax) increased considerably (Table 11.4), probably as a result of the patches of bare ground which the grazing animals created. The greater abundance of annuals in the heavily grazed plots, compared with the less intensively grazed plots, is probably explained by the higher proportion of bare ground in the former. Changes in the frequency of species in the grazed plots, other than annuals, were small. Studies of the diet of Blackface sheep by Martin (1964) and of Border Leicester Cheviot crosses by Hawes (1971), using faecal analysis techniques, have shown that grasses and sedges constitute more than 80 per cent of the sheep diet throughout the year, herbs forming a significant part of the diet only in late spring and summer. Sheep apparently control the dominant grasses, and allow lower growing herbs to thrive. Sheep grazing at high densities on chalk grassland can effectively

Table 11.3 Summary of the factors for consideration in the selection of a grazing technique for semi-natural grasslands used for amenity in lowland Britain

Type of management	Advantages	Disadvantages	Situation when appropriate
Grazing	(i) Attractive feature in countryside. (ii) Potential source of income. (iii) Saves costs of cutting. (iv) Can be used on steep slopes where cutting is impossible.	(i) Requires experienced labour, fencing, additional machinery, etc. (ii) Potential risk of stock fatalities (litter and dogs) (iii) Livestock might create unpleasant mud, smell, flies, etc.	(i) Grassland with water and fencing and where visitor pressure is not too great nor is there a dog problem.
(a) Sheep	(i) Maintain floristic diversity. (ii) Safe with people. (iii) Traditional animal on certain grassland types. (iv) Saleable products—animals, carcase, wool. (v) Attractive feature of interest for visitor, especially lambs.	(i) Susceptible to dog worrying. (ii) High level of husbandry required, especially when breeding. (iii) Disease-prone on wet, poorly-drained areas. (iv) Unsuitable on very productive grass swards over 100 mm (4 in).	(i) Chalk, limestone grassland especially steep slopes. (ii) As component of mixed grazing on meadow, parkland, rough grazing (iii) Low–medium public use, or intermittently on high public use areas when alternative grazing is available. (iv) Ancient earthworks and hill forts, etc.
(b) Cattle	(i) Maintain floristic diversity. (ii) Safe with people.	(i) Calves susceptible to dog worrying.	(i) Chalk/limestone grassland, not steep slopes.

Advantages	Disadvantages	Situation
(iii) Not susceptible to dog worrying (excluding calves).	(ii) Minority of public may be scared by their 'inquisitive' behaviour.	(ii) Meadow land.
(iv) Saleable products—animals, carcase, hides.	(iii) Can cause erosion on steep slopes.	(iii) Parkland.
(v) Attractive, moving feature in landscape.	(iv) Can poach grass in wet weather.	(iv) Control of long, coarse grass.
(vi) Attract subsidy in certain cases.	(v) Can damage cars.	(v) Reclamation management.
(vii) Certain breeds are ideal for reclaiming rough pasture.	(vi) Cow pats most offensive type of dung.	
(c) Deer		
(i) Exceptionally attractive feature in country parks.	(i) Very high costs involved in erecting and maintaining deer-fence.	(i) Established parkland with deer fence.
(ii) Very hardy, requiring minimum maintenance.	(ii) Requires specialized labour with knowledge of deer husbandry.	
(iii) Saleable products—venison, hides, antlers.	(iii) Tends to reduce floristic diversity.	
(iv) Docile and harmless to public.	(iv) Occasional 'rogue' stag may be potentially dangerous in latter stages of rut.	
(v) Less susceptible to dog worrying.		
(d) Horse		
(i) Attractive feature in parks.	(i) Temperamental behaviour, especially if annoyed—may kick or bite.	(i) Confined to paddock with public/horse interface at fence.
(ii) May be used for rides for public which may bring in revenue.	(ii) Very selective grazer, can spoil the floristic composition of sward—behavioural habits associated with dunging.	(ii) Larger open areas where they can retire away from public.
	(iii) High initial expense.	

Table 11.4 Changes in the mean percentage frequency of *Euphrasia nemorosa* (eyebright), *Linum catharticum* (purging flax) and *Crepis capillaris* (smooth hawk's-beard) during 1964–73 in control plots (ungrazed) and in plots grazed at 1 and 3 sheep acre⁻¹ (respectively equivalent to 2.5 and 7.4 sheep ha⁻¹)

	Euphrasia			Linum			Crepis		
	Control	1 acre^{-1}	3 acre^{-1}	Control	1 acre^{-1}	3 acre^{-1}	Control	1 acre^{-1}	3 acre^{-1}
1964	0	1	6.3	4.0	5.6	6.0	0	1.0	3.6
1965	9.3	3.6	9.3	2.6	2.6	2.6	0	6.3	7.3
1966	12.0	5.3	16.0	10.6	11.0	14.0	0	17.3	12.6
1967	6.6	14.0	19.9	6.6	13.0	18.6	0	17.6	18.3
1968	4.0	10.0	33.0	4.0	11.3	21.0	2.6	19.0	25.0
1969	0	4.3	30.0	4.0	3.6	16.3	4.0	7.0	23.6
1973	2.6	7.6	39.3	0	6.6	33.6	5.3	16.0	35.0

control coarse grasses like *Zerna erecta* (upright brome), but appear to be unable to control *Brachypodium pinnatum* (tor grass).

Sheep have been used for some years effectively to manage grassland in a number of country parks (e.g. Queen Elizabeth Park, Hampshire) and, despite the danger from occasional attacks by dogs, are now established as effective graziers of amenity grass. Where visitor pressure is highly seasonal, as at many amenity sites, late autumn and winter grazing, when visitors are mostly absent, may be the best system to adopt. As a result of the Aston Rowant experiments, it has been clearly established that hardy breeds of sheep, such as the Border Leicester × Cheviot, are able to survive the winter without supplementary feed, except in the most severe winter, provided that animals with initial body weights of at least 50 kg (110 lb) are used. Body weights follow an annual cycle under these conditions with considerable loss of weight from December until late March, but these losses are restored when the spring flush of growth begins.

Much more is required to be known about the effect of season of grazing on vegetation and it may be that special types of 'amenity sheep' may be bred in the future (see Large & Spedding, 1976).

Deer

Although deer have, to a varying degree, been an attractive feature of the English countryside since ancient times, surprisingly little is known in detail about the diet of these animals or about the effect that they have on vegetation. At present, deer are only used for managing amenity grassland in six country parks in which deer are kept in old deer parks, all with good perimeter fences. The high cost of deer fencing is likely to be prohibitive in introducing deer grazing into new areas, although increasingly, the sale of deer products such as venison, antlers and hides can generate income to offset high initial capital investment. It should also be borne in mind that deer greatly enhance the visual appearance of amenity grassland and, except for the occasional 'rogue' buck, are safe grazing animals in areas of high public use.

Horses and ponies

These animals cannot at present be recommended for areas used frequently by the public as their behaviour is unpredictable, especially when kept within the confines of a paddock. They may be a potential danger to visitors. Many breeds need considerable care during the winter months, but some of the hardier native ponies, such as the New Forest type, require less attention and have been used on an experimental basis for managing chalk grassland. Horses are said to be highly selective graziers, and often produce structurally contrasting vegetation within small areas, but little detail is known and the effect of horse grazing on vegetation is another topic which requires attention.

Rotational grazing

Here, parts of an area are grazed, while others are not. This is probably the best way of managing grassland for a diverse fauna and flora. Instead of the short, uniform grassland which is such as feature of many areas of amenity grass, especially in country parks, rotational grazing offers the opportunity of establishing different structural formations, each with its own characteristic spectrum of plants and animals. At the same time, by regulating stocking rates and time of grazing, and by using different classes of livestock, it is possible to prevent the more aggressive and dominant grasses from overwhelming the slower-growing species. The disadvantages of rotational grazing are mostly economic and are well-known—more fencing, more water points, more gates. These costs will also increase with the complexity of the rotational system.

Cutting in general

Cutting or mowing differs from grazing in three respects. First, it is non-selective, all vegetation above the level of the cutting blade being severed. Secondly, while dung and urine are returned to the sward by the grazing animal, cutting makes it possible to remove nutrients in the form of hay or else return them in part, if the cut material is left as clippings. Third, the cutting machine does not exert the same localized pressure on the ground as do the hooves of cattle and sheep. The advantages and disadvantages of mowing are summarized in Table 11.5, while many of the problems and costs associated with mowing have been discussed in Chapters 9 and 12. Only two questions concerning cutting will be raised here. First, can mowing be used as an effective substitute for grazing, and if so, in what situation should it be used? Second, is the removal of cut material either desirable or necessary?

Grazing versus cutting

It is not unreasonable to assume that plants commonly found in hay meadows but not in grazed pastures show some form of adaptation to cutting and are unable to withstand grazing. Thus Baker (1937) in his classic comparison of Port Meadow and Pixey and Yarnton Meads, the former grazed and the latter cut for hay since 1085, found *Arrhenatherum elatius*, *Bromus commutatus* (meadow brome), and *Sanguisorba officinalis* (great burnet)

Table 11.5 Summary of the factors for consideration in the selection of a mowing technique for semi-natural grasslands used for amenity in lowland Britain

Type of management	Advantages	Disadvantages	Situations when appropriate
Cutting	(i) Eliminates cost of fencing. (ii) Potential saleable product/rent from cutting rights. (iii) Can be used at all intensities of public use. (iv) No dog worrying problem. (v) No dung, smell, flies. (vi) Management has control over the type of finish on the grass, time, and frequency of cut.	(i) Costs money to purchase, run, maintain, and repair machinery. This has increased considerably in recent years (ii) Can create a rather uniform and uninteresting landscape, more typical of recreation grounds. (iii) Cannot be used on steep slopes. (iv) Advantages of livestock foregone. (v) Labour on cutting could be more profitably employed elsewhere.	(i) Situations when livestock requirements cannot be provided, or public pressure is too high for livestock. (ii) Games and certain picnic areas. (iii) Formal areas.
(a) Gang mowing	(i) Can cover large areas quickly. (ii) Leaves ideal finish for sports areas, etc.	(i) No income can be generated, only costs incurred. (ii) Creates uniform and uninteresting sward. (iii) Needs to be cut regularly—gang mowers cannot cope with long grass. (iv) May produce undesired 'town park' appearance in country parks. (v) Clippings left on ground. (vi) Ground must be fairly level.	(i) Games areas and certain picnic areas. (ii) Areas of high public pressure.
(b) Flail, rear-mounted, and rotary cutter	(i) Maintain large areas of grass in once/twice year cuts. (ii) Can cope with long, coarse grass or scrub. (iii) Versatile—can readily be adjusted.	(i) No income generated. (ii) Clippings left on ground. (iii) Can leave uniform and uninteresting appearance to park.	(i) Topping grass swards. (ii) Forestry rides. (iii) Light–medium scrub control. (iv) Sports grounds.

Table 11.5 (continued)

Type of management	Advantages	Disadvantages	Situations when appropriate
(c) Hand-operated machines	(i) Can be used in places where tractor-powered machinery is unsuitable.	(i) Small rates of cut. (ii) High labour requirement.	(i) On slopes—small areas. (ii) Surrounding trees, car parks, etc. (iii) Formal areas.
(i) Cylinder mowers			Formal gardens, flower beds, bowling greens, etc.
(ii) Rotary mowers			Areas surrounding trees, car parks, small picnic areas, etc. Grass banks. Areas around trees, car parks, etc.
(iii) 'Flymo'			
(iv) Portable bush saw			Clearing scrub off steep slopes.
Agricultural cutting machinery—operated by farmers, or as part of country park's own management programme	(i) Reduce costs of grassland maintenance. (ii) May provide income—sale/rent. (iii) Feed value of grass can be utilized instead of wasted.	(i) Lack of precise management control. (ii) Litter may be incorporated into livestock feed. (iii) May have to leave grass longer than otherwise, e.g. if using maintenance equipment.	(i) Large areas of grassland at present cut by maintenance machinery. (ii) Management can utilize/sell the product. (iii) Suitable for farmers willing to operate their own machinery.
(a) Hay-making equipment, cutter bar, tedder, baler plus carting bales.	(i) Traditional technique may be vital for maintaining floristic interest of sward.	(i) Bales may be knifed by visitors if left around too long.	(i) Fairly highly productive grass—low intensity of public use.
(b) Forage harvester	(i) Can be used more regularly, e.g. every 6 weeks in growing season.		(i) All types of grassland on a terrain suitable for the machinery.

abundant at Pixey and Yarnton, but absent from Port Meadow. D. A. Wells (personal communication) has found the effect of changing from cutting for hay to grazing to have a dramatic effect in reducing the numbers of *Fritillaria meleagris* (fritillary)—a plant closely associated with hay meadows of the upper Thames basin. On the other hand, there are many species common both to grazed and to cut grassland which appear to be adapted to both management regimes. Different ecotypes may be involved, but so far no evidence has been produced to support this possibility.

On grasslands that have in the past been grazed, cutting seems to be, at least in the short term, an effective substitute for grazing. In a 6-year comparison of the effects of cutting chalk grassland one to three times a year, Wells (1971) showed that cutting caused no loss of species. Although cutting at a certain time of the year caused a decrease in certain species initially, it was noticeable that this trend did not continue and after 4 years of cutting each species achieved a fairly constant level in the contribution it made to the vegetation in the plot. This suggests that the effect of cutting on the total flora is to produce a balance in the vegetation, which may be different from that achieved by grazing, but which nevertheless appears to maintain a similar degree of richness and diversity. Much more research is needed on this subject as it appears from present evidence that grasslands on different soils, containing different species, may react to grazing and cutting in a variety of ways.

Return versus non-return of cuttings

Cut vegetation left lying on a sward has two effects: (a) it smothers underlying vegetation, preventing light penetration and thereby photosynthesis; (b) it returns nutrients to the grass/soil system. The relative importance of these two processes depends on a number of factors of which amount of vegetation, state of division of returned material (i.e. as finely divided clippings or as a swathe), age and nutrient status of returned vegetation, and time of year when cut are probably of most importance. Green (1972) argued that returning clippings leads to eutrophication and adds to the total nutrient pool, this process encouraging the establishment of nitrophilous species and eventually leading to seral changes. The evidence for this was based on the vegetation which resulted when a 2 m (6.6 ft) stand of *Ulex europaeus* (gorse), representing about 12 years' standing crop, was cut with a forage harvester, leaving the cut material in a finely divided form on the soil. Non-replicated soil samples taken from beneath the cut *Ulex* showed increases in soil nitrogen of about 700 kg N ha^{-1} (624 lb acre^{-1}) which were attributed, not unreasonably, to nitrogen present in the cut *Ulex*.

In an experiment at Knocking Hoe NNR on chalk grassland, Wells (1976) found no difference in floristic composition in plots which were cut once,

Table 11.6   Total nutrients (N, P, K, Ca, Mg, and Fe) (a) removed or (b) returned, in 10 years (1965–74), from plots which were cut annually (i) once in May, (ii) twice, in May and June, and (iii) three times, in May, June, and July. Each value is the mean of four plots

| Element | Weight of nutrient (kg ha^{-1})† | | | | | |
| | Cut once | | Cut twice | | Cut three times | |
	(a)	(b)	(a)	(b)	(a)	(b)
N	347	362	302	327	273	283
P	23	23	18	20	17	17
K	318	333	275	300	240	250
Ca	205	217	190	207	182	192
Mg	38	40	35	38	32	33
Fe	12	12	17	18	8	8

†1 kg ha^{-1} = 0.892 lb acre^{-1}.

twice, and three times a year and from which the cut material had been removed for 10 years, compared with those to which it was returned in a finely divided form. This result may appear surprising at first, until the quantities of nutrients returned and removed are calculated. Table 11.6 is a summary of these quantities based on the chemical analysis of plant material from 1965–74, multiplied by the annual yield of vegetation for each

Table 11.7   Mean annual yield (g m^{-2})† in 1965–78 of plots (a) from which clipped vegetation was removed annually, and (b) to which cut material was returned. Each value is the mean of 12 plots

Year	(a)	(b)
1965	215.7	229.6
1966	180.1	182.4
1967	259.3	264.3
1968	172.9	188.3
1969	215.1	234.0
1970	149.9	162.9
1971	160.2	192.7‡
1972	233.6	247.6
1973	130.1	147.9§
1974	128.1	143.7
1975	129.7	174.8§
1976	86.8	113.0‡
1977	183.3	224.0‡
1978	152.5	193.3§

†1 g m^{-2} = 0.205 × 10^{-3} lb ft^{-2}.
‡Significant increase at $P < 0.05$.
§Significant increase at $P < 0.01$.

Table 11.8 The mean chemical composition of the 0–50 mm (0–2 in) zone of the soil in 1973 of plots receiving the following treatments annually since 1965: (a) control (not cut), (b) cut once (in May), (c) cut twice (in May and June), and (d) cut three times (in May, June, and July)

	Cut material removed				Cut material returned		
	Control†	Cut in May‡	Cut in May and June‡	Cut in May, June, July‡	Cut in May‡	Cut in May and June‡	Cut in May, June, July‡
pH	7.69	7.78	7.75	7.73	7.66	7.64	7.62
	(0.013)§	(0.016)	(0.011)	(0.012)	(0.015)	(0.014)	(0.012)
Loss-on-ignition (%)	14.20	14.17	14.21	14.56	14.81	14.80	15.32
	(0.245)	(0.328)	(0.342)	(0.245)	(0.424)	(0.351)	(0.406)
Nitrogen (%)	0.71	0.77	0.77	0.74	0.72	0.71	0.73
	(0.009)	(0.021)	(0.018)	(0.011)	(0.011)	(0.012)	(0.009)
Potassium (mequiv. 100 g^{-1})	0.34	0.34	0.35	0.36	0.30	0.31	0.36
	(0.016)	(0.024)	(0.016)	(0.017)	(0.014)	(0.013)	(0.014)
Sodium (mequiv. 100 g^{-1})	1.38	1.35	1.31	1.38	1.08	1.13	1.10
	(0.046)	(0.042)	(0.041)	(0.042)	(0.067)	(0.067)	(0.071)
Manganese (mequiv. 100 g^{-1})	0.05	0.05	0.05	0.05	0.05	0.06	0.06
	(0.003)	(0.004)	(0.005)	(0.004)	(0.002)	(0.004)	(0.003)
Magnesium (mequiv. 100 g^{-1})	1.78	1.56**	1.43**	1.56**	1.72	1.86*	1.69
	(0.057)	(0.054)	(0.046)	(0.057)	(0.106)	(0.071)	(0.086)
Phosphate (mg 100 g^{-1})	3.89	2.80**	3.22*	2.92**	3.91	4.37	4.33
	(0.154)	(0.103)	(0.238)	(0.191)	(0.148)	(0.125)	(0.195)

Square brackets enclose pairs of samples which are significantly different at *$P < 0.05$ or **$P < 0.01$.
†Mean of 40 samples.
‡Mean of 20 samples.
§Values in parentheses indicate standard errors.

treatment. The quantities of nutrients returned or removed each year was small. Some of these losses would have been replaced by nutrients in incoming rainfall. Nitrogen would also have been replaced by legumes, such as *Hippocrepis comosa* (horse-shoe vetch) and *Anthyllis vulneraria* (kidney-vetch), which occurred extensively in the plots. The mean annual yield of plots to which nutrients were returned in cut vegetation was slightly higher (Table 11.7) than that of plots from which the vegetation was removed, but a significant series of results was established over the last 4 years (1975–8).

Detailed soil analyses made in 1973 (Table 11.8) provide evidence that the return of cut material is not enriching the soil. The removal of vegetation annually for 10 years only causes a significant decrease in extractable phosphate and exchangeable magnesium, other nutrients being replaced either from primary minerals in the soil or by fixation by micro-organisms. Clearly, long-term removal of vegetation must deplete soil nutrients, but for how long this must occur before responses are shown by the vegetation is not known. This long-term replicated experiment provides no evidence to support any general contention that it is necessary to remove cut material in the management of amenity grassland if eutrophication is to be avoided, although in the special case of scrub clearance (Chapter 9) the return of a large standing crop to the nutrient cycle will obviously have a marked effect.

Burning

Fire is an important ecological factor in many of the world's grasslands, particularly in semi-arid regions where burning, annually or every few years, is a well-established practice (Campbell, 1960). In amenity grasslands, burning is most likely to be used as a management tool for the reclamation of unmanaged grassland, or as a management practice in a rotational system. Burning usually takes place in February or March in England and Wales when many species are dormant with few above ground parts or with winter buds which are protected by bud scales or old leaf sheaths. Lloyd (1968), in one of the few detailed studies of the effect of fire on limestone vegetation, showed that fire, by killing the more open tussocks of *Festuca ovina* (sheep's fescue), enabled *Helictotrichon pratense* (meadow oat), which was unaffected by fire, to replace it. Clearly, burning is a means of manipulating the composition of amenity grassland. However, great care in its use is needed, as bracken usually an 'unwanted' species in amenity situations, is likely to spread in areas fired frequently, usually at the expense of other more desirable species.

References

Al-Mufti, M. M., Wall, C. L., Furness, S. B., Grime, J. P. & Band, S. R. (1977). 'A quantitative analysis of shoot phenology in herbaceous vegetation', *Journal of Ecology*, **65**, 759–91.

Baker, H. (1937). 'Alluvial meadows: a comparative study of grazed and mown meadows', *Journal of Ecology*, **25**, 408–20.

Beard, J. B. (1973). *Turfgrass: Science and Culture*, Prentice-Hall, Englewood Cliffs, N.J.

Campbell, R. S. (1960). 'Use of fire in grassland management', in *Working Party on Pasture and Fodder Development in Tropical America*, FAO, Washington DC.

Dempster, J. P. (1977). 'The scientific basis of practical conservation: factors limiting the persistence of populations and communities of animals and plants', *Proceedings of the Royal Society, London, B*, **197**, 69–76.

Duffey, E. A. G., Morris, M. G., Sheail, J., Ward, L. K., Wells, D. A. & Wells, T. C. E. (1974). *Grassland Ecology and Wildlife Management*, Chapman and Hall, London.

Green, B. H. (1972). 'The relevance of seral eutrophication and plant competition to the management of successional communities', *Biological Conservation*, **4**, 378–84.

Green, B. H. (1973). 'Practical aspects of chalk grassland management in the Nature Conservancy's South-east Region', in *Chalk Grassland: Studies on its Conservation and Management in South-east England* (A. C. Jermy & P. A. Stott, eds), Kent Trust for Nature Conservation, Maidstone, pp. 42–7.

Hawes, P. T. J. (1971). 'Changes in the botanical composition of chalk grassland resulting from dietary selection by sheep', M Phil thesis, C.N.A.A.

Large, R. V & Spedding, C. R. W. (1976). 'Agricultural use of amenity grassland', in *Amenity Grassland* (S. E. Wright, ed.), Wye College (University of London), Wye, Kent, pp. 16–26.

Lloyd, P. S. (1968). 'The ecological significance of fire in limestone grassland communities of the Derbyshire dales', *Journal of Ecology*, **56**, 811–26.

Lowday, J. E. & Wells, T. C. E. (1977). *The Management of Grassland and Heathland in Country Parks*, Countryside Commission, Cheltenham.

Martin, D. J. (1964). 'Analysis of sheep diet utilising plant epidermal fragments in faeces samples', *Symposia of the British Ecological Society*, **4**, 173–88.

Morris, M. G. (1971). 'The management of grassland for the conservation of invertebrate animals', *Symposia of the British Ecological Society*, **11**, 527–52.

NERC (1977). *Amenity Grasslands—the Needs for Research*, Natural Environment Research Council, Publications Series 'C', No. 19, London.

Way, J. M. (1973). *Road Verges on Rural Roads: Management and Other Factors*, Nature Conservancy, Abbots Ripton.

Wells, T. C. E. (1969). 'Botanical aspects of conservation management of chalk grasslands', *Biological Conservation*, **2**, 36–44.

Wells, T. C. E. (1971). 'A comparison of the effect of sheep grazing and mechanical cutting on the structure and botanical composition of chalk grassland', *Symposia of the British Ecological Society*, **11**, 497–515.

Wells, T. C. E. (1973). 'Botanical aspects of chalk grassland management', in *Chalk Grassland in Studies on its Conservation and Management in South-east England*; (A. C. Jermy & P. A. Stott, eds), Kent Trust for Nature Conservation, Maidstone, pp. 10–15.

Wells, T. C. E. (1976). 'A report on the effects of cutting, with and without the return of nutrients on the botanical composition of chalk grassland', Internal report to NCC, Abbots Ripton.

Williams, O. B., Wells, T. C. E. & Wells, D. A. (1974). 'Grazing management of Woodwalton Fen: seasonal changes in the diet of cattle and rabbits', *Journal of Applied Ecology*, **11**, 499–516.

Youngner, V. B. & McKell, C. M. (1972). *The Biology and Utilization of Grasses*, Academic Press, London.

Amenity Grassland: An Ecological Perspective
Edited by I. H. Rorison and R. Hunt
© 1980 John Wiley & Sons Ltd

12

Management problems of mowing on an intensive scale

J. C. PARKER *Kent County Council, Estates and Valuation Department, Springfield, Maidstone, Kent, England*

Introduction

Other chapters in this volume have emphasized the various biological factors at work in the growth and development of amenity turf. In contrast, I would like to put forward some of the practical constraints which sometimes limit the way in which turf can be managed.

In certain circumstances the manager can influence the rate of growth of swards, but the main factors of weather and soil type are not normally within his control. As a result, he is presented with a demand for mowing or growth control which is mainly based on the characteristic growth curve of most types of grass sward in this country (see, for example, Moore, 1966, p. 34).

This growth curve shows a peak rate, usually about mid-May to mid-June, and it is the needs of this 'harvest' period that normally dictate the scale and organization of the mowing arrangements, particularly on formal and sports swards where the height of the vegetation must be kept within fine limits. Assuming, then, that the grass has to be cut, and this may not always be so, the problem is quite simply one of getting the right machine to the right place with a competent driver, ensuring that both are in working order and then hoping that the weather will allow mowing to proceed. The task, though easily started, can be frustrated by many different events which can make the biological aspects of the operation fade into insignificance. It is, therefore, worth examining the methods that both the managers and operatives use to deal with the pressures of the peak mowing season.

Practical approaches

On playing fields and similar extensive areas of turf the cylinder mower (Plate 12.1) is usually the most effective tool both in terms of power inputs, speed of working, and overall costs per cut (see Table 12.1). However, the

Table 12.1   Comparative costs and performance rates of common types of mowing equipment (£ sterling, 1978 prices). See also Plates 12.1 and 12.2, and Figure 12.1

Equipment	Annual costs			Hours use per year§	Hourly costs				Cutting rate‖ (h ha⁻¹)	Cost per hectare
	Depreci- ation†	Repairs and service	Total‡		Depreciation and repairs	Fuel	Labour¶	Total		
Tractor equipment										
5-gang units	910	800	1710	750	2.28	0.4	2.64	5.32	0.9	4.8
Rear-mounted flail	590	400	990	750	1.32	0.4	2.64	4.36	5.1	22.2
Rear-mounted rotary	590	400	990	750	1.32	0.4	2.64	4.36	4.4	19.2
Triple motor mower	490	500	990	750	1.32	0.5	2.64	4.46	2.2	9.8
34 in (0.86 m) cylinder mower	105	125	230	600	0.38	0.3	2.80	3.48	7.6	26.5
20 in (0.51 m) cylinder mower	40	80	120	450	0.26	0.2	2.80	3.26	17.8	58.1
20 in (0.51 m) rotary mower	50	70	120	450	0.26	0.2	2.80	3.26	24.0	78.4
'Flymo' (on steep banks)	80	60	140	450	0.31	0.35	2.80	3.46	60.0	207.6

†Based on renewal lives from 10 years for tractors and tractor-mounted equipment to 2 years for small rotary mowers.
‡Tractor costs are included where appropriate.
§Based on 25–30 week season.
¶Based on manual worker wage rates in Local Authorities and including allowances for superannuation, National Insurance, leave, sickness, wet weather, and other lost time; also including supervision and transport to site where appropriate.
‖Based on work-study measurements carried out by Kent County Council and including allowances for routine servicing and adjustments, rest allowances, minor repairs, where appropriate, tractors travelling between sites.

Plate 12.1 (a) A 15-unit gang mower specially assembled for the Newmarket racecourse, giving a cutting width of 12.6 m (41.5 ft) and an all-inclusive cutting rate of 10.9 ha h^{-1} (27 acres h^{-1})

(b) A gang mower of more conventional specification: five units, giving a cutting width of 3.5 m (11.5 ft) (see Table 12.1). This model has a special golf-course towing frame adapted to extreme undulations and giving a small turning circle (photographs by Lloyds & Co. of Letchworth Ltd)

[facing page 198

cylinder mower has the disadvantage that it becomes progressively less effective as the grass gets longer, wetter, and more dense. Thick, wet grass of moderate length can often take 25 per cent longer to cut than a dry, sparse sward (Coventry City Council data) and once growth gets much above 120 mm (4.7 in) it becomes impossible to mow effectively in a single pass. Because of these constraints the manager is extremely anxious to avoid a situation where, because of wet weather, breakdowns, or sickness, the grass gets out of hand, can no longer be cut with a cylinder mower, and has to be mown with a much slower rotary or flail machine. The prudent manager will, therefore, plan to cut his growth rather more frequently than is necessary. In addition, particularly for the operator, there are distinct advantages if he cuts the grass low. First, the severe defoliation of the low cut will reduce the plant's vigour and therefore ease the cutting next time; second, the mower needs less careful adjustment if it is to cut close. In practice, even a badly worn mower can often produce a reasonable finish if it meets the grass close enough to the ground, i.e. where the plant is stiffer and more resistant.

As a result, much intensive amenity grassland is cut too close, and sometimes too often, and a very weak, open, and weedy sward can develop, with a very poor wearing capacity. This is usually the opposite of what is required and often, when the situation becomes critical, attempts are made to restore the turf with applications of herbicide, which depress grass vigour further, and surface dressings of fertilizer that tend to encourage shallow-rooted plants that will quickly succumb to the next drought.

In order to reduce the overall demand for mowing, it has been suggested that lower-growing, more prostrate cultivars should be sown as they require less frequent cutting throughout the year (Shildrick, 1977). Such an ideal is obviously worth pursuing and certainly shows great promise where a taller sward can be tolerated, for example, on rugby pitches. It is not likely to be so effective a solution on, say, cricket outfields. In most instances it will only ease the manager's main problem if the cutting frequency can be significantly reduced in the peak growing period. Reduced cutting requirements throughout the rest of the year are of less value as the 'fixed' costs of manning and machinery levels have to be set for the peak season.

A mechanical approach to the problem is to use rotary mowers or flails which have the advantage of being able to cope with much longer growth and, in addition, cannot usually be adjusted to cut very close to the ground. Because of these advantages, tractor-mounted rotary mowers are ideal for the first year of maintenance of a new sward. They are, however, much slower to operate and can be four times more expensive per cut (Kent County Council data). Yearly costs are, therefore, much higher unless the cutting frequencies and the standard of maintenance are very much reduced (Figure 12.1). This costing is, however, based on the 1.82 m (6 ft) wide mowers that are

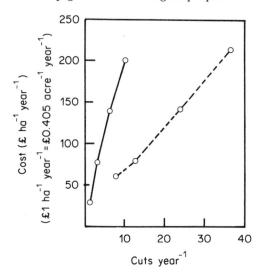

Figure 12.1 Annual costs of mowing by
tractor, shown in relation to frequency of cut.
——, Rear-mounted flail; - - -, gang mower
(1978 prices)

currently in use and it may be possible to improve rotary mowing
performance by the development of wider-cut machines similar to those
which are in use for orchard mowing.

In addition, it may be possible to improve the basic design of cylinder
mowers: first, as cutting tools and second, in their ease of adjustment. The
advent of the hydraulic-frame mower within the last 10 years has been a
considerable improvement, particularly when dealing with wet mowing
conditions, but many of the current mowers are over-laborious to adjust for
height and precision of cutting. For instance, on one common model, 20
separate nuts and bolts have to be undone, re-located, and re-tightened in
order to change the cutting height. No wonder that the operator will often
leave his mowers set to the lowest height regardless of the state of the sward.

On road verges, country parks, and similar informal areas it is usually
highly undesirable to cut frequently because of the effect on other flowering
plants within the sward. However, particularly on fertile soils and assuming
that some growth control is needed, the volume of herbage that results from
infrequent cuts can be a considerable problem, even if it has been macerated
by the flail mower. There are, therefore, positive practical advantages in
mowing more frequently, particularly if high-capacity gang mowers are
available which, as Figure 12.1 shows, prove to be cheaper overall. In addition,
such frequent cutting may well be condoned by the public-at-large, many of

whom seem to prefer the formality and neat appearance of a closely-cut sward. This is particularly so on urban fringes where longer grass often seems to encourage dumping of litter and rubbish.

In many of these situations a so-called low-maintenance mixture (Chapters 4 and 11) can be a considerable advantage. Reasonably attractive swards can be maintained with only two or three cuts per year. However, such a cutting regime will often not be sufficient to maintain a low-growing sward on fertile soils where more vigorous indigenous species will soon establish.

A positive reduction in soil fertility can, therefore, be an advantage and it has been suggested that this could be done by removing cuttings from the surface continuously (Chapter 9). Forage harvesters provide a relatively easy method of removing the cuttings and, ideally, a local farmer would be only too pleased to cut and cart the crop for its feed value. Alternatively he might be happy to cut and bale a hay crop. The difficulty is that such ideal situations do not always exist and, particularly in public areas, the feed value may be very low and the 'crop' often contaminated with plastic bags, broken bottles, and other roadside debris, and possibly polluted with lead. However, the extra labour requirements for carting or for slower machinery can be much less of a problem if the mowing does not have to be done in the peak growing season. Systems requiring only a single cut in late summer or early autumn would, therefore, be attractive to many organizations.

Personnel and their attitudes

It may be felt that I have been unduly pessimistic about the problems of adopting low-maintenance methods. I am, nevertheless, reasonably satisfied that, given sufficient will, there is enough technical information available for these methods to be adopted on a much larger scale. The problem is that relatively little of this information is available to the majority of managers and grounds staff. As a result, I feel that this lack of technical knowledge could well be the main factor that is limiting the development of the art of amenity turf management in this country, both for fine and for informal turf.

To illustrate this point I will describe what I suspect to be a typical supervision and management regime in local authorities, who collectively are estimated to be responsible for about 40 per cent of amenity grassland maintenance in this country (NERC, 1977). Starting at just above the 'grass roots' level, the men who cut the grass are usually grouped together in teams of two to four, each under the control of a chargehand. Some of these men will spend nearly all of their summer working-time on mowing, while others will carry out associated routine tasks such as pitch-marking, hoeing, hedge-clipping, sweeping, and tidying. Some teams will be mobile, moving from site to site by van or lorry, others will work full-time on a single large site.

In many cases these men will be working to some sort of bonus incentive scheme which either sets strict targets for the completion of certain items of work or pays a variable bonus which depends on how much work is completed in a given time. For all of them, their basic rate of pay will be that which is paid to all the other unskilled or semi-skilled manual workers in local government, e.g. dustmen and road sweepers. Any training that these men receive is likely to be geared towards the operation, adjustment, or servicing of their machinery, its safe operation, or the development of basic manual skills.

For some of these men an incentive bonus scheme will dominate their attitude to the work; for all of them, mowing will probably be a far-too-familiar routine task. It will have to be completed, as quickly as possible to earn a high bonus, or in order to get on with more interesting work. Any job-satisfaction which they derive from mowing will probably come from their pride in seeing a 'neat and tidy' finish. Hence, many will regard long or uncut grass as something undesirable: the attitude that 'God made grass for cutting' is prevalent. Again there are strong incentives to cut grass too short and the concept of informal, semi-natural swards is largely unappreciated.

The chargehand who supervises each group is likely to have similar attitudes. He is likely to be paid on a slightly higher rate, as a skilled gardener or groundsman, and also receive a small responsibility allowance, currently (1978) around £4 per week, in return for supervising his gang. He will probably have been trained in a range of skilled gardening tasks and have a special interest in 'growing plants' although most of his working time is taken up with the routine, almost 'caretaking', task of grounds maintenance. His main concerns about his work are likely to include bad weather, machinery breakdowns, dog fouling, and vandalism.

The next stage in the line of command is likely to be a foreman, who is possibly on the lower grades of a local government officer's scale. Nevertheless, his actual earnings are often only marginally above those of his working chargehands. He is likely to have been promoted up from a chargehand and to have a good basis of practical experience. His main task is supervision; the majority of his time is spent on checking that work is done, checking that staff are working when they should be, dealing with machinery breakdowns, issuing petrol and stores, collecting time sheets, and dealing with a host of other records and returns. Many foremen will cover a geographical area of up to 250 km^2 (100 square miles) supervising around 15 men who look after perhaps as many as 100 sites totalling around 80 ha (200 acres).

The foreman is generally responsible to an area supervisor, a maintenance officer, or a parks superintendent. Such an officer is what might be termed the 'middle manager' in the organization. He will have a total responsibility of at least 50 men covering 300 ha (740 acres) and probably spread over as

Plate 12.2 A cylinder mower for fine turf such as the golf green shown here; its cutting width is 0.53 m (21 in) (photograph by Lloyds & Co. of Letchworth Ltd)

[*facing page 202*

many as 400 sites and a geographical area of perhaps 800 km² (320 square miles). He will almost certainly have some practical experience and he will also have had some formal education in horticulture. However, his working life is likely to dominated by problems of day-to-day manpower management (including work-study), health and safety at work, staff recruiting and discipline, and an endless round of paperwork. As a result he will have little opportunity to use his technical knowledge and, indeed, his regular contact with technical matters may only be through reading trade publications and attending meetings with representatives from machinery and chemical firms. Such contact is, of course, desirable but is unlikely to present a balanced view of the total requirements of turf culture.

At a more senior level in the organization there will be Directors of Parks, County Playing Field Officers, and others who will normally have had a thorough education in biological sciences and horticulture. Alternatively, they may have been trained in landscape architecture, but they are all likely to be working predominantly as managers of staff and as liaison officers with other departments and Member committees. They will probably be responsible for thousands of hectares of amenity turf and large numbers of staff.

I have described this typical structure in some detail in the hope that it will be appreciated that, first, the number of technically-qualified staff is very small in relation to the areas involved and that second, what staff there are are too much involved in the day-to-day problems of managing men and machinery to be able to give more than casual attention to the technical problems at the 'grass-roots' level. Thus, for instance, routine monitoring of fertilizer requirements, pH status, and floristic composition is almost unknown. Even conscious reviews of mowing routines are a rarity.

The situation in commercial horticulture or agriculture is rather different. In 1970 less than 10 per cent of agricultural holdings in England and Wales employed more than eight full-time-equivalent workers (Nix, 1977). Consequently, owners or managers are much more able to concentrate their time on the technical needs of their crop or stock; indeed, they have to in order to remain in business. In addition, they have the very good back-up of the ADAS advisory service.

Recommendations for the future

The current local-government system has evolved into its present form only during the last 10 years or so, mainly as a result of increased financial pressures and increasing work-load. The increased use of work-study techniques has also had a big influence and, although it has been blamed for many things, work-study has been a major factor in developing much more effective organizations that have in turn brought about considerable increases in labour productivity. The overall system is therefore an efficient one in financial terms. But there has not generally been a corresponding improvement in the application of technical knowledge to the management of amenity turf, although there are, of course, a few examples where dedicated managers have combined the two.

As a first step, it would appear desirable to have much better technically qualified foremen and supervisors. Various colleges offer a range of suitable courses, but the salaries offered at the foreman level rarely provide a satisfactory career grade after such training. Relatively few of the trainees are anxious to devote their lives to the rather thankless task of production management—in our case, getting the grass cut on time. I understand that there is a similar problem in manufacturing industry. Running the production line does not appear so attractive as 'research and development' or 'overseas sales'.

This is, however, only one part of a whole range of socio-economic problems concerning the actual processes of management that influence the practical work on the ground. As far as I am aware there has not been any co-ordinated research into these management matters. I, therefore, propose that such research should be instituted, including investigations into

(1) the levels of technical knowledge among the existing supervisors and managers of amenity turf;

(2) the desirable staff levels, organization, and technical ability that are necessary for the proper technical management of amenity turf;

(3) the current and desirable career prospects for the managers of turf;

(4) the ways in which the biological requirements of turf can be given sufficient emphasis to balance the financial and other incentives of those who use and maintain it;

(5) how the results of research can best be developed into practical techniques that can be adopted on a large scale by those responsible for turf management;

(6) the effectiveness of existing organizations and the need or otherwise for a central-government-based advisory system that would provide good practical advice on turf and other amenity horticulture matters, bearing in mind the high proportion of such work which is carried out by public bodies in the country.

I feel that the need for such research was not given sufficient emphasis in NERC (1977) and it should now be given some priority, particularly as very little of the biological research can become of practical benefit without effective participation from the managers of amenity turf.

Acknowledgements

I thank the Kent County Council for the opportunity of presenting this chapter, but the views I have expressed are my own and not necessarily those of this employer. Lloyds & Co. of Letchworth Ltd kindly supplied photographs of some of their mowing machinery.

References

Moore, I. (1966). *Grass and Grasslands*, Collins, London.
NERC (1977). *Amenity Grasslands—the Needs for Research*, Natural Environment Research Council, Publications series 'C', No. 19, London.
Nix, J. (1977). *Farm Management Pocket Book*, Wye College (University of London), Wye, Kent.
Shildrick, J. P. (1977). 'Less work and more play—trends in turf grasses', *Report of 17th Askham Bryan Horticultural Technical Course, Jan. 1977.*

Part V
TWO OVERVIEWS

Amenity Grassland: An Ecological Perspective
Edited by I. H. Rorison and R. Hunt
© 1980 John Wiley & Sons Ltd

13

Economic and aesthetic evaluation

D. R. HELLIWELL *Waterloo Mill, Wotton-under-Edge, Gloucestershire, England*

Introduction

Within limits, it is a fairly easy matter to ascribe costs to the establishment and maintenance of grassland for amenity purposes, and to estimate the cost of various alternative management strategies. What is less easy to calculate is the benefit provided. Assessment of benefit is required at two levels: firstly, in order to decide how much effort, money, or resources should be spent on the provision of amenity areas, as opposed to other requirements such as medical services, schools, or transport, and, secondly, to decide how best to divide this provision between floral displays, close-mown turf, rough grass, sports turf, shrubs, trees, and paved areas. While the estimation of *costs* requires no great feat of economic versatility, the estimation of *values* is fraught with fundamental difficulties.

Price (1978) discusses at some length the ways in which an economist can approach the valuation of landscape, and it would be wrong to try to repeat all of his discussion here, even in abbreviated form. Suffice it to say that the problems are considerable and, in relation to amenity grassland, centre around the following points:

(1) The values associated with landscape are, in general, non-marketable, so there is no *direct* means of ascertaining the value which people place on them.
(2) The value of amenity grassland is only a part of the value of the total landscape, which, in turn, contributes only a part of the total value of a holiday, day-trip, game of golf, or evening stroll.
(3) The value of one particular area is dependent, to some extent, on the proximity and availability of other similar, and dissimilar, areas.
(4) The physical arrangement of various elements in the landscape can be aesthetically pleasing or displeasing. An area of close-mown turf, for example, may be attractive in some circumstances but less so, or not at all, in others.
(5) What is aesthetically pleasing to one person may not be so to another.

It may, therefore, be instructive to look at each of these five points in turn before returning to the question of relative and overall values of amenity grassland, and landscape in general.

Problems of measurement

Non-marketable benefits

The fact that something can not be bought and sold on the open market is not necessarily any great hindrance to its valuation (Sinden, 1967; Grayson, 1974; Price, 1978). If people are prepared to spend time or effort to obtain something, or are willing to forgo other things which do have a market value, the value of the non-marketable item can fairly easily be ascertained. In other cases, however, valuation is not so easily accomplished. One reason for this is that many non-marketable benefits fall into the category of *public*, as opposed to *private* 'goods'. A 'public good' is something which is not consumed in use by the individual, but remains for the benefit of others. The enjoyment of a fine view, or the use of a public footpath, may be cited as examples. The enjoyment of the view or the use of the path does not preclude their use by other people, as does the use of 'private goods' such as fish and chips, beer, shoes, a private motor car, or a private garden. It is, therefore, difficult to measure 'consumption' in any direct way. One can measure hours of use, numbers of people, etc., but that is not necessarily a measure of enjoyment or benefit. Ten minutes spent viewing a glorious sunset may be more valuable than an hour spent looking at a tranquil lake, or vice versa. However, there are similar problems involved in valuing commoditites for which a market price does exist; for example, a 10p ice-cream may be worth 10p to one purchaser but another purchaser might have been willing to pay 30p. The lack of a market price is not, in itself, an insurmountable obstacle to soundly-based valuation.

Separation of values

This second point can present more fundamental difficulties. It may be possible, for example, to place a value on a visit to a recreational area, but the relative contribution of various facilities or characteristics of the area may be much more difficult to assess. Each area is unique in at least some respects, making it impossible to compare it exactly with other areas which lack such facilities or characteristics. The number of variables and the inter-relationships between them make the use of statistical techniques such as multiple regression very difficult, often leaving as much variability unexplained as that which can be accounted for.

Interdependability of sites

The values associated with landscape have been described by Price (1978) under the following headings:

(1) landscape quality, judged in aesthetic terms;
(2) familiarity with the landscape;
(3) peculiarity.

The last two of these three are both very much related to the proximity and extent of other areas of landscape. Landscapes with which one is familiar have a certain attractiveness due to past associations and the feeling of permanence engendered by them, while landscapes which have peculiar qualities provide a contrast with other landscapes. To some extent, therefore these factors are in conflict when areas which resemble surrounding areas may feel familiar, and areas which are different from surrounding areas may provide a pleasing contrast. In general, familiarity will be related to specific areas of landscape, rather than to general types of landscape, and there will tend to be benefit in having some degree of contrast between areas, provided that the actual process of creating such contrast does not cause greater loss than gain, due to loss of familiarity.

Arrangement of landscape elements

The mere listing or quantification of elements does not give any clear indication of the aesthetic quality of that landscape. As Fairbrother (1974) stated, 'a good designer can make . . . a whole series of different landscapes by using the same dozen common plants' and the way in which landscape elements are arranged is of fundamental importance in determining the type and quality of the landscape. Where it has, in some cases, been found possible to assess landscape quality in terms of features measured on a map (e.g. Robinson *et al.*, 1976) the result may be purely fortuitous, and is not necessarily a statement about the intrinsic value of trees, grassland, water, or other elements in creating aesthetically pleasing landscapes. Trees, for example, may enhance many landscapes, but not all; and the presence of water may enhance most landscapes, but could ruin some, if placed in an obviously artificial position. Similarly, the arrangement and treatment of 'amenity grassland' can be of vital importance. Some areas of 'amenity grassland' would be more appropriate to a concentration camp than to the schools and public buildings which they surround, and it is obvious that the aesthetic value of some such areas is small in relation to the resources devoted to them.

Personal preferences

Having said that some areas are less pleasing aesthetically than others, it may be possible to find someone who actually prefers the 'concentration camp' landscape to a more obviously pleasing one. It is conjectured that such a preference would be related to 'familiarity' or 'peculiarity' rather than aesthetic quality. There will always be valid reason to avoid undue rapidity of change or undue uniformity in design styles. Although there may be some variation in taste, even within the realm of pure aesthetics, this variation is likely to be relatively limited (Zube *et al.*, 1974).

Measurement techniques

Counting heads

The simplest method of attempting to measure the value of an area of landscape is to record the number of people visiting the area and the amount of time that they stay there. A more sophisticated version of this (Clawson, 1959) is to record also the distance and cost of travel involved in getting there, and to construct a 'demand curve'. This may be a useful approach in some areas, particularly as a means of comparing one recreational area with another fairly similar recreational area, but it involves a number of dubious assumptions, and is of little use where the primary purpose of people's presence is other than recreational. Nor does it enable one to separate the contributions made by the availability of, for example, camping sites, the presence of trees, grass, mountains, wildlife, or the other elements which go to make up the landscape 'package'.

Behavioural studies

Rather more subtle than the mere recording of numbers of people, are studies of the behaviour of people within an area. These may take the form of plotting the routes that people follow and the places where they pause or stop; or the study of property prices in areas of contrasting landscape quality. Again, however, there are difficulties. People may stop where there is a parking space for their car or where there is a dry knoll on which to sit, or a wall behind which to shelter from the wind. Houses vary not only in the landscape which is visible from them, but also in the 'type of neighbourhood', the size of garden, the number of bedrooms, and distance from bus routes, shops, schools, etc. The problems mentioned earlier about the difficulties of separating inter-correlated variables will, therefore, be very relevant here, and the most that one is likely to learn from studies of this type are fairly obvious conclusions, such as the fact that people prefer to sit on the edge of a grassy slope rather than in the middle of a field or in the middle of a dense plantation. It may be possible to place a value on the *view of* a landscape as a contributory factor to the price of a house (although I know of no satisfactory study of this type to date). Even then, however, there are difficulties. Does it follow, for example, that the person who buys a cheaper house with no attractive view does not value such a view, or is it that he can not afford the extra price, or that he works every day in a near-by public park of great scenic quality and never looks at the view from his own house?

Attitude surveys

Whilst the counting of heads and the study of behaviour can provide useful, and possibly essential, information, a more detailed study of *attitudes* is likely to be needed if one wishes to assess the value which people place on aesthetic aspects of the environment. To take an extreme case, people may value highly the existence of pristine landscapes in Antarctica, even though they have no intention of going there or of buying a house with a view there. The mere knowledge of the existence of such landscapes may be a source of pleasure or comfort, which must be accorded some positive value.

There is an extensive literature on different types of attitude surveys (see Helliwell, 1976), stemming partly from the study of psychology and partly from environmental studies. All are again surrounded by difficulties. If one gives a respondent free rein to express himself, it is difficult to relate his views to those of other respondents, and if one constrains him to reply to pre-determined questions one can not be sure that the same questions mean the same thing to all respondents, or cover the whole field of a particular respondent's perceptions or preferences. Additionally, it is not always easy to assess how important an expressed preference is to the person in question. He may say quite firmly that he prefers birch trees to spruce trees (Kellomäki, 1975), but, in fact, will prefer a particular spruce forest to a particular birch forest if the canopy-structure of the spruce forest is more diverse. In theory, one should be able to assess the relative importance of tree species and canopy-structure, but the two variables may not be completely independent, and there may be other variables which are ignored, forgotten, or too numerous or complex to assess.

The fact that there are difficulties in measurement should not, however, deter us from attempting to progress some distance along the path of quantification. As Price (1978) reminded us, 'in the land of the blind the man with one eye is king'. If one is dealing with a resource which absorbs many millions of pounds worth of resources every year (£140 million at 1973 prices; NERC, 1977) it would be wrong not to attempt to assess the values which people derive from this resource. Only then could one try to assess the appropriateness of the overall level of expenditure, and its allocation between different operations.

Categories of amenity grassland

Types of ownership

Amenity grassland may be classified in terms of its ownership:

(1) private;
(2) semi-private;
(3) public.

The value of grassland in private gardens or grounds should, in theory, be fairly easy to ascertain, as the users of each area are fairly clearly defined and few in number. The increased value of property with large, rather than small, gardens should be somewhat simpler to ascertain than the question of the value attributable to wider views of the landscape. This, however, says nothing about the relative value of grass compared with tarmac or paving as an area on which to 'sit out', or of grass compared with flower-beds or orchards as an area to look at from the house. The use of some sort of attitude survey is required even here.

The value of semi-private grounds around schools, hotels, offices, or hospitals, must be determined almost entirely from attitude surveys, as the market for such properties is absent or is not closely related to the quality and extent of the surrounding grounds. The people who view them often have no real choice concerning their presence there; one rarely changes schools, hotels, offices, or hospitals just because their grounds are unpleasant to look at.

In some cases it may be possible to estimate the value of public open space by counting heads or studying behaviour, as people are able to exercise a certain amount of choice in being there. However, as outlined above, even here there may also be a need to study attitudes and preferences.

Types of maintenance and use

The term 'amenity grassland' covers a large range of maintenance types from grassland cut only once every year or two to closely-grazed or closely-mown turf cut several times per week. The cost of maintaining these may vary by a factor of twenty or more (see Table 1.2) and the selection of an appropriate management regime is obviously very important.

Some types of usage demand certain standards of maintenance. The decision to create a bowling green, a cricket square, or a golf green will imply the maintenance of those areas to very exacting standards, and will often be paid for by the users in some fairly direct way. Similarly, the use of grassland as football or hockey pitches or as tennis courts will also require certain types of maintenance. The value of such areas for physical recreation is not usually in very much doubt (although I, personally, would question the apparent obsession of state schools in Britain with team sports, and the almost total exclusion of any aesthetic considerations in the design and management of their grounds). It might be interesting to investigate the value of grassland for physical recreation, but that would be partly an aspect of physical health rather than a question of aesthetics, and the aspect which most concerns us in this paper is the appearance of such grassland and its contribution (be it positive or negative) to the overall quality of the landscape. It is possible to keep in good physical condition by running along a road or track, utilizing a gymnasium or playing games on artificial surfaces; grass is not essential for that. The added enjoyment or benefit which is presumably obtained from the use of grass would, again, need to be assessed by studies of attitudes.

The aesthetic contribution of amenity grassland will, as mentioned earlier, depend on the way in which the various elements in the landscape are arranged, as well as on the quantities of each element present. In this context it would seem likely that the law of diminishing returns will often apply. Ten per cent of an area maintained very intensively may give an aura of urbane gentility, but 20 per cent so maintained would not double this effect; and intensive management over all of the area may give a very bleak effect indeed.

In this field, therefore, there is much scope for the critical appraisal both of the design of new areas and of the management of existing areas of amenity grassland, particularly where physical recreation is not the main or only use of an area. If the area is not walked upon there will frequently be more pleasing, and often less expensive, ways of maintaining it than by the ubiquitous use of close-mown grass, either by having trees or shrubs, or by letting the grass grow longer. In areas where there is only light usage for walking or sitting, the mowing of 'paths' within a matrix of longer grass may be an appropriate method of maintenance.

Overall values and sensible sub-division

Having outlined at some length the problems of valuing amenity grassland, it is evident that we will never have a completely accurate, reliable, or easy method of achieving a valuation. However, a near approximation is better than nothing; that is the best we can hope for.

In placing an overall value on, for example, the prevention of a fatal accident on the roads, Williams (1971) has argued with some cogency that it is perfectly defensible for society to postulate a figure, which need not have any relationship to material or market values, but is simply a statement about the worth of something as seen by society. Such postulated values must be arrived at by political rather than by economic methods. In this

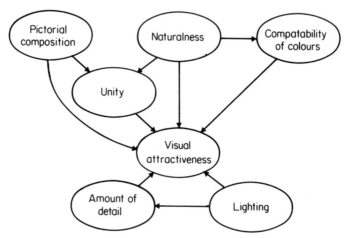

Figure 13.1   Relationships between various aspects of the environment and its visual attractiveness (taken, with some modification, from Helliwell, 1978; reproduced by permission of the editor, *Landscape Research*)

instance, therefore, it would be possible for society to say that it valued the visual appearance of the landscape of a part of Cornwall more than it valued an international airport in that location, but less than it valued food production, and in some rather muddled way, guided by studies of attitudes and preferences and by political pressures of various sorts, to say that it valued the landscape of that area at around, let us say, £50 million. This overall value could then be divided between areas of greater and lesser landscape quality and between areas of greater and lesser usage; guided, again, by studies of attitudes and preferences. The fact that such studies are not yet very far advanced should provide a stimulus to further research in this field. It should not be an excuse for assuming that close-mown grass is always very valuable!

Attempts to sub-divide benefits that are not easily quantified, in as logical a manner as possible, have been made in other fields, such as the valuation of trees for amenity (Helliwell, 1967; Tree Council, 1976) and the valuation of wildlife (Helliwell, 1980), but there may be greater difficulties in the present field than in others (Helliwell, 1978). Figure 13.1 demonstrates some of the complexities of the situation.

Conclusion

In the context of this volume, this overview of the problems of valuation has necessarily been fairly superficial, as the field of aesthetic evaluation is, possibly, as large as that covered by all the other chapters combined. A list of the relevant literature would in itself take up more space than this short chapter, but would have been out of place. All that has been attempted here is a statement of the importance of this topic (a fact which at the Sheffield meeting came up in the discussion following several of the contributions), and some general indication of the difficulties involved in dealing with it.

Unless the question of valuation is faced, at least partially, there can be little sound basis for the development of efficient management techniques, new cultivars, or the design of areas of amenity grassland. As Fischer (1975) pointed out 'environmental quality . . . has little to do with market transactions or exchanges' and is therefore difficult to measure. Tuan (1974) remarked that attitudes towards landscape can also vary from place to place or from time to time, but Byrom (1974) held that

> 'when all the material is assessed it is difficult to escape the conclusion that, while the precise nature of environmental quality may be difficult to define, people as individuals think they have a fairly shrewd idea of what it is all about, of when a [housing] estate has it or does not, and of the extent to which it is important or otherwise.'

It should not, then, be impossible to obtain some measure of the value of environmental quality, or the contribution made by amenity grassland.

References

Byrom, C. (1974). 'Perceptions of environmental quality on housing estates', in *Environmental Quality* (J. T. Coppock & C. B. Wilson, eds), Scottish Academic Press, Edinburgh, pp. 165–77.

Clawson, M. (1959). 'Methods of measuring the demand for and value of outdoor recreation', Reprint No. 10, Resources for the Future Inc., Washington DC.

Fairbrother, N. (1974). *The Nature of Landscape Design*, Architectural Press, London.

Fischer, D. W. (1975). 'Willingness to pay as a behavioural criterion for environmental decision-making', *Journal of Environmental Management*, **3**, 29–41.

Grayson, A. J. (1974). *Assessing the Contribution of Non-market Benefits*, 10th Commonwealth Forestry Conference, Forestry Commission, London.

Helliwell, D. R. (1967). 'The amenity value of trees and woodlands', *Journal of the Arboricultural Association*, **1**, 128–31.

Helliwell, D. R. (1976). 'Perception and preference in landscape appreciation—a review of the literature', *Landscape Research News*, **1**, 4–6.

Helliwell, D. R. (1978). 'The assessment of landscape preferences', *Landscape Research News*, **3**, 15–17.

Helliwell, D. R. (1980). *Planning for Nature Conservation*, Packard Publishing, Chichester.

Kellomäki, S. (1975). 'Forest stand preferences of recreationists', *Acta Forestalia Fennica*, **146**, 36.

NERC (1977). *Amenity Grasslands—the Needs for Research*, Natural Environment Research Council, Publications Series 'C', No. 19, London.

Price, C. (1978). *Landscape Economics*, Macmillan, London.

Robinson, D. G., Wager, J. F., Laurie, I. C. & Traill, A. L. (eds) (1976). *Landscape Evaluation*, Department of Town and Country Planning, University of Manchester, Manchester.

Sinden, J. A. (1967). 'The evaluation of extra-market benefits: a critical review', *World Agricultural Economics and Rural Sociology Abstracts*, **9**, 1–16.

Tree Council, The (1976). *An Evaluation Method for Amenity Trees*, The Tree Council, London.

Tuan, Y. (1974). *Topophilia: A Study of Environmental Perception, Attitudes, and Values*, Prentice-Hall, Englewood Cliffs, N.J.

Williams, A. (1971). 'Cost–benefit analysis: a basic exposition of its intellectual foundations', in *Recreation Cost–Benefit Analysis* (Seminar Report), Countryside Commission, London, pp. 9–13.

Zube, E. H., Pitt, D. G., & Anderson, T. W. (1974). 'Perception and measurement of scenic resources in the South Connecticut River Valley', *University of Massachusetts Publication No. R-74-1*.

Amenity Grassland: An Ecological Perspective
Edited by I. H. Rorison and R. Hunt
© 1980 John Wiley & Sons Ltd

14
Ecological aspects of management—a perspective

R. W. SNAYDON *Department of Agricultural Botany The University, Reading, England*

Introduction

It is perhaps surprising that in none of the foregoing chapters have contributors attempted to define 'ecology'. It was obviously assumed that all readers shared the same concept. This is a doubtful assumption, so I shall make my interpretation explicit to prevent any initial or fundamental misconception. My definition of ecology is 'the study of interactions between organisms, and between organisms and their environment'. This definition, like most of the previous ones from which it is closely derived, does not restrict the term to organisms and environments that are not influenced, manipulated, or managed by man. The term 'management' used in the title I take as synonymous with 'agronomy', i.e. 'the management of land'.

My intention is to look broadly at the place of ecology in the management or agronomy of amenity grasslands, using previous chapters as a background. As my title implies, I shall consider the importance of ecological principle in management, but I shall also indicate those aspects of management where ecology is not especially relevant.

Ecology and agronomy

From a functional point of view, one major difference between ecology and agronomy is that the former is theoretical, i.e. 'pure', ecology, while the latter is essentially practical or 'applied' ecology. However, agronomy is not simply 'applied ecology;' there are additional, non-ecological, components in agronomy. In particular, economic and aesthetic considerations are important in the management of amenity grassland (Chapter 13) and so is the management of non-ecological components, e.g. labour and equipment (Chapters 7 and 12).

Explanation and prediction

One important consequence of the theoretical approach of the ecologist, as opposed to the practical approach of the agronomist, is that the ecologist is often satisfied by general explanations that are made *post hoc*. On the other hand, the agronomist is only satisfied by formulations that have a high predictive value under specified conditions. The agronomist must be confident that his intervention, his manipulation of plants and environment, will lead to a specified outcome. At present, the application of ecology to the management of amenity grassland does not usually give sufficient predictive power. As a result, on the one hand, many agronomists seem to doubt the value of ecological principles and approaches in management and, on the other hand, many ecologists decry the agronomist's largely pragmatic approach. As an applied ecologist, somewhere between both groups, it seems to me that ecology has much to offer agronomy and vice versa. The relationship between ecologists and agronomists should be mutualistic, based on a two-way exchange of information and ideas.

Is ecology relevant?

If ecological principles, often derived from studies of natural or semi-natural vegetation, are to be applied to managed grassland and if, conversely, information derived from managed grassland is to be used in defining ecological principles, then it must be assumed that natural and managed vegetation are governed by the same ecological principles. This assumption seems to be doubted, at least implicitly, by various ecologists and agronomists, both in previous chapters and elsewhere.

The ecologist's view

Ecologists, on the one hand, seem to consider that managed plant communities (swards, crops, forests) are not proper subjects for ecological study. There are signs of this in some previous chapters, but it is even more apparent in recent texbooks, where attention is most heavily focused on vegetation that is least affected by man, and where agricultural crops and grasslands are rarely, if ever, mentioned. This criticism is equally true of introductory texts (e.g. Clapham, 1973; Odum, 1975; Ricklefs, 1978; Dajoz, 1977), of advanced general texts (e.g. Odum, 1971; Krebs, 1972, Collier *et al.*, 1973), and of more specialist texts (e.g. Etherington, 1975; Bannister, 1976). Most of these do briefly consider human influence, but it is usually peripherally, usually in separate chapters, and usually concentrating on the damaging effects of human interference (e.g. pollution and depletion of resources). None deals with the more positive side of human interference, in increasing the amenity value of vegetation and the landscape, and in increasing human food supplies. Billings (1972) devotes only one page to ecological aspects of agriculture and horticulture, but does state that 'An agronomist is a crop ecologist; his success in increasing productivity depends upon the knowledge he has of the principles and data of physiological, population and ecosystem ecology for his particular crops'. This implies that ecological principles are relevant to agriculture. Harper (1977) seems to be the only ecologist who has freely used data from crops, grasslands, and other managed communities to examplify and define ecological principles.

The agronomist's view

Many agronomists seem to assume that, because environmental conditions, species composition, and genetic constitution are all at least partially under human control in managed grasslands and crops, ecological principles are invalid. This attitude seems to be most rife when the human influence is most intense, since few doubt the relevance of ecological principle to range-lands or rough grazing. Textbooks reflect this attitude: although there are several on crop physiology which deal extensively with the effects of environ-mental factors on crops (e.g. Milthorpe & Moorby, 1974; Evans, 1975), there are few texts on crop ecology. However, some textbooks on grass-lands (e.g. Davies, 1954; Spedding, 1971) have taken a clear ecological approach, and a more ecological approach to crops is now apparent (e.g. Alvin & Kozlowski, 1977).

An objective view?

Plant species respond to the physical environment (climate and soil) and to other organisms (competing plants, pests, and pathogens) regardless of whether or not one or more of these factors are influenced or manipulated by man, or whether or not the species have been sown by man. Human interference modifies environmental conditions, it may even modify the plants' response to those conditions (e.g. by breeding), but it does not make the plant, population, or community immune from the influences of the environment and other organisms. Human interference, whether by management or in experiments, does not negate ecological principles; indeed, many ecological principles have mainly been derived from experimental studies, often of crop and grassland species, and from studies of the more simple managed communities and ecosystems.

Contrasting approaches

Ecologists and agronomists have tended to use different approaches to the study of ecosystems, plant communities, and populations. These different approaches may be the result of, or may cause, their different viewpoints.

The ecological approach

Ecologists have concentrated heavily on field surveys, especially of vegetation types and of individual species (Chapter 2). More recently, this has been extended to studies of individual plants, i.e. demography (Chapter 2; Harper, 1977). Experimental studies are now more common, but they are mainly carried out under controlled conditions, e.g. Grime's 'screening experiments' (Chapter 2). These experiments are designed to elucidate field observation, though great care should be exercised in extrapolating from these controlled conditions to the field.

Remarkably few 'pure' ecologists, working on semi-natural vegetation, have carried out experiments in the field. Perhaps this is related to the 'pure' ecologists' apparent dislike, or disdain, of managed or modified vegetation.

The agronomic approach

Conversely, agronomists have relied heavily on field experiments, studying the effects of fertilizers, lime, cutting, grazing, irrigation, drainage, pesticides, and herbicides, on the yield and composition of grasslands and other crops. Such experiments were started as early as 1856 (Brenchley & Warington, 1958). These field experiments have been supported by numerous studies under more controlled conditions.

Surveys have also been carried out, ranging from mapping broad categories of grassland types (Davies, 1941) to detailed surveys of the distribution of individual species and their correlations with environmental factors (e.g. Kruijne *et al.*, 1967).

Information and its uses

These various studies, both by ecologists and agronomists, have produced a wealth of data, but each group has tended to disregard the work of the other, partly because each uses a different range of specialized outlets for publication.

Ecologists and agronomists also tend to use the available information in rather different ways. Ecologists tend to use data to construct conceptual frameworks or principles: these are usually fairly flexible, dynamic, and often individual (e.g. Chapter 2). New items of information can be fitted within the framework, or the framework modified to accommodate new information. This is in general agreement with the accepted scientific method of observation → hypothesis → test → new hypothesis, though the test has more often been done by accumulation of more observations than by direct experimental investigation. The approach of the agronomist is both more empirical, i.e. relying on experiment rather than theory, and more pragmatic, i.e. recognizing facts with reference to their practical value. However, without the basis of a dynamic conceptual framework, there is a danger that this empirical and pragmatic approach may degenerate into a body of dogma. The danger is heightened by a constant demand to provide quick answers to practical problems, usually on the basis of inadequate information.

A synthesis

Some may regard these descriptions as caricatures of ecologists and agronomists, though there is certainly evidence of their validity in previous chapters. However, there is also evidence of some welcome cross-fertilization between ecology and agronomy (e.g. Chapters 3, 5, and 11). The most important function that this volume could serve would be to help convince each that the other has something important to offer. Ecologists should recognize the vast wealth of relevant information obtained by agronomists, mostly from carefully executed experiments. Agronomists should recognize that the conceptual frameworks constructed by ecologists, which are flexible and dynamic, have considerable value in interpreting and synthesizing information and in constructing management plans.

Definition of principles

It is easy to make sweeping statements about the importance of conceptual frameworks, or ecological principles: it is more difficult to define and demonstrate their value. Grime (Chapter 2) has made a bold, and often successful, attempt to do both but he has concentrated on life-cycle strategies. I shall take a broader approach, perhaps at the risk of stating the obvious.

Ecological principles

There seem to be three broad principles of ecology that are relevant to the management of amenity grassland. The first is that all plant communities, including various amenity grasslands, are part of larger interacting systems—ecosystems. Ecosystems include not only plant communities but also the animals, micro-organisms, climate, and soil, interacting with plants and with each other. Bradshaw (Chapter 5) emphasizes this in relation to mineral nutrition, where the effects of climate, soil, animals, and micro-organisms, and interactions between plants, all influence the mineral nutrition of the sward. These complex interactions are also important in relation to other aspects of sward management, e.g. cutting/grazing, weed control, pest and pathogen control, and the selection of species and cultivars.

Change in any aspect of management (e.g. fertilizers, cutting, control of earthworms) is likely to have repercussions in other parts of the system. Spedding (1971, 1975) has developed this ecosystem approach for agricultural grasslands. The approach is less common in relation to amenity grassland, though Schmidt & Blaser (1969) consider some aspects.

The second broad principle is that each species and genotype is adapted to a particular range of environmental conditions. Knowledge of the response pattern of various grassland species to various environmental factors is fragmentary. Reviews of the differences between grassland species in response to temperature, light, water, and nutrients have been made by McWilliam & Ludlow, Turner & Begg, Andrew & Johansen, and Robson & Loneragan, respectively (see Wilson, 1978, for references). Knowledge of these differences is important both in selecting suitable species and cultivars for specific conditions and in modifying conditions to suit them. In general, the information is most useful if it has been obtained under relevant field conditions; data obtained under controlled and artificial conditions should be used with great caution.

The third broad principle relevant to amenity grassland is that plant communities are dynamic: their composition and structure are changing, often quite rapidly, in response to changing conditions. These changes may be externally-induced, e.g. by management, by disturbance, or by natural changes in environmental conditions, or may be intrinsic, i.e. the result of natural processes and changes occurring within the community. Various aspects of this broad principle have already been considered (Chapter 2). It would be difficult to overemphasize the importance of this principle in grassland management. Davies (1954) points out its importance for agricultural grassland and Wells (Chapter 11) for amenity grassland; both emphasized that almost all grasslands in lowland Britain are plagioclimaxes—highly unstable and rapidly changing in response to cutting/grazing, fertilizers, and climatic conditions.

Agronomic principles

It is even more difficult to define broad principles of agronomy. Such principles, if they can be said to exist, are functional steps in management rather than theoretical concepts. It seems that there are four or five. The first principle, or step in management, is to define the objectives of management. In the case of amenity grassland, these objectives are primarily determined by the type of use that is proposed. The second principle is to define the available resources; these include not only ecological resources, i.e. soil and climate (the site), and species and cultivars, but also non-ecological resources, i.e. finance, labour, and equipment. The third principle is to define the management variables, i.e. the practices that can be used to modify the environment or the vegetation (e.g. fertilizers, irrigation, cutting, and species selection). The fourth principle is to match the resources and management variables to the proposed objectives. Most managers would add a fifth principle—do it!

Principles of management

The agronomic principles, or steps, just considered can be expressed diagrammatically (Figure 14.1). I have made the ecological component, which involves matching the species to the environment and vice versa, the central core of this functional system (Chapter 1), not only because of its importance, but also because it is the subject of this volume.

'Hardware' and 'software'

The ecological resources (climate, soil, species, and cultivars) and the non-ecological resources (finance, labour, equipment) can be regarded as the 'hardware' of the system. Together they set the ultimate or potential limits on the achievement of objectives. The actual limits are more often set by our knowledge of the systems, and our ability to devise management plans to manipulate them, i.e. by the 'software'. In the absence of the necessary knowledge and conceptual framework, management is often by trial and error, precedent or intuition, rather than by rational decisions. Trial and error management is indicated in Figure 14.1 by the feedback loop:

management → outcome → evaluation → management.

Such a process is usually an essential part of any rational management plan, but can be hazardous when decisions are made on the basis of the immediately previous reactions of the system and when the conditions that produced those reactions have changed. Management by precedent can also be hazardous, especially when the previous experience was gained under different conditions, or when information is inadequate or misinterpreted. In addition, management by precedent is usually not sufficiently flexible, and too often leads to dogma.

The management of the various types of amenity grassland has certainly improved in recent decades, especially as a result of improved 'hardware', e.g. equipment, fertilizers, and cultivars, and the availability of finance, all of which allow more management options. In my opinion, further improvements are limited by 'software', especially by our lack of knowledge of the systems, and by our limited ability to utilize the available knowledge to construct rational management plans. Advances in these areas will require closer links between theory and practice, i.e. between ecologists and agronomists. One useful starting point is a clearer definition of objectives.

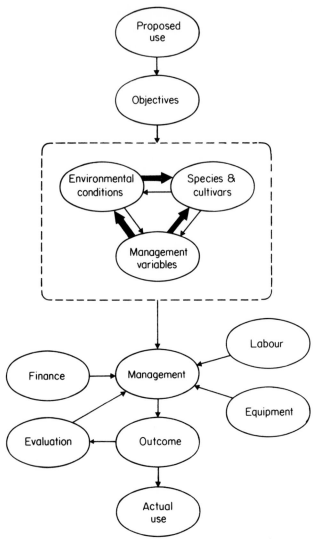

Figure 14.1   Diagrammatic representation of the place of the ecological component (boxed) in the management of amenity grasslands

Objectives of management

The objectives in managing amenity grassland depend upon the proposed use (Figure 14.1). Two classifications are presented in Table 14.1. The first (Table 14.1(a)), which is commonly used (e.g. NERC, 1977), is based on the amenity which is served; this is not very useful in defining objectives. A

Table 14.1 Classification of the uses of amenity grassland according to (a) the amenity served, and (b) the form of use (not exhaustive)

(a) Amenity served	(b) Form of use
(1) Visual	(1) Type of use
(i) Broad landscape	(i) Wear
Reservoirs	Pressure
Parks	Tear-wear
Verges	(ii) Visual
(ii) Detailed landscape	(iii) Control of erosion
Lawns	(2) Amount of use
(2) Nature Conservation	(i) Intensity
(i) Plant communities	(ii) Frequency
(ii) Plant species	(3) Time of use
(iii) Animal species	(i) Winter
(3) Sports	(ii) Summer
(i) Race courses	(iii) Year-round
(ii) Soccer, rugby, hockey	
(iii) Cricket	
(iv) Golf	
(v) Tennis	
(vi) Bowls	
(4) Other uses	
(i) Watersheds	
(ii) Airfields	

better classification is shown in Table 14.1(b). Both can, of course, be extended or refined.

Many amenity grasslands provide several amenities, e.g. most urban open spaces are used both visually and for sport or play, and many sport areas are used for several sports (e.g. soccer and cricket). In addition, an area used for a single amenity, e.g. bowls (Plate 1.2), may have several 'forms of use', e.g. play and visual enjoyment, and the form and amount of use may vary considerably over the area. In particular, various areas within soccer/rugby pitches, tennis courts, and bowling greens are subject to wide differences in use. In some cases, the type of sward and its management are varied to match the use (e.g. golf greens, fairways, and rough; cricket infield and outfield), but more often the sward or management is uniform, in spite of these spatial differences in requirements. A more careful definition of use, along the lines of Table 14.1(b) and of the variations in use in time and space, is necessary if management objectives are to be clearly defined.

Objectives in the management of amenity grassland are classified in Table 14.2. Again, this can be extended and refined. The relative importance of the various objectives will, of course, depend upon the proposed use (Table

Table 14.2   Objectives in the management of amenity grassland

(1)   Appearance
   (i) Cover
   (ii) Colour
   (iii) Structure
       Uniformity/diversity
       Species/height
(2)   Durability
   (i) Resistance to wear
   (ii) Resistance to mis-management
(3)   Persistence
   (i) Resistance to environmental extremes, e.g. drought, waterlogging, cold/heat
   (ii) Resistance to other organisms, e.g. pests, pathogens, weeds
(4)   Ease and cost of management
   (i) Establishment
       Soil preparation
       Seed
   (ii) Established sward
       Cutting
       Fertilizer
       Lime
       Weed contol
       Pest control

14.1). Most of the objectives are obvious and some, e.g. wear (Chapter 8), have already been considered in detail.

Criteria in evaluation

In addition to defining objectives, it is necessary to develop criteria to evaulate the success of any management practice in achieving those objectives. Canaway (Chapter 8) considered detailed criteria for one specific objective, resistance to wear, while Shildrick (Chapter 4) more broadly considered the criteria for assessing species and cultivars. Helliwell (Chapter 13) assessed economic and aesthetic values as criteria for management in general. These three examples represent highly contrasting approaches to the problems of defining criteria, ranging from highly specific and detailed to broad and non-specific. They raise interesting questions:

(1) Is it possible to use objective criteria for aesthetic objectives?
(2) How is it possible to integrate the various criteria to provide an overall assessment of the management practice?
(3) Is it possible to devise an evaluation 'package' that can be used as the basis for day-to-day management decisions for a specific amenity use?

It seems likely that devising valid criteria for evaluation will prove even more difficult than defining the objectives that they will serve. However, both these processes are essential if rational management plans are to be devised.

The ecological component

The main purpose of the ecological component is to fit species and cultivars to the environment, and vice versa, so as to meet set objectives (Figure 14.1). This is achieved by manipulating the various management variables, and must be carried out within the bounds set by non-ecological factors, e.g. finance, labour, and equipment.

So far, I have tried to put this ecological component, i.e. the boxed area in Figure 14.1, into the general perspective of management. Many of the previous chapters have dealt with specific aspects of the ecological component. Bradshaw (Chapter 5) and Stewart (Chapter 6) have dealt with soil factors. Shildrick (Chapter 4) and Humphries (Chapter 3) have dealt with the selection and breeding of species and cultivars. Most of the other authors (in Chapters 7, 9, 11, and 12) have dealt with the effects of management, mainly cutting/grazing, on species composition, while Grime (Chapter 2) has dealt with broad ecological concepts.

A wide range of management variables can be manipulated or controlled (Table 14.3). These give the manager considerable control both over environmental conditions and, directly or indirectly, over species and cultivar

Table 14.3 A classification of management variables that can be manipulated or controlled in amenity grassland management

(1)   Environmental modification
    (i) Fertilizers (N, P, K, etc.)
    (ii) Drainage
    (iii) Soil replacement
    (iv) Irrigation
    (v) Soil heating
(2)   Cutting and grazing
    (i) Frequency
    (ii) Intensity
    (iii) Timing
(3)   Control of weeds, pests, and pathogens
    (i) Herbicides
    (ii) Pesticides
    (iii) Fungicides
(4)   Sowing/planting
    (i) Choice of species
    (ii) Choice of cultivars
    (iii) Sowing/planting method

composition. A great deal of the ecological skill in managing amenity grassland lies in the ability to define the factors which stand in the way of the set objectives, and then to manipulate the management variables so as to achieve those objectives. This is made more difficult, on the one hand, by insufficient information on the potential effects of the manipulation and the unpredictable nature of some environmental conditions, e.g. climate, and, on the other hand, by the limitations set by non-ecological factors. It is also made difficult by requirements for several, often conflicting, objectives. As a result, management is usually by a series of compromise solutions, frequently varied in response to continual changes in both the ecological and non-ecological variables. In the light of these difficulties, it is perhaps not surprising that management is often by trial and error, by precedent, or by dogma.

There is obviously scope for a more rational approach to management, that will include a large ecological component. This will require a closer understanding between the theoretical ecologist, on the one hand, and the practical agronomist, on the other. It will also require closer definition of objectives (Table 14.2) and more satisfactory criteria for evaluation (Table 14.3). There is also need for more detailed knowledge of the response of swards, both single-species and mixed-species, to environmental factors and to management variables. Perhaps what is needed most of all are clear conceptual frameworks on which to hang all this information. More thought is needed in defining what is to be done, why it is to be done, and how; this is the area in which the ecologist has most to offer, but he must recognize the constraints within which the agronomist works.

References

Alvim, P. & Kozlowski, T. T. (1977). *Ecophysiology of Tropical Crops*, Academic Press, New York.

Bannister, P. (1976). *Introduction to Physiological Plant Ecology*, Blackwell Scientific Publications, Oxford.

Billings, W. D. (1972). *Plants, Man and the Ecosystem*, Macmillan, New York.

Brenchley, W. E. & Warington, K. (1958). *The Park Grass Plots at Rothamsted 1856–1949*, Rothamsted Experimental Station, Harpenden.

Clapham, W. B. (1973). *Natural Ecosystems*, Macmillan, New York.

Collier, B. D., Cox, G. W., Johnson, A. W. & Miller, P. C. (1973). *Dynamic Ecology*, Prentice-Hall, Englewood Cliffs, N.J.

Dajoz, R. (1977). *Introduction to Ecology*, Hodder & Stoughton, London.

Davies, W. (1941). 'The grassland map of England and Wales', *Journal of the Ministry of Agriculture, London*, **48**, 112–21.

Davies, W. (1954). *The Grass Crop*, Spon, London.

Etherington, J. R. (1975). *Environmental and Plant Ecology*, Wiley, London.

Evans, L. T. (ed.) (1975). *Crop Physiology*, Cambridge University Press, Cambridge.

Harper, J. I. (1977). *Population Biology of Plants*, Academic Press, London.

Krebs, C. J. (1972). *Ecology*, Harper, New York.

Kruijne, A. A., de Vries, D. M. & Mooi, H. (1967). 'Bijdrage tot de oecologie van de Nederlandse graslandplanton.' *Verslagen van Landbouwkundige Onderzoekingen*, 696.

Milthorpe, F. L. & Moorby, J. (1974). *An Introduction to Crop Physiology*, Cambridge University Press, Cambridge.

NERC (1977). *Amenity Grasslands—the Needs for Research*, Natural Environment Research Council, Publications Series 'C', No. 19, London.

Odum, E. P. (1971). *Fundamentals of Ecology*, Saunders, Philadelphia.

Odum, E. P. (1975). *Ecology*, Holt, Rinehart & Winston, New York.

Ricklefs, R. E. (1978). *The Economy of Nature*, Chiron Press, Portland.

Schmidt, T. E. & Blaser, R. E. (1969). 'Ecology and turf management', in *Turfgrass Science* (A. A. Hanson and F. V. Juska, eds), American Society for Agronomy, Madison, Wisc., pp. 217–39.

Spedding, C. R. W. (1971). *Grassland Ecology*, Oxford University Press, Oxford.

Spedding, C. R. W. (1975). *The Biology of Agricultural Systems*, Academic Press, London.

Wilson, J. E. (ed.) (1978). *Plant Relations in Pastures*, CSIRO, Melbourne.

Abstracts of poster contributions

Grasses and legumes for hill land improvement

D. A. DAVIES *Welsh Plant Breeding Station, Plas Gogerddan, nr Aberystwyth, Dyfed, Wales*

One-third of the agricultural area in the United Kingdom is classified as hill and upland. Future development is dependent on land improvement either by ploughing or surface seedling. Evaluation of herbage plants involves detailed study of responses to many interacting climatic, edaphic, and biotic ecological factors. Since 1961 over 300 varieties of 19 grass and six legume species have been screened at a number of contrasting sites in mid-Wales. The main characteristics assessed included establishment vigour, persistence and winter hardiness, tolerance of infertility, waterlogging and drought, earliness and stability of production, compatability with clover, freedom from disease, and feeding value.

Only *Festuca rubra* (red fescue), *Lolium perenne* (perennial ryegrass), *Phleum pratense* (Timothy), and *Trifolium repens* (white clover) were regarded as suitable for wetter hill conditions. *F. rubra* has particularly advantageous spring growth and winter hardiness and *P. pratense* shows good 'animal' performance. *T. repens* has long been regarded as the cornerstone of hill land improvement because of its dual importance in nitrogen fixation and feed quality.

Considerable genetic variation exists in most of the characters examined and the potential for special purpose varieties is being explored. Since many of these attributes are equally important in amenity areas, joint breeding programmes could be developed.

Cultivar evaluation on colliery spoil

C. O. ELIAS *Derelict Land Reclamation Research Unit, Department of Biology, University of York, York, England*

The Derelict Land Reclamation Research Unit of the University of York was set up in 1974 to investigate long-term maintenance problems on colliery spoil, particularly in relation to nitrogen, phosphorus, and species/cultivars. The Unit is funded by the Department of the Environment and the EEC.

The work has involved the use of field trials, glasshouse experiments, and controlled-environment studies. Some of the results relating to species/cultivars were presented. The experimental work concerned the use of agricultural and amenity species (and cultivars) such as *Lolium perenne* (perennial ryegrass), *Dactylis glomerata* (cock's foot), *Festuca rubra* (red fescue), and *Agrostis tenuis* (common bent-grass). In view of the high maintenance costs in terms of fertilizer input and management, there has recently been greater interest shown in the use of amenity cultivars for reclamation. There is a growing realization that agriculture is not always the most suitable use for restored land.

The display showed the main results of a preliminary continuous-flow experiment and an extensive glasshouse trial in which the growth of agricultural and amenity grass cultivars were compared on two contrasting colliery spoils at three levels of nitrogen and phosphorus. It outlined the field trials work in progress throughout the country.

PP333—a new grass growth retardant

D. J. F. ENGLAND *Imperial Chemical Industries Ltd, Plant Protection Division, Jealott's Hill Research Station, Bracknell, Berkshire, England*

PP333 is a potent growth retardant active on a wide range of species commonly present in amenity grassland. In worldwide evaluation trials in 1978, mowing frequency has been reduced significantly (40–60 per cent), especially in the peak growing period, with relatively low rates of application (1–4 kg ha^{-1} (0.9–3.6 lb acre^{-1})). The chemical is mainly soil-acting and its initial activity is dependent on soil moisture.

Timing is not critical but treatment at, or just before, the onset of spring growth seems most effective, although associated with more phytotoxicity. Initially there can be leaftip damage, but subsequently the grass darkens, the sward develops a coarser appearance with shorter, thicker leaves and a more prostrate habit. Finer grasses are retarded more than coarse ones leading to a temporary change in species composition or apparent dominance. Additionally, reduced fresh green growth, a property of any retardant, gives more visual prominence to the normal processes of death and senescence in lower leaves and stolons, resulting in a longer 'post-mown' appearance. Seedheads are reduced in number and height but are not normally eliminated.

The 1978 programme concentrated on timing of a single dose to give season-long control. Preliminary tests using sequential low doses have indicated the possibility of further savings in cutting costs, an extended period of moderate growth, and fewer adverse effects.

This work will be continued and expanded, to include the possibility of improving seedhead suppression with mixtures, in the various types of amenity grassland, to determine the most effective combination of management practice and chemical treatment.

An unmaintained amenity grassland area

R. GULLIVER *York Educational Settlement, Holgate Road, York, England*

York cemetery has not been maintained for 12 years, though the paths are kept clear. The site is now dominated by a tall grass community, with areas of *Rubus fruticosus* (bramble), *Polygonum cuspidatum* (Japanese knotweed), and *Rubus idaeus* (raspberry). There is active colonization of the site by *Acer pseudoplatanus* (sycamore) and some *Fraxinus excelsior* (ash). There are also 160 individual established trees that were originally planted.

The area supports a large small-mammal population. This in turn provides food for tawny owls, kestrels, stoats, and weasels. The area has thus become an excellent nature reserve. As the paths are maintained, the graves can still be visited. The ornamental trees can also be seen and admired.

The site has low maintenance costs but represents high amenity value. It may not be a model many land managers would wish to follow but it is an interesting example at one extreme of the range of options available.

Field wear trials of acidic, neutral, and basic amenity grasslands in London's Green Belt

C. HARRISON and S. WALKER *Department of Geography, University College London, Gower Street, London, England*

Field trials using known trampling levels were described for a range of neutral and acidic grassland and acidic grass-heath sites in London's Green Belt. All sites were currently managed for informal recreation, and some were mown annually, but the treatment plots had not previously been trampled. Our objective in these trials was to rank different sites in terms of their capacity to recover from similar usage.

In order to establish the recovery capabilities of different sites, plots on each of five sites were trampled during a summer period of 6 weeks and allowed to recover for a further 7 weeks. A second season of treatment and recovery was due to be applied during the winter and spring of 1979. Results of the first treatment and recovery period were presented. During this period all treatment strips exhibited a decline in absolute cover. Live cover reached a minimum between 1200–1600 passages. Percentage bare ground on all sites was low, suggesting that, for these sites and environmental conditions, the trampling treatments did not lead to the marked changes in cover values that have been recorded by other workers.

Recovery of treatment on all sites over a 7-week period in September and October 1978 was good, with most sites achieving a live cover similar to that recorded at the start of the treatment. The ranked order of sites, based on rates of recovery, parallels the acid–neutral gradient in soil pH. Acidic grassland and grass-heathlands showed slower recovery rates than neutral grasslands on clay with flints although this pattern was also influenced by the different management regimes. The performance of certain species on the different plots during treatment and recovery was also displayed.

UCPE vegetation surveys

J. G. HODGSON and J. P. GRIME *Unit of Comparative Plant Ecology (NERC), Department of Botany, The University, Sheffield, England*

The floristic composition of all the major habitats, both semi-natural and artificial, is now described for the Sheffield region. Standardized ecological information is available for 270 of the commoner species and will shortly be forthcoming for another 600 species.

Roadside soils and vegetation

A. JONES *Department of Biological Sciences, Lanchester Polytechnic, Coventry, England*

This poster presented some results of an investigation into aspects of the ecology of the verge vegetation of dual-carriageway roads. The major effect on plant growth conditions in these verge soils was that of salt application for de-icing. The resulting accumulation of sodium and chloride ions, with their effects on the physical and chemical characteristics of the soils, produced conditions hostile to plant growth. These effects were reflected in the distribution of plant species in the verge vegetation. Species found growing nearest to the road were salt-tolerant and/or annual species which are able to take advantage of the reduced salinity which exists during the summer.

Agropyron repens (couch-grass) was commonly found in pure stands at the roadside, and is known to exhibit salt tolerance. Experiments have shown that germination of *A. repens* seed is less inhibited by high sodium chloride concentration than seed of other common roadside grasses, and it is thus better able to colonize soils adjacent to roads. Once established, the vegetative reproduction of *A. repens* is advantageous since young plants are able to obtain ample supplies of water and nutrients from the parent plant, thus avoiding the detrimental effects of sodium chloride during early stages of growth. Flowering is frequently prevented by mowing of verges; thus vegetative reproduction is again advantageous.

Germination experiments with other common roadside species showed good correlation between ability to withstand high sodium chloride concentrations during germination, and ability to grow near roads.

The effects of climatic abnormalities on performance of turfgrass cultivars in Great Britain

R. W. LAYCOCK *Sports Turf Research Institute, Bingley, West Yorkshire, England*

Multi-centre trials of turfgrass cultivars have shown how some important local climatic factors such as drought and winter conditions can affect plant performance, While these factors have been severe at particular centres and in some years, it was possible for resilient cultivars to recover subsequently. Deviations from the national pattern of cultivar performance, while locally important, have not usually been sufficient to change the ranking of cultivars averaged over all five centres in the trials network (see *Journal of the Sports Turf Research Institute*, **55**, in press).

Structure and dynamics of populations of *Holcus lanatus* L. (Yorkshire fog)

S. P. McGRATH and Y. D. Al-MASHHADANI *Unit of Comparative Plant Ecology (NERC), Department of Botany, The University, Sheffield, England*

This investigation was centred on a grassland site in Sheffield dominated by the perennial grass *Holcus lanatus* L. Vegetation samples were taken during the period April–November 1978.

Fluctuation of above-ground biomass, individual species contributions to standing crop, weight-structure of the *Holcus* population, fluctuation in seedling numbers and seed banks were studied on five sampling occasions in each of five 0.25 m² (2.7 ft²) quadrats. Several other sites in the region were also sampled for comparative purposes.

Numbers of individuals per unit area showed strong seasonal fluctuation, with highest numbers recorded in spring and autumn and lowest in mid-summer. The minimum number corresponded with the period of maximum standing crop. Catastrophic declines in the number of small individuals in late spring and autumn suggested that recruitment to the population from seedlings is a rare event in sites which have high standing crop and little bare ground.

Rapid growth rate, high seed output when uncut, and the presence of dormant seeds of this species in the soil all contribute to the good ground cover which results from vegetative expansion or colonization of gaps by seedlings. *Holcus* has a wide environmental tolerance and, taken together, these attributes confirm the potential of this species for low-maintenance amenity grassland uses.

Grassland management in countryside recreation areas

W. A. REES *Countryside Commission, John Dower House, Crescent Place, Cheltenham, Gloucestershire, England*

A tapeslide presentation outlined, in simple terms, the options available to managers of grassland recreation areas. It was based on a report prepared for the Countryside Commission by T. C. E. Wells and J. E. Lowday of the Institute of Terrestrial Ecology, Monks Wood.

The influence of aspect on the climate in ungrazed limestone grassland

I. H. RORISON and F. SUTTON *Unit of Comparative Plant Ecology (NERC), Department of Botany, The University, Sheffield, England*

Photographs and computer traces were used to illustrate some of the equipment used and the results obtained by the UCPE, which is currently logging continuous measurements of soil and air temperatures on the north- and south-facing slopes and the plateau grassland of a Derbyshire dale, and the total direct and diffuse radiation of the plateau.

Variation in both soil and air temperature, and in solar radiation and moisture level is more extreme on south-facing slopes than on north-facing slopes, both in summer and winter. The resulting north-sward resembles a lush alpine meadow and the south-, a stunted, open downland.

An automatic translation, storage, and data retrieval system has been developed and the computer traces of temperatures recorded in the field and inside a chamber show that by linking a tape reader to the laboratory, the simulation of selected field climates can be achieved. Climatic influences on plant performance are currently being assessed, one aim being to provide relevant data for sites where aspect is a significant factor (see Rorison, I. H. & Sutton, F. (1976). 'Climate, topography and germination', in *Light as an Ecological Factor*, vol. II, (G. C. Evans, R. Bainbridge & O. Rackham, eds), British Ecological Society Symposium no. 16, Blackwell Scientific Publications, Oxford, pp. 361–83).

What is a good cultivar worth?

J. P. SHILDRICK *Sports Turf Research Institute, Bingley, West Yorkshire, England*

It is important to put user values on the improvements made by breeders in recent years. There are two main benefits for which calculations might be made—reduced mowing frequency as a result of less growth, and improved durability under wear.

Trial results from the Sports Turf Research Institute and elsewhere illustrated that recent improvements have been of the order of 25 per cent. A few examples were given, to translate this into potential financial benefit. Local authorities and other major users were invited to help research by examining their own experiences to confirm or contradict these theoretical calculations.

Artificial mosaics of grassland species

A. SMITH and P. J. ALLCOCK *Grassland Research Institute, Hurley, Maidenhead, Berkshire, England*

The demonstration consisted of a brief outline of the reasons for sowing mosaics of grassland species, a summary of the methods used, and a description of the types of mosaic currently under investigation. While the objectives of the work were agronomic, the subject had ecological and amenity implications.

The aim was to evaluate indigenous grasses for agricultural production. It was intended to determine which type of plant community is best adapted to each of a series of contrasting management techniques. The adapted swards would contain one or more species, and their quasi-stability would be of agronomic value.

The communities would be obtained by sowing a mixture and allowing a succession to take place towards a stable state appropriate to each constant management regime. The direction of these successions would be influenced by the ingress of unsown species and the time taken to achieve stability might depend on invasion rates. Thus, to accelerate the changes, all suitable species (i.e including those grasses naturally available for colonization) ought to be present from the start.

The establishment of genetically heterogenous populations involves the technical difficulty of avoiding excessive competition between species (and variants) during the year following sowing. In tests, initially using seven species, the problem has been overcome by sowing in strips, each strip being of a single species or a mixture of two. A hand-propelled fertilizer spreader has been modified to broadcast parallel bands of species simultaneously. Other apparatus has been made for sowing mosaics. In one mosaic, individual species were sown in strips (each *c*. 110 mm (4.3 in) wide). The spreader had been modified to broadcast parallel strips simultaneously, without mixing the species. A mosaic consisting of a matrix of pair-mixtures and monocultures has also been created by criss-crossing strips. Other apparatus has been made for sowing circular colonies of hexagon-based mosaics in which boundary interactions between all species are identical.

These techniques should be of some interest in amenity grassland where the simulation of natural vegetation patterns is desirable. In conservation work they may also be of value when introducing a new species to a habitat.

Turfgrass mixtures trials at STRI

T. A. WATT *Sports Turf Research Institute, Bingley, West Yorkshire, England*

The wear-tolerance of mixtures containing up to five turfgrass species is being studied under a sub-contract with NERC. Sixteen mixtures were sown, during spring 1975, at three sites in Britain. These mixtures received artificial, football-type wear during the following winter but the proportions of the species which *established* in any one mixture varied greatly between the sites. Where irrigation was possible during the dry period following sowing, the intended range of mixture compositions was achieved. Otherwise, *Lolium perenne* (perennial ryegrass) dominated the mixtures in which it had been sown.

Mixtures with a high proportion of *L. perenne* with *Poa pratensis* (smooth-stalked meadow-grass) and *Phleum pratense* (Timothy) tolerated wear best. *Agrostis tenuis* (common bent-grass) and *Festuca rubra* (red fescue) did not tolerate wear successfully.

More research is needed in order to be able to explain the behaviour of these species in terms of species × environment and interspecific interactions. Meanwhile, the effects of

(1) length of time of establishment before wear,
(2) using *L. perenne* in monoculture, and
(3) using a newer *L. perenne* cultivar ('Manhattan') on wear tolerance

are being examined in a new series of mixtures trials at the same three sites.

Verge management by the use of selective herbicides and growth regulators

A. J. WILLIS *Department of Botany, The University, Sheffield, England*

Research work over a period of 20 years on the vegetation of wide roadside verges in an area of the Cotswolds, Gloucestershire, has shown the long-term effects of sprayed chemicals on the growth and composition of the sward.

The selective herbicide 2,4-dichlorophenoxyacetic acid (2,4-D) acting alone leads to a grassy turf, in which *Poa pratensis* (smooth-stalked meadow-grass) and *Festuca rubra* (red fescue) become increasingly prominent, *Arrhenatherum elatius* (oat-grass) declines and many broad-leaved species are eliminated. The regulator maleic hydrazide (MH) alone results in a low vegetation of diverse composition containing a number of dicotyledonous plants (e.g. *Galium cruciata* (crosswort)) but in which *F. rubra* progressively increases, although its flowering is suppressed. The mixed spray of MH + 2,4-D applied once in spring leads to a grassy sward dominated strongly by *P. pratensis*, which remains short all the year.

Similar spray treatments on a tall herb-rich community containing woody species (*Prunus spinosa* (sloe), *Rubus fruticosus* (bramble)) in Derbyshire (Staveley) lead to fairly similar changes (Plate 10.3). Where shrub species are removed initially, *F. rubra* assumes dominance when the mixed spray or MH alone is supplied. Where *Pteridium aquilinum* (bracken) is present this declines, and *F. rubra* gradually increases; in some areas the bracken community has progressively changed to a grass cover.

List of registered participants

Mr C. E. ANDERSON
Education Playing Fields Service, Nottinghamshire County Council, County Hall, West Bridgford, Nottingham NG2 7QP, England

Mr J. C. BAINES
City of Birmingham Polytechnic, School of Planning and Landscape, Franchise Street, Perry Barr, Birmingham, England

Dr A. J. M. BAKER
Department of Botany, The University, Sheffield S10 2TN, England

Dr F. G. A. BASSI
Hurst Crop Research and Development Unit, Great Domsey Farm, Feering, Colchester, Essex CO5 9ES, England

Dr J. J. BATCH
Plant Protection Division, Imperial Chemical Industries Ltd., Jealott's Hill Research Station, Bracknell, Berkshire RG12 6E7, England

Professor A. D. BRADSHAW
Department of Botany, University of Liverpool, PO Box 147, Liverpool L69 3BX, England

Dr E. L. BREESE
Welsh Plant Breeding Station, Plas Gogerddan, nr Aberystwyth SY23 3EB, Wales

Mr M. B. BROWN
Department of the Environment, Royal Parks Division, Bog Lodge, Richmond Park, Richmond, Surrey, England

Mr C. BURTON
Department of Botany, University of Liverpool, PO Box 147, Liverpool L69 3BX, England

Mr P. M. CANAWAY
Sports Turf Research Institute, Bingley, West Yorkshire BD16 1AU, England

Mr G. P. CHALLENGER
Peak District National Park, Aldern House, Baslow Road, Bakewell, Derbyshire DE4 1AE, England

Dr A. H. CHARLES
Welsh Plant Breeding Station, Plas Gogerddan, nr Aberystwyth SY23 3EB, Wales

Mr C. COLLINS
Education Playing Fields Service, Nottinghamshire County Council, County Hall, West Bridgford, Nottingham NG2 7QP, England

Mr H. P. CONLON
Department of Landscape Architecture, The University, Sheffield S10 2TN, England

Mr G. J. F. COPEMAN
Grassland Husbandry Division, North of Scotland College of Agriculture, 581 King Street, Aberdeen AB9 1UD, Scotland

Mr I. DANIELLS
Sports Turf Research Institute, Bingley, West Yorkshire BD16 1AU, England

Mr D. A. DAVIES
Welsh Plant Breeding Station, Plas Gogerddan, nr Aberystwyth SY23 3EB, Wales

Mr K. DAWSON
Rolawn (Turf Growers) Limited, Elvington, York, England

Mr A. P. DUNBALL
Department of Transport, 25 Savile Row, London W1, England

Mr P. L. K. DURY
Education Playing Fields Service, Nottinghamshire County Council, West Bridgford, Nottingham NG2 7QP, England

Mr L. W. EDWARDS
Rolawn (Turf Growers) Limited, Elvington, York, England

Dr C. O. ELIAS
Derelict Land Reclamation Research Unit, Department of Biology, University of York, Heslington, York YO1 5DD, England

Mr D. J. F. ENGLAND
Plant Protection Division, Imperial Chemical Industries Ltd., Jealott's Hill Research Station, Bracknell, Berkshire RG12 6EY, England

Mr J. R. ESCRITT
Sports Turf Research Institute, Bingley, West Yorkshire BD16 1AU, England

Mr B. EVANS
Planning Department, Gwent County Council, County Hall, Cwmbran, Gwent NP4 2XH, Wales

Mr C. J. FORESTIER-WALKER   *Goldsmiths Seeds, Bury St. Edmunds, Suffolk, England*

Mr J. H. FRANKS
British Seed Houses Ltd., Bewsey Industrial Estate, Pitt Street, Warrington, Cheshire WA5 5LE, England

Dr O. L. GILBERT
Department of Landscape Architecture, The University, Sheffield S10 2TN, England

Mr A. J. P. GORE
Institute of Terrestrial Ecology, Monks Wood Experimental Station, Abbots Ripton, Huntingdon, Cambridgeshire PE17 2LS, England

Dr B. H. GREEN
Countryside Planning Unit, School of Rural Economics and Related Studies, Wye College (University of London), nr Ashford, Kent TN25 5AH, England

Mr J. O. GREEN
Grassland Research Institute, Hurley, Maidenhead, Berkshire SL6 5LR, England

Dr J. P. GRIME
Unit of Comparative Plant Ecology (NERC), Department of Botany, The University, Sheffield S10 2TN, England

Dr R. GULLIVER
York Educational Settlement, Holgate Road, York, England

Dr R. J. HAGGAR
ARC Weed Research Organization, Begbroke Hill, Yarnton, Oxford OX5 1PF, England

Dr C. M. HARRISON
Department of Geography, University College London, Gower Street, London WC1E 6BT, England

Mr R. J. M. HAY
Grasslands Division DSIR, Private Bag, Gore, New Zealand

Mr D. R. HELLIWELL
Waterloo Mill, Wotton-under-Edge, Gloucestershire GL12 7JN, England

Mr J. H. HEMSLEY
National Trust, Phoenix House, Phoenix Way, Cirencester, Gloucestershire, England

Mr A. D. HODGSON
Room 409 Property Services Agency, Department of the Environment, DHRS/B, Apollo House, Wellesley Road, Croydon CR9 3RR, England

Dr J. G. HODGSON
Unit of Comparative Plant Ecology (NERC), Department of Botany, The University, Sheffield S10 2TN, England

Mr J. C. HOLBORN
 National Playing Fields Association, 25 Ovington Square, London SW3 1LQ, England

Dr M. O. HUMPHREYS
 Welsh Plant Breeding Station, Plas Gogerddan, nr Aberystwyth SY23 3EB, Wales

Dr R. HUNT
 Unit of Comparative Plant Ecology (NERC), Department of Botany, The University, Sheffield S10 2TN, England

Mr C. INGRAM
 Department of Botany, University of Liverpool, PO Box 147, Liverpool L69 3BX, England

Miss V. JACKSON
 Department of Biological Sciences, The University, Keele, Staffordshire ST5 5BG, England

Mr R. JEFFERIES
 Department of Botany, University of Liverpool, PO Box 147, Liverpool L69 3BX, England

Mr M. A. JOHNSON
 W. W. Johnson & Son Limited, Seed Growers & Merchants, Boston PE21 8AD, England

Mr H. JONES
 D. J. Van der Have B. V., The Barn, Westfield Road, Oakley, Bedford MK43 7SU, England

Dr T. KAVANAGH
 Kinsealy Research Centre, Malahide Road, Dublin 5, Republic of Ireland

Mr H. J. KILLICK
 Natural Environment Research Council, Polaris House, North Star Avenue, Swindon, Wiltshire SN2 1EU, England

Mr R. LAYCOCK
 Sports Turf Research Institute, Bingley, West Yorkshire BD16 1AU, England

Mr D. J. McMAHON
 Department of Botany, University of Liverpool, PO Box 147, Liverpool L69 3BX, England

Mr A. MIDDLEMISS
 Rose Cottage, West Poplars, Kirk Hammerton, York, England

Dr A. L. MORGAN
 Derelict Land Reclamation Research Unit, Department of Biology, University of York, Heslington, York, YO1 5DD, England

Dr A. M. MORTIMER
 Department of Botany, University of Liverpool, PO Box 147, Liverpool L69 3BX, England

Mr M. K. NICHOLLS
 Department of Botany, University of Liverpool, PO Box 147, Liverpool L69 3BX, England

Mr J. P. PALMER
 Department of Biology, University of York, Heslington, York YO1 5DD, England

Mr J. PARKER
 Estates and Valuation Department, Kent County Council, Springfield, Maidstone, Kent ME14 2LL, England

Mr T. W. PARR
 Institute of Terrestrial Ecology, Monks Wood Experimental Station, Abbots Ripton, Huntingdon, Cambridgeshire PE17 2LS, England

Mr J. W. PATRICK
 National Exhibition Centre Ltd, Birmingham B40 1NT, England

Mr K. M PEARSON
 DAFS, Agricultural Scientific Services, East Craigs, Edinburgh, Scotland

Mr M. PETERSEN
 PO Box 185, DK-5100 Odense C., Denmark

Dr A. POLWART
 Department of Biological Sciences, The University, Keele, Staffordshire ST5 5BG, England

Dr D. POPE
 Department of Environmental Design, Manchester Polytechnic, Loxford Tower, All Saints, Manchester M15 6HA, England

Mr R. J. PROBERT
 Royal Botanic Garden, Wakehurst Place, Ardingly, Haywards Heath, Sussex RH17 6TN, England

Dr J. G. PUSEY
 Directorate of Research Policy, Department of the Environment, Room S9/20, 2 Marsham Street, London SW1, England

Dr P. D. PUTWAIN
 Department of Botany, University of Liverpool, PO Box 147, Liverpool L69 3BX, England

Miss W. A. REES
 Countryside Commission, John Dower House, Crescent Place, Cheltenham, Gloucestershire GL50 3RA, England

Mr T. O. ROBSON
 ARC Weed Research Organization, Begbroke Hill, Yarnton, Oxford OX5 1PF, England

Dr I. H. RORISON
 Unit of Comparative Plant Ecology (NERC), Department of Botany, The University, Sheffield S10 2TN, England

Dr R. H. D. ROWLING
 W. W. Johnson & Son Limited, Seed Growers & Merchants, Boston, Lincolnshire PE21 8AD, England

Mr C. SAXON
37 Maesceinion, Waunfawr, Aberystwyth, Dyfed, Wales

Mr S. J. SHEARING
Plant Protection Division, Imperial Chemical Industries Ltd, Jealott's Hill Research Station, Bracknell, Berkshire RG12 6EY, England

Mr J. P. SHILDRICK
Sports Turf Research Institute, Bingley, West Yorkshire BD16 1AU, England

Dr A. SMITH
Grassland Research Institute, Hurley, Maidenhead, Berkshire SL6 5LR, England

Miss D. B. SMITH
198 Adamsrill Road, Sydenham, London SE26, England

Dr R. W. SNAYDON
Department of Agricultural Botany, The University, Reading RG6 2AS, England

Mr R. J. STEPHENS
School of Biological Sciences, University of Bath, Claverton Down, Bath BA2 7AY, England

Dr V. I. STEWART
Soil Science Unit, University College of Wales, Aberystwyth SY23 3DE, Wales

Dr A. TASKER
Department of Biological Sciences, Lanchester Polytechnic, Coventry VC1 5FB, England

Mr G. S. TAYLOR
W. W. Johnson & Son Limited, Seed Growers & Merchants, Boston PE21 8AD, England

Mr P. R. THODAY
Department of Horticulture, University of Bath, Claverton Down, Bath BA2 7AY, England

Dr R. L. THOMAS
7 Whittall Street, King Sutton, Banbury, Oxfordshire, England

Dr W. D. THOMAS
Plant Protection Division, Imperial Chemical Industries Ltd., Jealott's Hill Research Station, Bracknell, Berkshire RG12 6EY, England

Dr K. THOMPSON
Department of Botany, Science Laboratories, University of Durham, South Road, Durham DH1 3LE, England

Mr B. F. TYLER
Welsh Plant Breeding Station, Plas Gogerddan, nr Aberystwyth SY23 3EB, Wales

Ir J. P. van der HORST
Nederlandse Sport Federatie, Obrechtlaan 16, Ede, Netherlands

Ir H. VOS
RIVRO, Postbox 32, Wageningen, Netherlands

Mrs S. E. WALKER
Department of Geography, University College London, Gower Street, London SC1E 6BT, England

Mr D. P. WATERHOUSE
Parks Office, City Engineer's Department, Civic Centre, Royal Parade, Plymouth PL1 2AA, England

Dr T. A. WATT
Sports Turf Research Institute, Bingley, West Yorkshire BD16 1AU, England

Dr J. M. WAY
Room S10/02A, Department of the Environment, 2 Marsham Street, London SW1P 3EB, England

Mr T. C. E. WELLS
Institute of Terrestrial Ecology, Monks Wood Experimental Station, Abbots Ripton, Huntingdon, Cambridgeshire PE17 2LS, England

Mr H. WILLIAMS
Plant Protection Divison, Imperial Chemical Industries Ltd., Fernhurst, Haslemere, Surrey, England

Professor A. J. WILLIS
Department of Botany, The University, Sheffield S10 2TN, England

Professor C. E. WRIGHT
Department of Agricultural Botany, Queen's University, Newforge Lane, Belfast BT9 5PX, Northern Ireland

Author Index

Numbers in *italics* indicate those pages on which references are listed

Systematic Index

Subject Index